Religion and Family
in a Changing Society

PRINCETON STUDIES IN CULTURAL SOCIOLOGY

EDITORS: *Paul DiMaggio, Michèle Lamont,*

Robert Wuthnow, Viviana Zelizer

A list of titles in this series appears at the back of the book.

Religion and Family
in a Changing Society

Penny Edgell

PRINCETON UNIVERSITY PRESS

PRINCETON AND OXFORD

Published by Princeton University Press, 41 William Street, Princeton, New Jersey 08540
In the United Kingdom: Princeton University Press, 3 Market Place, Woodstock,
Oxfordshire OX20 1SY

Library of Congress Cataloging-in-Publication Data

Edgell, Penny, 1963-
Religion and family in a changing society / Penny Edgell.
p.   cm.—(Princeton studies in cultural sociology)
Includes bibliographical references (p.) and index.
ISBN-13: 978-0-691-08674-3 (cl.)—ISBN-13: 978-0-691-08675-0 (pb. : alk. paper)
ISBN-10: 0-691-08674-5 (c1. : alk. paper)—ISBN-10: 0-691-08675-3 (pb. : alk. paper)
1. Family—Religious life—New York (State)   2. Church work with families—New York (State)
3. New York (State)—Religious life and customs.   I. Title.   II. Series.

BV4526.3.E33 2006
306.6'09747—dc22   2004058631

British Library Cataloging-in-Publication Data is available

This book has been composed in Minion

Printed on acid-free paper. ∞

pup.princeton.edu

Printed in the United States of America

1 3 5 7 9 10 8 6 4 2

We live in the description of a place,
and not in the place itself.

———————————————

WALLACE STEVENS

CONTENTS

TABLES

Tables

ACKNOWLEDGMENTS

MY FIRST THANKS go to the people in the four communities in upstate New York—Tompkins County, Seneca County, Liverpool, and Northside—who co-operated so generously in this research, making their time available for a telephone survey, in-depth interviews, and focus groups and allowing me and a team of researchers to visit local congregations for fieldwork.

This research was made possible by a grant from the Lilly Endowment (1996 1880—000). Additional support was provided by the Alfred B. Sloan Foundation (96-6-9, Phyllis Moen, principal investigator). The Center for the Study of Religion at Princeton University provided a year of fellowship—in all senses of that word—that materially advanced the conceptualization and writing of this manuscript, and the Cornell Careers Institute provided support for summer salary and research assistants.

I could not have completed the project without hardworking research assistants. Thanks to Pawan Dhingra, the lead project research assistant, for all of his hard work and his significant intellectual contribution, and to Heather Hofmeister, who made the transitions from student to coauthor to colleague with grace. Elaine Howard Ecklund, Evelyn Bush, and Sonja Williams contributed to the fieldwork and data analysis. At Cornell, Kristen Schultz, Jessica Ellel, Lynley Schulman, Virginia Page, Camarra Barrett, Leah Horowitz, Julia Renedo, Anne Heyn, Stephanie Manning, Ronald Johnson, Barbara Vivas, Jasmine Abdul-Khalik, and Chris Sullivan provided invaluable help, as did Eric Tranby at the University of Minnesota.

Colleagues have contributed to this research in numerous ways. Jim Lewis, Steve Warner, Nancy Ammerman, Chris Ellison, Chris Smith, and Heather Haveman gave feedback on the early ideas and project design. Marin Clarkberg and Lindy Williams provided help with various parts of the data analysis, and Yasamin DiCiccio, the director of Cornell CAST (Computer-Assisted Survey Team) helped design the pastor and community resident survey instruments. Many colleagues have read all or part of the manuscript and provided the encouragement, ideas for revision, blunt criticism, and intellectual "spark" that keeps a project going. For this, thanks to Douglas Hartmann, Kathleen Hull, John Wilson, Mary Blair-Loy, Paul Lichterman, Ram Cnaan, Fred Kniss, Marie Griffith, Darren Sherkat, Roger Finke, Mark Chaves, Steve Ellingson, Nancy Eiesland, Brad Wilcox, Kevin Christiano, Nancy Nason-Clark, Helen Rose Ebaugh, Phyllis Moen, Elaine Wethington, Pam Tolbert, Chris Ellison, Steve Warner, Nancy Ammerman, and Marin Clarkberg.

Opportunities to present this research greatly sharpened my ideas, and I appreciated being invited to speak at the Groves Conference on Marriage and the Family (Chautauqua, 2002); at departmental colloquia series at Duke University, Swarthmore College, Rutgers University, and Northwestern University; at the Politics and Culture Workshop at the University of Wisconsin and at the Center for Community Partnerships at the University of Pennsylvania; at Hartford Seminary; and at two conferences at Princeton University, the Religion and Family in Contemporary America Conference and the Cultural Dynamics Conference. Members of the Congregational Studies Team have talked through these ideas many times with me and thus enriched the project and my broader thinking about religion and family in countless ways.

Perhaps most crucial to completing this work has been the support of good mentors and ongoing conversation partners. Phyllis Moen took me under her wing as a new faculty member at Cornell University, providing lots of practical support and help and, in the process, becoming a real friend. Nancy Ammerman, Wendy Griswold, and Robert Wuthnow gave advice on negotiating major and confusing decisions about work and life. Ronald Breiger pushed me to think about things in new ways and examine my taken-for-granted assumptions. Paul Lichterman and Nina Eliasoph talked with me about culture, sociology, politics, and community. Thanks also to Peter Marsden, Christian Smith, Steve Warner, Roger Finke, Ann Swidler, Michele Lamont, Henry Walker, Martin Marty, and Heather Haveman. Colleagues at the University of Minnesota have been friendly and welcoming, and their creativity, vitality, productivity, and civility have energized me as I completed this book. Mary Drew, Hilda Daniels, Carol Rachac, and Yoonie Helbig make mountains of paper move and office arrangements work like magic. At Cornell, Debra Kastenhuber provided the same efficiency, cheerfulness, and hard work.

Life is more than work, and good friends and family have provided the bulwark of my sanity as this project unfolded amid many other demands, concerns, and decisions. Anita Kline, Lisa Sideris, Marie Griffith, Darren Sherkat, Anne Mini, Prema Kurien, Evelyn Bush, Marin Clarkberg, Lindy Williams, Elaine Wethington, Carol Krumhansl, Pam Tolbert, Lyn Wiles, and Tom Hirschl were incredibly supportive, as were Tim Edgell, Joy Gillette, and Cathy Edgell, who have always been friends as well as family. Rhys Williams went above and beyond the call of duty to share professional responsibilities that proved too daunting given everything else that was going on.

Many of the strengths of the work result from the support of the communities and institutions of which I have been fortunate to be a part. The flaws and oversights are mine alone.

Religion and Family
in a Changing Society

Chapter One

CONTESTED CHANGES—"FAMILY VALUES"

IN LOCAL RELIGIOUS LIFE

CHANGES IN FAMILY LIFE have transformed our society in the last thirty years. One of the biggest has been the virtual disappearance of the male-breadwinner lifestyle and the emerging dominance of the dual-earner couple. Working wives and mothers face questions about the effects of their choices on their children's welfare and their own health under the strain of the "second shift," while their husbands confront—and respond to in a variety of ways—new opportunities to construct a masculine identity not focused exclusively on breadwinning. Leaders in education, business, and government debate what policies should be in place to help people manage their work and family lives and who should bear the cost of work-family management.[1]

Changing patterns of family formation and disruption have also created widespread concern and vociferous policy debates, forming a major theme of the "culture war" between liberals and conservatives. High divorce rates raise questions about the effects of divorce on children's well-being and future success and how to make "blended" families work. The problems facing single-parent families have become a focus of policy makers, religious leaders, and the national media. Debates about homosexual unions have led to battles over gay and lesbian marriage in a number of states and many local controversies over what legal rights should be extended to homosexual partners. Delayed marriage and childbearing mean that more American households comprise single adults and childless couples, and remaining childless throughout life has become much more common, fueling concern among some about the decline of the family.[2]

All of these changes have led to an increasing pluralism in family life and a new consensus that there are many kinds of loving, caring families.[3] Most Americans spend some portion of their adult lives outside of a nuclear family, forming and re-forming familylike connections periodically over the course of their lives, causing many to rethink long-held assumptions about the necessity of marriage and parenting for adults' happiness, security, and well-being. But this pluralism is intensely contested and debated for both moral and social philosophical reasons. Not everyone agrees about what constitutes "the good family" and what kinds of families are morally legitimate. Many Americans see the family as the bellwether of our society and find the rapid and numerous changes in family life over the last few decades to be troubling. Some argue that a devaluing of family life, and especially of lifelong, heterosexual marriage, inevitably leads to a decline of the nation.[4]

These debates also focus on questions of resources and inequality. Who has access to the rights that marriage confers? Why does divorce lead to a reduction in women's and children's standard of living, and what can be done to change that? The culture war is real and has real policy implications, and in our national discourse, a liberal/conservative divide has largely organized debates about the family. But a focus on divisions between liberals and conservatives obscures both the presence of consensus across these lines on many issues and the other sources of division that come into play as we argue over what constitutes a good family today.[5]

Changes in family life have been a central concern for religious leaders, activists, and local communities of faith. Throughout American history, religion and family have been intertwined and interdependent institutions.[6] Congregations, parishes, and synagogues have provided an important context for families to spend time together and have shaped the religious education and moral development of children and youths. Sociologists have long noted that marriage and parenthood make religion more important to people and increase their participation in local congregations.[7]

The constancy of the link between religion and family can obscure the fact that "the family" participating in local congregations has varied markedly over time and in different social contexts. Religious familisms, or ideologies about the nature of "the good family," have also varied over time and among different religious traditions. For example, the 1950s saw a century-high peak in U.S. church attendance rates and religious institution building, coinciding with the beginning of the baby boom and burgeoning of a postwar family-oriented lifestyle.[8] The religious expansion of the 1950s was organized around a particular kind of familism, central to which was the middle-class, male-breadwinner, suburban family profiled in classic sociological works such as William H. Whyte's *Organization Man* and idealized in the popular media through productions such as *Ozzie and Harriet.* The historical irony is that almost as soon as mainstream religious institutions had developed official discourse and local ministry to facilitate this particular form of the family, rapid and fundamental changes in work and in family life began to transform our society.

How have local religious communities responded to this period of rapid change in family life? And how have these changes transformed Americans' involvement in local religious communities? This book begins to develop answers to these questions about the religion-family link today through a study of four communities in upstate New York, ranging from rural to small-town to urban environments, and including middle-class and working-class areas. From 1998 through the summer of 2002, I collected data on the religious congregations in these communities through a survey of 125 local pastors, participant-observation with a team of graduate students in twenty-three con-gregations, and focus groups with almost fifty pastors. At the same time, a tele-phone survey of just over one thousand community residents and eighty follow-up in-depth interviews provided a wealth of information about how people's family lives and work arrangements influenced their religious partici-pation. The combination of qualitative and quantitative data on congregations and community residents provides rich detail about the interconnections between religion and family in these upstate New York communities. The ap-pendix explains in detail why these communities were chosen and how the project data were collected.

These communities are not a microcosm of America or of American reli-gion in the 1990s. They are about 94 percent white and have a religious ecology dominated by the mainstream religious institutions that one would have found in abundance here—and across America—for much of the twentieth century. Rather, these communities are an excellent location to study that por-tion of the religious landscape that was dominant in the 1950s and 1960s—the mainline Protestant, Catholic, and evangelical institutions that grew so rapidly in the postwar religious expansion and organized their ministry so particularly around the middle-class, nuclear, male-breadwinner family with children. These mainstream religious institutions helped to establish the Ozzie and Har-riet family as a pervasive cultural ideal, one that still inspires nostalgia today.[9] Although mainstream congregations and denominations today face increasing competition from newer religious forms,[10] they still encompass the majority of churchgoing Americans and have major financial and material resources. And they are highly influential players in the American cultural scene, exerting public leadership in national and local debates about gay marriage, single-parent families, policies to help with work-family management, and other "family values" issues.

The story of how these religious institutions have transformed what they say about the family (rhetoric) and how they provide ministry to families (prac-tices) sheds light on central questions in the sociology of religion. How does religious ideology change over time? How do the institutional routines estab-lished in a period of expansion and growth shape the capacity for religious or-ganizations and leaders to act in the future? How do religious leaders maintain moral authority as society changes, and how do individuals make decisions about the meaning and relevance of religious participation in their own lives when they confront institutions that may be slow to respond to contemporary family realities? How do institutions that defined and defended the ideal of the suburban male-breadwinner family define the good family today, and how do they welcome—or exclude—people whose lives do not fit the former ideal?

These questions concern not only sociologists, but anyone who wants to understand the role that religious institutions play in society, how they main-tain moral authority and exercise cultural power, how they thrive or decline in the face of rapid social change, and how people judge them to be relevant, meaningful, and welcoming places. Throughout the book, I will argue that these communities provide a useful lens through which to examine the question of how a particular set of religious institutions have responded to changes in family life and how changes in the family have reconfigured religious commitment.

THE IMPORTANCE OF THE LOCAL—FAMILY IDEOLOGY AND LIVED RELIGION

When we think about religious responses to family-related issues, our minds turn immediately to televised images of evangelicals picketing local abortion clinics, chanting and carrying signs, perhaps being dragged away by the police. Or we remember hearing an interview with a Catholic bishop who weaves his views on abortion, gun control, and opposition to the death penalty into a consistent ethic of life. We may recall a newspaper article on the briefs filed by liberal religious leaders with the Massachusetts Supreme Judicial Court supporting the right of same-sex couples to marry. Religious leaders do not directly make policy but they do exercise a great deal of cultural power in American society—the power to bring issues to national attention, to shape policy debates and media coverage, and to change individuals' hearts and minds.[11]

But most Americans do not encounter religious discourse about what is good, moral, and appropriate in family life solely, or even primarily, through news coverage or base their understandings on the pronouncements of religious elites and activists. People encounter religious ideas about the good family in the sermons and parenting workshops and adult education forums in their local congregations. They think anew about the centrality of family in women's lives when the church's annual Mother-Daughter Banquet is renamed the Women's Banquet and a speaker is invited to talk about women's contributions to local businesses and voluntary organizations. They confront the issue of whether homosexual unions are really "families" when they debate whether to become a congregation that is open and affirming to gays and lesbians.[12] Evangelical men confront what it means to be the "spiritual head" of the family in the intensive workshops on being a good husband and father run by their pastor or in a Promise Keepers group.[13]

People also encounter taken-for-granted assumptions about the centrality and importance of the family—and about what counts as a family—through the programs and ministries local congregations offer. Churches send messages about appropriate family lifestyles when they offer support groups for single parents or parenting classes designed for men. When the women's group meets at 10 A.M. on a Wednesday, women who work outside the home may conclude that traditional church-based women's groups are not relevant to their lives and not responsive to their concerns—and may either "vote with their feet" and go elsewhere or become involved in a different set of church-based activities. A proliferation of intergenerational programs designed to include people in all life stages and family arrangements may make singles or childless couples feel that their choices are supported and recognized as legitimate, and offering babysitting during the Parish Council meeting facilitates the participation of adults in dual-earner and single-parent families.

There are more than three hundred thousand local religious congregations in the United States, and what happens in these congregations shapes the moral debate about the meaning and legitimacy of changes in the family and shapes who feels included or excluded from practicing their religious faith. Churches and synagogues influence individuals' choices about marriage and parenting and how women and men divide responsibility for paid work and family caretaking. They influence people's attitudes about the morality of divorce and single parenting and gay and lesbian lifestyles. They provide social capital, connection, and belonging that help ameliorate the disruptive effects of family transitions on people's lives.

Local congregations do not simply reproduce official religious doctrine on family issues, but are creative arenas where new moral understandings are produced.[14] Local congregations balance two moral imperatives when they confront changes in the family. Members and leaders want to do "what is right," to be faithful to the authoritative teachings of their faith traditions. They also want to do "what is caring," to be loving and inclusive of the real people and real families they encounter. Both are integral parts of lived religion, the basic moral requirements of religious community. Lived religion blunts the sharp edge of ideological zeal while new understandings of the good family evolve. This lived religion is what most Americans encounter and what shapes hearts and minds.

Understanding how face-to-face religious communities have responded to changes in family life and work-family arrangements is important for sociologists who analyze how religious institutions change over time and for anyone who wants to understand how religious institutions exercise cultural power and moral influence in American society. Understanding the "family values" that organize local congregational life is crucial for anyone who cares about the survival of faith communities in a changing world and the meaning of religious involvement for those who do not fit the Ozzie and Harriet family around which the last great religious expansion was organized.

This study was designed to uncover the moral frameworks through which local congregations grapple with the meaning and implications of the changing family. To some extent, the moral frameworks I found in these upstate New York communities do mirror the "culture wars" division between liberals and conservatives. This was particularly true when religious leaders were asked about general themes ("family ministry" or "changes in family life") as opposed to specific issues. This excerpt from one pastor focus group conducted in Tompkins County in June 2000 shows clear divisions among local pastors along liberal/conservative lines:

> The pastor of a thriving independent Baptist congregation has just explained that in his church they try to avoid the term "family ministry" because it makes people who are not part of traditional "two kids and a dog" families feel left out. The focus group leader asks, "What about the rest of you? Do you use the terms 'family ministry,' or 'family programming,' or something else?" The following exchange occurs:
>
> G.B., pastor of evangelical Lutheran congregation:
>
> ". . . the traditional nuclear family is not a bad thing. And it has been around for some time and it has a fairly significant endorsement from Scripture. The Lord knows the Bible is filled with a bunch of nontraditional families. . . . And you know, God loves people despite the weaknesses that have led them sometimes to do, to do what they've done. . . . But you cannot lose the fact that God still endorses the family. It is [pause] I think a strong, um, prescription that God advocates the marriage of a husband and wife and their allegiance to the children and the children's allegiance to the parents."
>
> R.H., pastor of a Unitarian congregation:
>
> "Um, personally I think that we, we try to speak of normal families in *comparison or in contrast to the Bible*, because to me the Bible is just filled with a bunch of stories about dysfunctional families. I [pause] can't look at a Bible and find a family I would hold up as a model." [emphasis in original]
>
> S.W., pastor of independent Baptist congregation:
>
> "I do hold up, you know Scriptural families as a model . . . and I say this, I'm very strongly convinced that whatever the Bible says is what is right, and I try not to change things because I think society's changing. . . . Someone said earlier God has established the family. He has, you can discover the groundwork in the Scripture for the family. He hasn't changed it, we have changed it, society's changed it."
>
> R.H., pastor of a Unitarian congregation:
>
> "You can go through the Bible and you just don't find any normal families that you would hold up as a model."[15]

However, differences between liberals and conservatives, although evident in some conversations and sermons and program materials, were not the main theme I found either in focus groups or in the fieldwork in local churches. More striking were the commonalities across conversations with pastors and lay leaders from disparate religious traditions—Catholic, mainline Protestant, and evangelical. Most of these conversations revolved around the time bind faced by dual-earner couples or the problems of scheduling programs for children in an era of multiplying extracurricular activities. And congregations from all traditions were experimenting with changes in rhetoric and in programming to make working women, single parents, single adults, childless couples, and empty nesters feel more welcome.

Chapter 5 explores the rhetorics found in local congregations and used by their leaders in responding to changes in work and family life, and shows the influences of a liberal/conservative divide on local religious familism but also the consensus on the core family issues facing local faith communities across religious traditions. Part of this consensus stems from a widespread commitment to being as caring and inclusive as possible when confronted with the complex realities of members' lives. Chapter 6 shows the range of family-oriented ministries that local churches offer and analyzes the factors that lead congregations to be more or less responsive to the various changes in family life that have taken place in their communities. In this chapter I argue that the "standard package" of family ministry developed in the 1950s still shapes the programming and practices of many congregations today. And I examine the combination of theology, resources, denominational structure, pastoral training, and triggering events that lead some congregations to become distinctively innovative in the ways that they think and talk about family life and in the profile of ministries they provide.

This study also sheds light on changes in the meaning of religious involvement in individuals' lives after a period of rapid social change and on the interpretive frameworks that individuals use to make sense of the links between their own family lives and their religious participation. Many residents of these communities believe that religious involvement and family life go hand in hand, primarily because of the moral and ethical support that congregations provide for raising children and because congregations provide family-oriented social activities. Rachel told me at length about how religion and family fit together for her:

> It's a rainy April afternoon. Over lunch at a dark little restaurant near the college campus, Rachel, a professional woman in her early thirties and the married mother of two, has just told me that her liberal Protestant church plays a central role in her family life. With worship services and religious education classes, potlucks and socials and monthly family nights with other couples from the church, her congregation not only provides a context in which her family spends time together, but also a network of church friends who provide emotional support and trade child care with her and her husband. When she pauses to eat a bite of her lunch, I ask her about her own religious beliefs. After a pause, she tells me that she considers herself an atheist but sees the value in a belief that God is in everyone, and feels sorry for people who don't have any kind of religion, because the rest of the world is all about "what makes money" or "what is efficient" or "what is trendy" but this is about "what is right." It's a caring and moral community that ponders, together, how to live a good life, and that's invaluable, and it's rare—"Most of the communities you're a part of aren't about that, and you need support for that."[16]

At least some single parents find the same kind of supportive environment in the congregations of these communities, especially single mothers. Jackie was typical of the single mothers we spoke to:

Jackie is a forty-nine-year-old divorced mother of three children who has attended her local Catholic parish regularly throughout her life. When she got married and started her own family she became even more involved and began teaching in the religious education program. She described the church as an "anchor" when her father was diagnosed with a brain tumor several years ago, and again when she went through her divorce. Now that her children are teenagers, she said that the parish and its activities bind them together at a time when it's hard even to get everyone to sit down for a meal at the same time. She told us that her faith is central to every major decision she makes. When she was offered a promotion to a job that would have meant more money and status but also more time spent at work, she decided that "as long as I can make ends meet, spending more time with my family is what's important." So she turned down the promotion, a decision she told us was rooted in what her faith has to say about the importance of family.[17]

Rachel and Jackie raise several issues that are discussed in more detail in chapters 3 and 4. One of these issues is how one's own experiences with family formation and disruption influence involvement in a local faith community. Chapter 3 shows that marriage and parenting still lead to increasing religious involvement and suggests that this is particularly true for men. However, local faith communities are also supportive environments for many single parents and those in blended families, and this is particularly true for women.

Chapter 4 begins to explore the question of the meaning of religious involvement in people's lives and describes two different interpretive frameworks, or schemas, that people in these communities bring to bear in thinking about the links between religion and family. Rachel and Jackie both have a family-oriented schema that interprets religious involvement as central to the construction of a good family life—even for those, like Rachel, who do not affirm a religious faith. But many people in these communities have a more self-oriented schema that sees involvement in a local congregation primarily as an expression of their own religious faith, values, and spirituality. A self-oriented schema weakens the connection between family formation and religious involvement. Counter to conventional wisdom about gender and religion, more women than men have a self-oriented schema, and chapter 4 explores how gender influences the different understandings of family and religion in these communities.

Taken together, chapters 3 through 6 provide a rich understanding of how the congregations in these communities provide moral frameworks for understanding what a family is and what kinds of families are "good families." They shed light on how local churches include or exclude people in various kinds of families and how they support or do not support people as they go through periods of family formation and disruption in their adult lives. They show the relationship between patterns of family formation and disruption and involvement in a local congregation and they provide a window into different interpretive frameworks that people use to make sense of the fit between their religious involvement and their family lives. These chapters are informed by an intellectual perspective that foregrounds the moral and cultural power that religious communities wield in shaping how people understand contemporary family life, through what is said (rhetoric) and what is done (local practices). I also highlight the importance of institutional culture and history in shaping contemporary religious responses to changes in the family.

Part of the purpose of this book is to provide a "map" of the religion-family links in one set of communities after a period of rapid social change. But the remapping that is at the heart of this project extends beyond describing the links between religion and family in these communities today. It also includes the development of a new conceptual map for understanding religious familism and for thinking about the processes and mechanisms through which religious institutions respond to social change. I draw on theoretical language from the sociology of culture and institutional analysis to highlight the role of interpretive frameworks—or cultural schemas—in mediating two different change processes. The first is the process through which family formation motivates religious involvement, discussed in chapter 4. The second is how the rhetorics about family life in local churches filter which social changes congregations collectively "notice" and respond to, and the moral value they place on the contemporary pluralism in family life (chapter 5).

This intellectual remapping also involves engaging with sociological debates about how and why family formation motivates religious involvement and how and why religious institutions change as society changes. Chapter 2 outlines three theoretical traditions in the sociology of religion. The first is a structural location tradition that sees religious involvement as a "natural" and automatic outcome of family formation—particularly of marriage and parenting. My analysis of the links between marriage, parenting, and involvement in local religious life suggests that the "natural" and automatic link between religion and family formation is not so automatic today, but rather depends on how people interpret the meaning of religious involvement and its relevance to their own lives.

Chapter 2 also outlines the market or religious economy framework, which has become a dominant way for sociologists to understand how religious leaders act and how religious organizations respond to a changing environment. In these upstate New York communities, I found that some religious organizations and leaders respond to changes in family life like entrepreneurs in a market. Others respond like professionals embedded within particular institutional routines, and some engage in value-oriented action that is more concerned with "what is right" and "what is caring" than with "what works to increase market share." Chapter 2 outlines the strengths of a cultural and institutional approach for understanding the processes and mechanisms through which change comes about in religious institutions. Finally, chapter 2 addresses the question of whether local religious responses to changes in family life indicate increasing secularization and a decline in religious authority. Instead of secularization, I propose that these responses are more accurately described as a form of evolving orthodoxy that sacralizes many new family arrangements.

What unfolds over the next several chapters is a snapshot in time, but it is also the end point of a story. The 1950s religious expansion was a defining moment in the history of the religious institutions that form the religious ecology of these four communities in upstate New York. It was the era of unabashed religious familism, and the programs and ways of doing ministry developed then became a template that is still influential today. The story of the congregations in these communities is for most a story of small, incremental changes from this "standard package" of family-oriented ministry established in the 1950s; the story of a few is a more radical innovation that is based on a different understanding of what a family is and of the centrality of the family in congregational life. The story of people in these communities is a story of the development of different interpretive frameworks for understanding how religion and family might or should be related in an era of individualism and family pluralism, where orientations toward a host of "traditional" institutions have come into question. I hope to give a sense of why these stories matter and why they unfold the way that they do.

In the final chapter, I provide a critical consideration of how this study can shed light on larger questions about the religion-family link today, given the choice to focus on this particular place and these institutions. I use this study of how one set of religious institutions have responded to changes in work and family life to explore questions of religion's role in society and how religious institutions change. My goal is to provide a language for how religious institutions change that does not assume that change is, itself, a sign of secularization or "accommodation" to secular values. The language of evolving orthodoxy provides this language of talking about change that judges whether secularization has occurred by some objective and a priori criterion and recognizes that change is a constant in all institutional arenas.

I also want to provide a language for describing American religion as an institutional arena that encompasses different logics of action as opposed to a market that operates by a single logic. Sometimes religious elites are entrepreneurs and some people do "shop" for a local church. But Rachel, quoted earlier, was right; religious institutions pour most of their members' time and resources into doing what is right and what is caring, pursuing values seen as good in and of themselves, and following traditions that are valued for their own sake. Changes in family life juxtapose all of these concerns for religious leaders—what will work (and lead to thriving congregations instead of declining ones), what is right, what is caring, and how have we always done things before?

RELIGION AND FAMILY—RELATIONSHIPS OF DEPENDENCY AND CONTROL

Throughout the history of the United States, religion and family have been linked together through relationships of dependency and control.[18] Mainstream religious institutions have responded to evolving family life and household arrangements by providing new ministries to meet families' needs in an ever-changing social context. New religious groups and movements such as the Shakers have formed around alternative family and household arrangements. But if changes in family life have had an impact on how religious institutions are organized, religious institutions have also provided moral guidelines that shape family practices, the organization of family life, and our perceptions of "the good family."

Religious institutions have depended on families to pass on the rituals and beliefs of a particular faith tradition. In colonial times, fathers, as heads of extended and production-oriented households, were often primarily responsible for the religious instruction of their wives and children, along with other dependents. In the nineteenth century, an industrial economy fostered more nuclear-family households and, in the latter half of that century, an emerging urban middle class with a male-breadwinner lifestyle. A new emphasis on mothers' responsibility for the religious well-being of children and husbands emerged in the context of home-centered religious education and devotional practices.[19]

In the late nineteenth and early twentieth centuries, Sunday School and other formal religious education programs were partly successful in moving the religious instruction of children out of the home and into the congregation or parish; these did not eliminate, but rather worked to reinforce, the home-based rituals central to religious socialization.[20] From the mid-nineteenth century onward, Protestant churches experienced ongoing tension and controversy over the "feminization" of religion. In the twentieth century a similar tension developed in the Catholic church, with religious elites working to retain religious authority in the face of home-centered religious practices that often deviated from officially endorsed ritual and doctrine.[21] This tension became heightened in post–World War II America, as Protestant and Catholic churches thrived in the rapidly expanding middle-class suburbs. As local congregations organized numerous—and popular—ministries for women and children, religious leaders warned anew that the "feminization" and "privatization" of religion were taking time and resources away from more important "public" goals such as social justice and outreach to the poor.[22]

If families have influenced religious institutions, they have also depended on them for the moral socialization of children, for reinforcing a sense of ethnic identity and continuity, and for important rituals that mark life-course transitions—weddings and funerals, bar and bat mitzvahs, baptisms and brises. Confirmation and Sunday School classes welcome children into moral adulthood. Methodist and Baptist churches pass out Bibles with students' names stamped in gold letters on the front to seniors in celebration of high school graduation, and priests bless the celebration of girls' *quince años* in Mexican American communities. Religious involvement, many argue, has been functional for families, associated with lower rates of divorce and higher levels of satisfaction in marriage, parenting, and other family relationships.[23]

These relationships of mutual dependency have also had an aspect of social control. Religious institutions in the United States have promoted familism, the ideology that the family is the central, most fundamental unit of social order in a society.[24] Familistic ideologies are historically specific and vary over time and place. They do not promote the idea that any kind of family is equally valid, but rather tend to idealize certain forms and functions of the family, defining them as legitimate, valuable, and morally correct, even essential for the health of the nation.[25]

A few utopian religious communities have experimented with forms of communal organization that do not rely on some form of nuclear, patriarchal family as the basic unit of social organization. But generally, mainstream religious institutions in the United States have promoted stable, monogamous, heterosexual marriages that produce children. They have bolstered parental authority and have discouraged premarital and extramarital sex. Religious institutions have contributed to a normative consensus in our society, stronger in some times and places than in others, that being an unmarried adult, deciding to remain childless, or living in a same-sex union are at best unfortunate states in which to find oneself, and at worst irresponsible, deviant, or immoral choices that should be sanctioned.[26] For much of American history, religious institutions have promoted ideologies that interpret men's and women's natures as fundamentally different, and they have encouraged the development of various versions of the ideology of separate spheres, with male activity concentrated in the realm of work and civic life (defined as public) and women's activity concentrated in the home and church (defined as private). Many mainstream religious groups today endorse various forms of traditionally gendered family roles.[27]

Of course, the specific forms of family behavior and specific ideals of the good family have varied over time and according to ethnicity, social class, and religious tradition. Churches in the African American tradition have found ways to value extended, maternal-based family networks, although they have also sought to bolster male familial authority in the context of a society that systematically disempowers black men.[28] In the 1960s, sociologists documented large Catholic/Protestant differences in childrearing and other family behaviors, with Catholics favoring more extended family networks and emphasizing the importance of obedience and conformity in children. By the 1980s, such differences had largely disappeared as Catholics experienced upward social and economic mobility.[29] The major differences in childrearing norms and behaviors were between those who attended church (any church) and those who did not. Church attenders were more likely to favor conformity in children and traditional gender roles—a convergence around a male-breadwinner nuclear family ideal.[30]

In the 1990s, sociologists began to argue that the major differences in family ideology and behavior today are driven by the presence of a distinct conservative Protestant subculture, which endorses an ideology of male household headship and a preference for obedience in children. A historical treatment, however, shows that the label *conservative* is too broad to characterize the response of those on the religious right to post-1950s family change. Fundamentalist Protestants, the most conservative end of the spectrum, have resisted any rhetoric that embraces equality between men and women and have maintained a strict focus on paternal authority and obedience in children in practice as well as in rhetoric. More moderate evangelicals, while maintaining a rhetoric of the man as "spiritual head" of the house, have been more flexible and adaptable on questions of women's labor-force participation and have remained more egalitarian and nurturing in practice than in rhetoric.[31]

Such religiously based family norms affect behaviors within families, but some have also become overtly politicized. One of the major grounds of the "culture war" has been family norms and behaviors.[32] Some have argued that two different cultural models of the family not only are linked to liberal/conservative differences in the areas of birth control, abortion, gay marriage, and other "family values" issues, but also underlie many other culture war policy differences, including different ideas about economic development, welfare, and access to political representation. Because liberal and conservative models of the family are based on and uphold fundamentally different understandings of the division between the public and the private, they foster different understandings of the link between family behavior and citizenship.[33]

It is important to draw out and examine the public nature of religious institutions, because most scholars have treated religion and family as being in the private sphere.[34] As Stephen Hart argues:

> Both provide values; both provide a context where one is valued (more than elsewhere) as a whole person rather than on the basis of specific contributions; both provide companionship, support, and non-material pleasures; both help people who do not find much meaning in their work lives feel that their lives are meaningful; and both provide a framework for seeing oneself as a good person and one's life as basically good, independent of the success that one has in acquiring money, fame, or power. Both are "private" spheres in contrast to work or politics and one's relation to the state, and as such are felt to be spheres of individual autonomy and dignity, free of the constraints one's job or government imposes. (Hart 1986, pp. 51–52)

But I argue that it makes more sense to see religion and family as encompassing aspects of both private and public life. Families link the individual to broader connections with the workplace, with civil society, and the state. The way in which families are defined has important public implications. To take just one example, comparable worth policies historically have found less support among those who endorse a religiously based view of the man as the family breadwinner.[35] Today, welfare policies are formed by a policy elite that wants to discourage single-parent families not just on practical grounds regarding children's well-being, but also because many find such families to be morally illegitimate. Feminists have long argued that families are not naturally "private" but are defined as such, in part by religious institutions.[36] Defining family as "private" systematically deemphasizes the importance of women's typical daily lives and concerns in the political arena. As a result, women are not in practice treated as full citizens in the same sense as men are, and they are vulnerable to the violation of their rights, including in some cases the very basic right to physical safety within their homes.

Religious institutions are also public in the sense of being a part of civil society not controlled by the state. They provide a public arena of moral discourse and a location for building "community" and the social capital that entails. Religious institutions provide ideologies and identities that mobilize people for political and social action on a wide range of issues. The role of religious leaders in the controversy over gay marriage is a concrete example of how religious institutions mediate the relationship between the family and the state. Conservative religious leaders have lobbied to block legal recognition of same-sex marriages at both the state and national level, providing a moral rationale for laws that designate heterosexual marriage as a specific kind of legal status with publicly enforceable obligations while not providing that status for same-sex unions. Liberal religious leaders have advocated for legal same-sex marriage on religious and moral grounds. And gay and lesbian couples engage in joining ceremonies in churches in part because they view this as an alternative way to gain a form of legal, public sanctioning of a union that the state does not recognize.[37]

The assumption that religion and family are private institutions has dominated scholarship in the sociology of religion, but it is clear that these institutions operate in both the public and the private sphere as these traditionally have been understood. It is more analytically useful, then, to think of both religion and family as institutions that connect individuals to public life and to ask questions about how those connections are conceptualized and practiced in different times and places. Three kinds of questions seem especially helpful in designating a location from which to begin a different kind of scholarly inquiry into the religion-family link. Do religious institutions today define the family, in practice and in rhetoric, as a private institution? What cultural model of the family are contemporary congregations organized around? And does the historical association between religious institutions and a privatistic, "separate spheres" family ideology make them a less comfortable fit for contemporary men and women, who have experienced within one or two generations rapid changes in work and family roles?

The 1950s Religious Expansion and Post-1950s Family Change

These questions become even more central because the last great religious expansion in the United States institutionalized programs and ways of doing things that facilitated a revival of a form of familism that defined the family as a private "haven in a heartless world" and assumed a traditionally gendered division of labor in the home.[38] The 1950s saw rapid growth in organized religion and century-high levels of church attendance, as new congregations sprang up overnight, especially in the booming postwar suburbs. This 1950s religious revival was driven by changes in commuting patterns, rising marriage and birth rates, changing child-rearing patterns, and prosperity, which allowed more and more families to adopt the male-breadwinner lifestyle.

Congregations embraced these developments with enthusiasm, expanding their programs for children, teens, and women and developing social activities for the whole family. Such programs became a "standard package" of family ministries, a template that was widely disseminated, borrowed, and reproduced.[39] This standard package not only assumed a two-parent family, but was based on a specific middle-class male-breadwinner version of it. Of course, the male-breadwinner family did not describe a majority of Americans even in the 1950s. But it was upheld as an ideal, and congregational practices and rhetoric were organized around supporting the middle-class, suburban, organization-man lifestyle.[40] For example, the increasing numbers of women's ministries generally met during the daytime. This made them largely unavailable to women who worked outside the home. But for stay-at-home mothers, daytime United Methodist Women meetings (or the Altar Guild at the Catholic parish or the Sisters Group at the local temple) meant evenings that were free for spending time with their families or watching the children while husbands went to evening church (parish, temple) council meetings.

It is important to emphasize that the profamily rhetoric, the organization of local church life to promote a male-breadwinner family, and concerns about conformity and purity in teens—features that we associate today with evangelical Protestantism—were promoted with great vigor by mainline Protestant and Catholic churches in the 1950s and were part of a very public effort to endorse a particular kind of family lifestyle.[41] In her excellent study *Growing Up Protestant*, the historian Margaret Bendroth argues that the public, overt familism of mainline Protestants and Catholics in the 1950s paved the way for the mainstreaming of evangelical religious familism a decade later. Moreover, the ideal family of 1950s mainline Protestant and Catholic churches was not so different from the ideal family of evangelicals today; across these traditions an emphasis on a patriarchal family that was nevertheless loving and nurturing— a kind of "domesticated" patriarchy—was a common theme.[42]

The male-breadwinner lifestyle must have seemed not only right but even inevitable to many church leaders in the 1950s. The proportion of households comprising two married parents and one or more children peaked, reaching a century-high level of 43 percent with the postwar baby boom. But what may have seemed like historical inevitability turned out to be only an anomaly, and a relatively short-lived one at that. By the 1990s, the male-breadwinner family was only a memory to most Americans, surviving in a few of the most affluent suburban enclaves. Congregations found themselves facing an entirely different landscape.

Post-1950s Changes in Family Life

Family life today is very different than it was in the 1950s for the vast majority of Americans.[43] Table 1.1 shows some of these differences at a glance. The dual-earner family has become the most common family form. A large and growing literature on the dual-earner couple supports the idea that a specific dual-earner lifestyle, based primarily on the values of middle-class managers and professionals, is becoming culturally normative in our society, and that other institutions are beginning to adapt to this lifestyle.[44]

Of course, the dual-earner couple is not a new family form. In 1950, both parents spent at least some time each year in the paid labor force in fully half of all families with children. But the dual-earner family has become much more common, and the number of joint hours spent at paid work by husbands and wives on a regular basis has rapidly increased.[45] And the dual-earner family form has spread widely throughout white, middle-class America, a marked change from the 1950s. Most mothers, even of very young children, now work outside the home for pay, and many work full-time. The change in the relationships among gender, work, and family is one of the most fundamental social transformations during this period.

There has been an ongoing debate about the effects of this transformation on family life. Some argue that the "time squeeze" encountered in dual-earner households has caused greater levels of stress and anxiety for women and various other problems in managing family life on a daily basis. Others argue that women who work outside the home have less stress and better relationships with their spouses and children, and point to the beneficial effects of having two jobs to buffer the family from economic uncertainty.[46] More generally, if Americans work more, they are also getting more education and working better jobs for higher pay.[47] And although most Americans still view

TABLE 1.1
Changes in Families and Households, United States, 1950–2000

Household Composition	1950	2000
Percentage of all households composed of married couples (with or without children)	78	53
Percentage of all households composed of married couples with children younger than eighteen	43	25
Percentage of all households composed of single-parent families	11	16
Percentage of all *family households*[a] composed of single-parent families	8	23
Percentage of all households composed of single adult, living alone	11	31
Family Labor-Force Participation	1970	2000
Percentage of married mothers with children younger than six who worked some time during the year	44	68
Percentage of married mothers with children younger than six who worked year-round, full-time	10	33
Percentage of families with children under 18 in which both parents had work experience	50	72
Percentage of families with children under 6 in which both parents had work experience	44	67
Percentage of families with children under 6 in which both parents worked year round, full time	7	28

Sources: Figures on household composition are taken from U.S. Bureau of the Census, http://www.census.gov/population/socdemo/hh-fam/htabHH-1.txt, accessed 02/17/04, and http://www.census.gov/population/socdemo/hh-fam/htabFM-1.txt, accessed 02/18/04; figures for 1970 labor-force participation are taken from Howard V. Hayghe and Susan M. Bianchi, "Married Mothers' Work Patterns," *Monthly Labor Review* (June 1994): 24–30; figures for labor-force participation for 2000 are taken from ftp.bls.gov/pub/news.release/History/famee.04192001.news, accessed 02/17/04.

Note: [a] Defined as two or more related persons living together.

the management of work-family conflict as a "women's issue," it is also true that marriage and parenting have become more central in men's lives and identities.[48]

In addition to the rise of the dual-earner household, there are more and more households not organized around two parents raising children. Much larger and more stable portions of the population remain unmarried or child-less throughout much of their adult lives than in the 1950s. More couples live together and raise children without being married. There are more single

parents; divorce and blended families are much more common. Gay and lesbian lifestyles, although still controversial in some parts of American society,
have gained a great deal of legitimacy and visibility. Frank Furstenberg, one of
the most prominent sociologists studying family life, argues: "Marriage is no
longer the master event that orchestrates the onset of sexual relations, parenthood, the departure from home, or even the establishment of a household.
These events have become . . . discrete moments in the life course" (1999: 148).
Although the large majority of Americans still aspire to marriage, many no
longer see marriage and parenting as necessary or automatic parts of establishing an adult life.

Accompanying the changes in family form and in women's roles in society
have been changes in people's attitudes and beliefs about gender roles. Prior to
the 1970s, polls show that most Americans agreed with statements like, "It's
better for everybody if the man earns the money and the woman takes care of
the home and family." Since the mid-1970s, Americans have displayed more
egalitarian ideas about gender roles and have come to favor not only fathers'
increased involvement in child rearing, but also policies that grant women greater
access to "public" goods—good jobs, equal pay, and political power. More generally, Americans have come to have an individualistic orientation toward
many institutions, including work, family, and religion, and to feel that assigning individuals roles in society based on ascriptive characteristics—gender and
race, for example—is wrong.[49]

As a result of these changes, mainstream religious institutions in the United
States have faced a large-scale and fundamental transformation in the institution to which their fate historically has been most closely tied. A period of
rapid religious expansion and institution-building in the 1950s was organized
around a form of family life that quickly peaked and rapidly faded away. It is
not that all families in the 1950s were of the male-breadwinner type; fully half
were not. It is not that suburbs, or even male-breadwinner families, have completely disappeared. But religious organizations that promoted a suburban
male-breadwinner lifestyle as ideal and organized themselves around this
model of the family found themselves with programs, rituals, and discourses
targeted to a rapidly decreasing proportion of the population. How have religious institutions responded? And has the response led to the maintenance of
the tight link between religion and family that was characteristic of the 1950s
religious expansion?

The Effects of Post-1950s Changes on Local Religious Communities

There has been relatively little work analyzing how local religious communities
have responded to these changes in work and family. In a case study of one
mainline Protestant church she calls Briarglen, Penny Long Marler (1995)
outlines what she believes may be a typical response of churches within that

tradition. Briarglen has been successful in attracting a younger generation of dual-earner families with children. These families have less time and more money than the previous generation of members, and their participation largely takes the form of writing checks to support ministries for their children, while an older generation provides the labor to make the ministries work. Marler asks whether the current generation of dual-earner parents will bother to stay with the church once their children are grown, and she raises the question of whether the mainline Protestant decline in membership since the 1960s may be linked to an inability to form a better response to changes in women's roles, work, and family. She also argues that the focus on two-parent families with children stems from a nostalgia for the 1950s and leads to the exclusion of the increasing numbers of single parents, long-term singles, and childless couples in our society.

Leaders of mainline Protestant and Catholic traditions share Marler's concerns and trace the problem to the historical development that Margaret Bendroth described in her book *Growing Up Protestant*. From the 1960s on, mainline Protestant denominations have poured energy into developing new ministries around more valued "public" outreach—peace, justice, and poverty ministries. A focus on family ministry is often seen as directly competing with more "public" forms of outreach for members' time, money, and effort. And this, some argue, has contributed to the decline of mainline Protestantism. Religious leaders and sympathetic academics from these traditions have called for members and leaders of mainstream religious groups to rejoin the public dialogue on family issues, which has largely been ceded to evangelical Protestants, who see the family as a central focus of mission, not a distraction from more important goals or activities.[50]

Evangelical leaders have responded to the increasing gender egalitarianism of American society by developing discourses that emphasize mutuality, caring, and sharing within the household rather than a strict exercise of patriarchal authority.[51] Case studies suggest that evangelical Protestant congregations have adapted well to dual-earner families, and that pastors from these traditions see the development of more contemporary forms of family ministry as a natural extension of their prior activities and a positive mission priority.[52] Case studies of Catholic parishes have also tended to show that they have adapted well to changes in women's work and family roles, although as with evangelical Protestants, there are limits to the kinds of contemporary families many Catholic parishes will embrace.[53]

Although scholars have focused a great deal of attention on the official responses of religious leaders to changes in work, family, and gender, looking at the rhetoric developed in advice books or other "official" texts, our knowledge about congregational response to family change is piecemeal. There have been a few case studies of individual congregations. But we have no good comparative studies of local congregations that would allow us to identify how and why they vary in the kinds of family ministry they provide, or the variation in the kinds of individuals and families that they attract. So it is hard to know if the congregations that case studies focus on are typical and what the range of response is within and across religious traditions. We know relatively more about evangelical Protestant congregations, but have little knowledge of what is going on within Catholic parishes, Jewish synagogues, or other religious communities.

In addition, we need to understand the impact of religious institutions' adaptations on their ability to attract contemporary families and individuals. Do those who are not in a male-breadwinner or intact two-parent family arrangement find religious organizations relevant and meaningful in their lives? Do they feel welcome in local congregations? What effect does religious involvement have on individuals' choices about work and family, or on child rearing, or on relationships between husbands and wives? Constructing a new map of the religion-family nexus requires understanding not only what religious institutions are doing, but also how religious institutions are linked to family formation and work for the contemporary families—and individuals—of the 1990s.

In terms of understanding the effect of changes in family and work on religious participation, scholars have looked at only a limited set of questions.[54] There has been little research on the effects of divorce and other forms of family disruption on religious involvement, and little research on the involvement of single parents, those in blended families, or long-term singles. We know that family formation is still associated with religious involvement, but we do not know if this is equally true for men and women because research on men's and women's involvement has focused almost exclusively on the "gender gap" in church attendance and not on the processes of religious affiliation or the meaning religious involvement has in men's and women's lives.[55] We know that paid employment increases men's religious involvement and that women who attend church regularly are more likely to work part-time when children arrive,[56] but there has been too little research on how religious involvement might affect individuals' decisions about the hours they spend at work or about accepting promotions or transfers to jobs with more travel.

If there are gaps in what we know about congregations and the religious commitment of individuals, there are also silences created by our conceptual categories. Most sociologists accept at face value the idea that religious involvement is functional for families, and this has consequences both for the interpretation of research findings and for what kinds of questions are asked. For example, scholars emphasize not the structural inequality between men and women in evangelical churches, but the negotiated and more egalitarian practices within evangelical families. We know from other research that work-family issues are treated largely as private matters in the United States, and that businesses off-load the costs of managing work and family onto individuals, thus "privatizing" the cost of coping with social change. Do religious institutions contribute to this idea that family is a private institution and that troubles managing work and family are private troubles, the costs of which should be borne by individuals, not companies or the state? There has been little or no research on questions such as these.

One of the main goals of this book is to understand how congregations have adapted to changes in work and family in their rhetoric, in their formal programming, and in their everyday practices. Another goal is to analyze how individuals' work and family contexts affect religious involvement in a way that includes an examination of family disruption, alternative life-course pathways, and nontraditional family arrangements. This will generate a good map of the current linkages between religion and family in these four communities. Put together, the answers to the questions posed here also add up to a larger pattern that can help us to refine our theoretical account of how religious institutional change comes about. This more theoretical analysis will allow for a critical examination of theories about the role of religion in the contemporary United States, as well as theories about the overall direction or outcome of religious institutional change.

THE RELIGION AND FAMILY PROJECT

In formulating a way to conduct research that would shed light on these questions, I made several key choices. First, I decided that such a study should be conducted in a way that would allow for simultaneously answering two kinds of questions. What has happened inside religious organizations and institutions faced with changes in work and family? And how are religious institutions intertwined with the lives of individuals and families in contemporary society? I decided the study must be an analysis of reciprocal relationships, examining how two historically connected institutions have changed over time.

In examining how religious institutions have adapted to changes in family life, it made sense to focus on local congregations. Religious elites make pronouncements about family life, and the scholarly discourse on religious groups' family ideologies is quite well developed. But local congregations directly provide ministry to individuals and families, and it is these organizations in which the vast majority of the religiously involved participate. Unlike some other, newer forms of local religious community, congregations were associated in the 1950s with a very specific work-family lifestyle, and so changes in work and family may pose particular challenges for them. Local congregations may fall in line with official pronouncements, but in fact they often do not, particularly in areas such as women's roles or lifestyle choices.[57] Yet our knowledge of how the religion-family link works at the level of the local congregation is limited to a few case studies.

A focus on the congregation excludes some new institutional forms that are increasingly common in the American religious landscape. Small groups such as the Promise Keepers and informal networks of religious practice that come together only occasionally for common rituals comprise increasingly more religious participants. Parachurch groups organized around single-issue policy, lifestyle, charitable, or activist causes have also grown in recent decades.[58] Any more comprehensive study of religious change would have to take the emergence of these forms into account. But congregations still comprise far more regular religious participants than any of these forms. And a focus on the congregation allows me to examine how those institutional forms that were dominant during the 1950s religious expansion have adapted to changes in work and family.

Another choice was to take an explicitly ecological approach to the research design. An ecological approach implies a focus on a few specific communities in order to understand how the local context influences processes of social change. Particularly important was the decision to pick communities that varied in socioeconomic status and in population density. Many studies of American religion have focused on a white, suburban middle-class environment, and although infinite variation is not possible in a small-scale study, some variation in resources and lifestyles is desirable because it prevents universalizing one particular set of middle-class experiences as "the" American religious experience. The changes in work and family that have occurred in the society at large matter less than local demographics and economics in driving the "demand" for voluntary organizations in general and churches in particular.[59] See box 1.1 for a brief description of the four communities chosen.

These four communities are described in more detail in the appendix, which also includes tables that compare census data from each community to national figures for both 2000 and 1960. These communities have experienced the same major transitions that most of the nation has experienced in that forty-year period, including the decline of farm-related jobs and the increase in white-collar managerial and professional employment, rising levels of education, a decline in the portion households composed of two parents with children, and a rise in dual-earner families. These communities differ from national averages, however, in some ways. They range between 90 and 97 percent white (the national average is 80 percent). This means that they contain no areas with significant nonwhite populations and no areas with a concentration of new immigrant groups. Tompkins County and Liverpool are more middle-class (well-educated, professional) than the national average, whereas Seneca County and Northside are considerably less educated and have fewer professionals that the U.S. population as a whole.

Box 1.1
Religion and Family Project–4 Communities

Liverpool, a metropolitan, white, professional/middle-class suburb outside of Syracuse. Liverpool contains both an older, more established middle class as well as a younger generation of managers and professionals who work for the major employers of the Syracuse metropolitan area.

Northside, a metropolitan, working-class neighborhood in Syracuse, with ethnic diversity and a history of economic decline, experiencing some influx of urban renewal money.

Seneca County, a nonmetropolitan county with a stable agricultural base and a largely working-class population, many of whom commute to a city in a neighboring county for service-sector jobs.

Tompkins County, a nonmetropolitan county with a large central town that is economically prosperous, Cornell University and other major employers, and a largely middle-class, professional population.

There is another form of ecological influence on congregational adaptation to social change, and that is the embeddedness of each congregation within a local organizational ecology, a network of interacting congregations and the other voluntary organizations. Congregations look to peers in their own communities for ministry ideas, borrowing through local networks of cooperation and information exchange. They also self-consciously define themselves against similar congregations in the community in order to establish a distinctive profile that will attract more members. In engaging in this kind of "borrowing and niching" processes within local networks of reference, congregational leaders are like other agents of organizational innovation.[60]

These ecological considerations prompted me to gather information through a census survey of all of the congregations in a four-community area. The survey instrument was designed to gather information about each congregation's history and programming, the pastor's own views on family-related issues, and congregational networks of peers and competitors. Follow-up fieldwork in twenty-three area congregations and focus groups with almost fifty local pastors not only allowed me to clarify and elaborate themes that emerged from the survey but also to discover issues and problems confronting local churches that the survey had not uncovered.

In the appendix, the religious ecology in these four communities is compared to the national sample of congregations drawn in 1998 for the National Congregations Study (NCS). Reflecting the history of these communities, the religious ecology is more heavily Catholic and mainline Protestant than the national average, and 76 percent of the congregations here were founded before 1965. Because these congregations tend to be larger than independent Baptist and nondenominational churches, and because smaller congregations were more likely not to respond to our survey, there are also more large congregations represented here than in the NCS sample.[61]

In order to examine the question of how local community residents think about and participate in local congregations, a random-digit-dial telephone survey of more than one thousand community residents was conducted by a professional survey team operating at Cornell University. This survey was followed by eighty in-depth interviews with survey respondents, split evenly between church-attenders and those not involved in a local congregation. The appendix describes the data collection in detail.

It is very common for those who do small-scale community or case studies to claim that, in effect, the world is reflected in a grain of sand. But it is perhaps more useful to understand the particular ways in which any given small-scale study is exemplary in order to understand the broader significance offered by a close analysis of a given locale. It is appropriate to treat these communities as exemplary of a particular kind of religious ecology that is still heavily influenced by the family ideology and the template for family ministry that was so formative in the 1950s religious expansion. In one sense, then, this is a case study of the continuing influence of the male-breadwinner family ideal and how nostalgia for this family form shapes and limits the capacity of voluntary organizations and local community institutions to adapt to changes in family life.

It is also a study of how and why some local organizations are able to adopt radically new understandings of family life in ways that nevertheless build on authentic aspects of their religious traditions. One of the broadly applicable insights from this study is that this kind of religiously authentic innovation leads to vitality and growth, whereas a nostalgic longing for the past leads to decline—for liberal and conservative, Protestant and Catholic religious communities. This is important for those who want to understand how the fate of religious institutions is tied up with the changing family.

It is also important to hear the voices of those in moderate and liberal religious traditions who continue to focus on the family as a centrally important religious issue and who have managed, at the local level, to adapt to changes in family life in a way that is consonant with the feminist and social justice strands of their religious traditions. Many Catholic and mainline Protestant congregations in these communities both acknowledge the painful effects of family disruption and provide a strong moral vision for family life. They do this while affirming egalitarian relationships between men and women, favoring more help from businesses and government for those struggling to balance work and family life, and endorsing the legitimacy of new forms of loving, committed relationship. At the national level, religious discourse on such family values issues has largely been ceded to conservatives. This impoverishes our ongoing national conversation on the changing family and leaves many Americans with the idea that all religious institutions are alike—to the point where some moderate Americans forsake any religious identification whatsoever.[62]

This study can also shed light on whether those in nontraditional families have access to the social support and social capital that flow from participation in local religious communities. The survey of community residents and in-depth interviews, as well, point to barriers facing single parents, the divorced, and those in blended families, for whom religion is very salient but who find it hard to participate in local religious communities because of pragmatic difficulties of timing and scheduling—difficulties that are structural and likely to be widespread in our society. Congregations provide an important arena of social support for those who participate. Social support can be crucial in ameliorating the most harmful effects of family disruption on both adults and children, establishing a future trajectory that leads to happiness, stability, and the capacity to form healthy relationships throughout life.[63]

These communities also provide a window on more theoretical questions about how a person's gender, work situation, and family context shape religious participation and how religious institutions change over time. For sociologists, perhaps the most important insight this study generates is the need to take into account how interpretive frameworks shape social action. Religious institutions adapt to changes in family life in a way that is shaped by interpretive frameworks that identify which issues to pay attention to and bundle those with different sets of practical and symbolic responses. The language of institutional analysis and evolving orthodoxy, outlined in the next chapter, is meant to provide a way to analyze these normal processes of change without resorting to an assumption that secularization is natural and inevitable. Likewise, individuals interpret the fit between religion and family differently, and this shapes both their patterns of religious participation and the meaning of that participation. This particular form of individualism is not new, but is rather a constitutive feature of the voluntarism and pluralism that have always characterized American religion.

The next chapter shows how this local study of the interconnection between religion and family can reshape our theoretical frameworks in the sociology of religion. The chapters that follow show the interpretive frameworks and daily practices that are reworking the religion-family link in these communities. Without the acrimony or fanfare of the culture war, these local religious communities are quietly going about the business of redefining the meaning of family, gender, and work and the centrality of the family in local religious life. And the individuals who live and work in these communities are making their own moral judgments about the fit between family and religion and the relevance of religious participation for their own lives. In upstate New York, the cultural contestation over the good family continues on a daily basis. Understanding how this cultural contestation plays out in these communities is a first step in better understanding religious familism in a changing society.

Chapter Two

RELIGIOUS INVOLVEMENT AND RELIGIOUS

INSTITUTIONAL CHANGE

MAX WEBER argued that in order to achieve adequate explanatory accounts, sociologists must do more than analyze the effects of social structural arrangements on social outcomes. They must also understand how individuals orient themselves to social structures through interpretive frameworks that have an independent effect on the individual behaviors that either reproduce or change these structures. Interpretive frameworks can privilege instrumental (means-ends) rationality or value rationality—the idea that some things are good in and of themselves, incommensurable, and to be pursued regardless of cost. In this way, Weber introduced the idea of value-rational action to sociological explanation, rejecting approaches that see action as overdetermined by social structural arrangements and providing a corrective to approaches that view social actors solely as agents who pursue goals or maximize a utility function through instrumental-rational action.[1]

Contemporary sociologists of culture take for granted that social actors engage in both value-rational and strategic (instrumental-rational) action. In addition, there has been a renewed emphasis in recent work on the routine and pragmatic dimensions of social action, or action that may be pursued without an elaborate reflection on ends and means. This work focuses on both routine forms of social practice and on the practical-evaluative dimension of action involved in short-term problem solving.[2]

Where do the interpretive frameworks that orient individuals toward value-rational, pragmatic, or instrumental-rational action come from? Contemporary scholarship on the question of culture and agency moves beyond a focus on individual meaning-making to analyze the institutional and structural embeddedness of cultural codes, symbol systems, and routines of action. Culture is understood as a simultaneously constraining and enabling ground of social action. Structural arrangements are understood to be organized around cultural "rules" that provide a template for action. At the individual level, social actors are understood as being able to achieve reflexivity vis-à-vis the larger structural arrangements in which they are embedded, either reproducing them or, at times, bringing about change.[3]

As Ann Swidler argues, this implies that there is a hierarchy of cultural forms, or levels of cultural analysis.[4] Some cultural forms anchor others. For example, the institutional arrangements of marriage anchor and shape our discourses on love. Or, cultural models of what a congregation might and should be like influence the framing and forms of argument surrounding conflict over particular issues and events within congregational discourse.[5] The rules (anchoring cultural forms) are durable but not immutable. For example, social movements can impose new anchoring frames in particular arenas of discourse, or new church members may bring with them and impose a different model of congregational life than the one previously in place.[6]

In this chapter, I outline a cultural approach to understanding the religious involvement of individuals that takes into account the insights about the links between culture, social structure, and agency outlined above. Previous work has emphasized the effects of structural location on religious belief, identification, and church attendance. Marriage, the birth of a child, and employment status are all seen as structural conditions that directly predict religious involvement. But I argue that, although these structural factors influence religious involvement, they do so in a way that is mediated by the interpretive frameworks that individuals bring to bear in understanding the meaning of religious involvement and the cultural schemas that determine how religion fits—or does not fit—with other aspects of adult lives, including work and family. In chapter 4, I argue that an individual's *religious involvement rhetorics* mediate the effects of structural location on choices to participate in local religious communities. These rhetorics capture different schemas that link religion and family life in different ways. In the current chapter, I develop the theoretical underpinnings for this analysis.

I also outline a cultural-institutional approach for understanding how congregations respond to changes in work and family. Standard accounts in the sociology of religion explain religious institutional change either as a reaction to ongoing secularization or as the result of the entrepreneurial activity of religious leaders in the religious economy. In chapters 5 and 6, I focus on how rhetorics that define "the problem of family ministry today," symbolic constructions of "the good family," and institutional routines of ministry shape congregational adaptation to new family forms and work-family strategies. These rhetorics and routines are anchored, I argue, in different *family schemas* that shape daily congregational life.

These arguments have implications for several standard interpretations of religious involvement and religious-institutional change in the sociology of religion, implications that are outlined in detail in the following pages. In place of a structural location account of individual religious involvement, I propose a cultural account that takes seriously how religious involvement schemas provide different ways to interpret the meaning and relevance of religious involvement for one's family life and family connections. In place of rational-choice and secularization accounts of religious institutional change, I propose a cultural-institutional framework that allows me to account for value-rational and routine forms of action and that does not impose a teleology of decline on all understandings of religious change. These arguments also have implications for the sociology of culture, by continuing the work of specifying the empirical relationships between levels of cultural analysis and the mechanisms through which some cultural forms anchor and influence others. In this case, the mechanisms flow from interinstitutional dependencies between religion and family in the U.S. context.

But these arguments are also relevant for those who are more concerned with empirical questions than with theoretical debates. Is religious participation becoming more privatized and individualistic? Have changes in work and family undermined religious involvement? How do women and men relate differently to religious institutions at various stages in the life course, and how is this linked to the gendering of local religious communities? In the face of rapid change in the family, do congregations operate as arenas of social inclusion for those in diverse family arrangements or as arenas of social exclusion based on family form and lifestyle? In the chapters that follow, I will show that a cultural and institutional approach can also shed light on these more substantive questions about the unfolding relationship between work, family, and religion in our society.

WORK, FAMILY, AND RELIGIOUS INVOLVEMENT

Religious institutions provide support for the moral socialization of children and a family-centered lifestyle. Structural location theories view religious involvement as flowing automatically from family formation, especially for those who view marriage and child rearing as central to their own identities.[7] Family formation effects are thought to account for women's persistently higher rates of religious involvement relative to men's, because women have, historically, been more involved in the family, particularly in child rearing, than are men.[8] This insight has also been applied to examining differences in individual levels of religious involvement. For both men and women, being older, being married, and having children in the home all predict higher levels of church attendance.[9]

Employment status is also understood as an aspect of structural location, although there have been debates about how it influences religious involvement. On the one hand, Mueller and Johnson (1975) link full-time paid employment to increased religious participation through the social class hypothesis, which postulates that church attendance is an expression of social status and economic security. On the other hand, de Vaus and McAllister (1987) argue that full-time labor-force participation may reduce religious involvement because it reduces discretionary time and exposes people to competitive values that have a secularizing effect, reducing religious participation.

Using General Social Survey (GSS) data from 1972 through 1990, Hertel (1995) finds that for all men and for single women, full-time paid employment increases religious involvement, supporting the social class hypothesis. However, for married women, full-time employment reduces both their own and their spouses' religious involvement. Hertel argues that, depending on life stage, full-time labor-force participation in an advanced industrial economy may increase women's individualism and decrease their willingness to assume traditionally gendered roles historically associated with religious institutions. He reintroduces an older debate about the role of "modern" values in explaining religious involvement.[10] He does not, however, include direct measures of the modernized values of individualism and egalitarianism that he believes are linked to religious involvement. He also does not control for other factors related to both "modern" values and religious involvement, such as age and religious subculture, which might influence the findings he reports.

Previous research identifies several dimensions of "modern" (or progressive) values possibly affecting religious involvement. The first is a belief in egalitarian gender roles for men and women, understood as a rejection of the idea that women ought to specialize in homemaking and family and that men ought to specialize in paid employment as breadwinners. Traditional attitudes toward gender roles or "conservative family attitudes" are linked to religious participation.[11]

Second, beliefs about religious institutions themselves may be linked to involvement. Religious individualism is a broad concept that has received a great deal of attention in the sociology of religion, but most scholars agree on the central importance of views of religious authority in influencing religious participation. A view that religious authority resides in the person's own judgment, not in a religious institution or its representatives, may also reduce religious involvement.[12]

Taking individuals' attitudes and beliefs into account is the first step toward a more interpretively adequate understanding of religious involvement and better predictive models. However, most of this work tends to see the values and attitudes in question as stemming directly and uniformly from a person's social-structural location. To put it another way, this work assumes that individuals in similar situations (or structural locations) interpret the world in similar ways. In contrast, an interpretive approach argues that individuals in similar structural locations may well see the world differently. For example, one thirty-five-year-old married Jewish woman with children may think that regular participation in a local synagogue is essential for a good family life, whereas another woman demographically similar in all ways may think that the synagogue is totally irrelevant to her family life.

Roof and Gesch (1995) provide support for this view as applied to religious involvement when they make the distinction between "family attenders" and others. Family attenders believe that family formation and religious involvement are tightly linked, and that people who are married or have children should attend church together as a family. They find that those who believe in the importance of families attending church together are more likely to actually attend church after marriage and the birth of their children than are others.[13] Drawing on a different theoretical tradition but supporting the same insight, Sherkat (1998) argues that religious schemas that link family formation and church attendance are likely to reinforce the behavioral connection between family formation and religious participation; the erosion of such schemas may lead to reduced participation.

Interpretive frameworks, or schemas, are not randomly distributed or idiosyncratic, but they are not determined by structural location, either. They reveal differences in institutionally based cultural repertoires that define appropriate activity. As Sewell (1992) argues, different structural locations provide individuals with exposure to different schemas for organizing action. But because people are exposed to multiple schemas and because schemas are transposable across arenas of activity, structural location influences but does not determine social action.

This work provides a theoretical language for raising questions about how individuals may exercise agency in applying alternative interpretive frameworks in assessing the implications of marriage, the birth of a child, and their employment situation for their religious involvement. It also suggests a more complicated causal arrangement than traditional structural location approaches imply. Paid work may expose people to more individualistic and secular schemas, thus eroding religious participation. But religious involvement and religious socialization may influence attitudes toward—and entry and exit from—paid employment, and traditional religious beliefs may predispose individuals to ignore the secularized and individualist values they learn in modern workplaces.[14]

The term *schema* is somewhat problematic because some uses of the word imply both a cognitive depth and a systematization that is difficult to verify with standard kinds of data sources such as surveys or semistructured interviews.[15] I use the term *schema* here more in the sense that Sewell (1992) employs: schemas are interpretive frameworks through which individuals assess how work, family, and religion fit together in their own lives. I am not arguing that these frameworks provide the deep cognitive structure implied by more social-psychological uses of the word *schema*. Schemas are social, embedded in social structures, they provide a template for action, and they are revealed in both the rhetoric and in practical routines of action that individuals encounter across institutional arenas.

In chapter 4, I argue that there are two different interpretive frameworks that individuals bring to bear in judging the appropriate relationship between work, family, and religion in these four upstate New York communities. A *self-oriented* rhetoric draws on a schema that interprets religious participation as the appropriate expression of an individual's own faith or spiritual journey and does not see religious involvement as dependent on work or family context. A *family-oriented* rhetoric draws on a different schema, which interprets religious participation as an appropriate expression of a family- and community-oriented lifestyle.

I will argue that the causal relationship between schemas and structural location is complex. On the one hand, in-depth interviews clearly show that marriage or the birth of a child are triggering events that lead many individuals to a different way of thinking about the meaning and relevance of religion in their lives. For others, a family-oriented religious involvement schema predates their own family formation. Regardless of the timing and causal direction, statistical models of various measures of religious participation show that religious involvement schema[16] are associated with variations in religious involvement regardless of employment status and family formation. Religious involvement schemas are not simply straightforward effects of structural location but have an independent effect on religious participation.

For women, the effects of family formation on religious involvement are mediated almost entirely through these religious involvement schemas. In chapters 3 and 4, I show that the links between work, family, and religion are different for men and women, in part because women's attitudes and beliefs about the appropriateness of religious involvement have a much larger effect on their religious participation than do men's. I argue that gender, then, is best understood not as another aspect of structural location, but as a set of experiences that lead women to be more critical than are men in judging the fit between religious institutions and their own lives.

How Religious Institutions Change

In developing a theoretical understanding of how changes in work and family have affected religious institutions, two kinds of questions need to be addressed. The first set of questions has to do with *the processes through which change occurs.* How have religious institutions adapted to changes in work and family? What are the processes and mechanisms through which religious leaders define some changes as relevant, decide on a response, and carry out that response?

Processes of religious institutional change can be analyzed using two different theoretical frameworks, both of which originate outside of the sociology of religion but which have been imported by scholars who found secularization theory, the dominant theoretical paradigm in the sociology of religion, to be inadequate. The first is a religious economy (market) framework, based on rational-choice theory. The second is an institutional framework drawn from organizational theory and the sociology of culture. These frameworks have been developed and applied in an effort to understand a wide variety of social processes across institutional realms.

The second set of questions has to do with the *overall result of the changes that have come about*. Are religious institutions still as tightly organized around family formation and family life as they were in the 1950s? Do they still have the same impact on family life that they did in the 1950s? What are the consequences of the changes in family and work for the ongoing vitality of religious institutions in American society?

The outcomes of religious institutional change have been understood through frameworks that are more centrally located within sociology of religion as a distinct discourse. The first framework is that of secularization theory, which has developed from the tradition of sociological theory inspired by the work of Max Weber. The second framework draws on the work of the French sociologist Pierre Bourdieu and conceptualizes religious institutional change as a process of defining and defending an evolving orthodoxy.

Processes and Mechanisms of Change: Markets versus Institutions

The idea of a religious "market," complete with consumers and entrepreneurs, borrows from rational-choice theory and classical organizational theory in sociology.[17] This framework understands individuals as consumers of religious goods and services, who make rational choices about participating in religious institutions that meet their socially influenced preferences. Religious goods are understood to be supernatural in nature—the salvation of one's soul and an eternal life in which believers are rewarded and unbelievers punished. Rational choices maximize benefits and minimize costs of religious participation in the face of existing limits on information.

How religious preferences are formed has received quite a bit of attention in the rational-choice approach to religion, and is often linked to family relationships.[18] For example, religious socialization into a particular tradition during childhood makes it familiar and lowers the costs of participation, leading to stability in religious preferences. For an adult, a spouse who attends a particular church may either exert a normative influence on one's own choice to attend or provide information that makes a particular church (or mosque, or synagogue, or Wiccan group) more familiar or more trusted, reducing the learning costs associated with participation.

This perspective lends itself to certain kinds of predictions about how changes in work and family may affect religious participation. For example, as families change, churches that make participation easier for those in new family arrangements—dual-earner families, single-parent families—will thrive and expand to occupy a greater market share by retaining a greater percentage of future generations of adherents. In fact, some rational-choice proponents have made this argument to explain the processes through which mainline churches have declined and evangelical Protestant churches have thrived over the last three decades.[19]

Like changes in family formation, changes in work may reconfigure religious participation. The long hours spent at work by managers and professionals caught up in the "time squeeze" make less time available for religious activities. Paid employment may provide women, who have typically been more religiously involved than men, with alternate venues for achieving status and other rewards they previously received from religious organizations, thus reducing religious involvement. On the other hand, early religious socialization may counteract these tendencies for some individuals.[20] And those with lower occupational attainment may turn to religious groups for status and other forms of affirmation they do not receive at work.

From this perspective, religious organizations also make rational choices to react to changes in the market for religious goods and services. Or at least, religious leaders do; most rational-choice perspectives emphasize the role of religious "entrepreneurs" who are relatively free, given the largely congregational structure of American religion, to innovate in ways that attract new adherents by providing services that religious consumers really want. This leads, proponents of this framework argue, to a vital and pluralistic religious landscape that provides an overall high level of quality and diversity in religious goods and services.

Rational-choice approaches do not see modernization as dangerous or damaging to religious organizations. From the rational-choice perspective, Weber's fears about the "disenchantment" of modern life have not been borne out. Modernization fosters the pluralism of unregulated religious markets and free religious choice, leading to vital religious belief and expression. Rational-choice theorists explicitly reject the teleology of decline that underlies secularization theory and argue that modernization has beneficial effects on rates of religious participation despite (in fact, because of) the weakening of official religious influence in government and other institutions.[21]

Rational-choice theorists would not predict an overall decline of religious participation in the United States resulting from changes in work and family. Religious demand is assumed to be relatively constant, and rates of religious participation are driven largely by changes in religious supply. In a society with a religious monopoly, changes in sociodemographics might lead to religious decline, but in the United States, with a fluid and pluralistic religious system that encourages religious entrepreneurs, rational-choice theory predicts that religious organizational change will facilitate high and stable levels of religious involvement. Instead of overall decline, "winners" and "losers" will emerge as consumer preferences change.

Who will win and who will lose? Stark and Finke (2000) predict that low-commitment churches[22] that have little tension with the larger society and demand little from their members will lose membership over time, giving way to newer groups (or newer movements within older, established denominations) that have more tension with the larger society. In reacting to changes in work and family, a rational-choice approach would predict that churches will thrive if they provide ways to retain young families in the face of changing work-family lifestyles and maintain a distinct "brand identity" by fostering tension with the society.

Rational-choice theories would tend to predict a great deal of change and adaptation among religious organizations in the face of changes in work and family, along with some shifting of *who* is religiously involved and where. Churches that do not adapt would lose members, and failure to adapt results from the same kinds of things that cause a failure of rationality in organizations more generally. These mostly center around blocks to effective communication of market demand or effective decision making in response to it. For example, a bureaucratic structure or a highly professionalized clergy, both of which remove religious leaders from the immediacy of consumer demands in a hierarchical denomination, might delay or forestall adaptation—and lead to decline. Churches that are more comfortable and society-affirming—less in tension—might decline, as well. So, for example, the comfortableness of more liberal churches with working women and egalitarian gender roles may not provide the same tension with society that evangelical discourses on male headship in the home provides.

In contrast to this picture of a highly adaptive market with rapid and responsive change, an institutional approach tends to emphasize stability and continuity of religious organizations. Religious institutions are bundles of ideas and practices that have come, over time, to be valued for their own sake. Current institutional arrangements guide and direct which social changes will be attended to and foster standard ways of responding to change; all of this may or may not be "adaptive" from a market perspective. As discussed earlier in this chapter, institutional approaches understand social actors to be influenced by the schemas embedded within the social structures they encounter (for example, in organizations or entire institutional arenas). This embeddedness influences action in particular ways, and much social action, in this perspective, takes the form of deploying standard routines of practice, or scripts, in a habitual way. Some actions are "traditional," or rooted in routines or goals that have come to be valued for their own sake, as evidenced in this quotation from a member of an Episcopalian parish profiled in Becker (1999): "We have always done it this way. We have *never* done it that way."

However, institutional theories do provide ways of thinking about when and how adaptation may occur. Theorists as diverse as Sewell (1992), Stryker (1994), and Friedland and Alford (1991) note that institutions change when they come into contact with other institutions that provide different frameworks for thinking about the world (what Sewell calls schemas) and different rules of appropriate action. In this, institutional theory makes a place for agents who, although not as unconstrained as the typical rational actor of market approaches, nevertheless have considerable scope for creativity and for affecting the organizations and institutions of which they are a part. Religious leaders can try to change their organizations or found new ones. Members of religious groups can encounter new ideas, whether from other religious organizations or other institutional arenas—such as work, education, or family— and can apply these to the religious organizations of which they are members, seeking change.

Adaptation, when it does occur, may not be an immediate and transparent response to members' or potential members' demands. And adaptation may not work; changes can be unresponsive to the needs of members and potential members. Institutional theories provide ways to think about the social processes that may influence the "how" of adaptation, like the desire to maintain institutional routines or protect the legitimacy, authority, or interests of those in power. Much adaptation, in this view, is undertaken to solve immediate problems, and there may be little attention to the long-term or unintended consequences of today's innovation. A conservative Baptist church board that votes to allow women to serve as elders one day may find itself pressured to rethink the issue of women pastors the next. "Innovator" churches may find themselves asked to continue to innovate in ways they did not anticipate; and congregational leaders may resist all innovation, knowing about the "slippery slope" they may encounter if they begin.

I will argue that an institutional approach provides a better framework within which to understand the dynamics of religious-institutional change in general, and in particular for understanding how religious institutions have adapted to changes in work and family life since the 1950s. This argument is based on two kinds of supports. The first is theoretical, the second substantive.

In terms of theoretical scope and power, market approaches suffer in comparison to institutional approaches. The first example of this is how both frameworks account for social embeddedness, or the influence of social relationships on decision making. Rational-choice accounts cannot explain without borrowing heavily from other theoretical approaches, including institutional theory, where preferences come from or why actors choose to maximize particular goods over others. Judgments differ in how serious a problem this is for rational-choice accounts. Ellison (1995) agrees that rational-choice theories need to draw on other approaches in order to specify how social location constrains, or sets limiting conditions on, rational action, but he finds this a useful addition to rational-choice theory and the theory itself a useful tool thus modified.[23]

In contrast, I agree with Karl Popper, who argued that theories that specify covering laws such as the rational-choice maxim "people pursue their own interests" or "religious groups grow when they meet people's needs and preserve a religious tradition" are not particularly useful because the covering laws cover those things that do not vary, and those things that vary are always specified in the side conditions of the theory. Ironically, the truest theoretical statements, from a rational-choice perspective, are the least interesting because they are true by definition and do not vary over time and social location. The theoretically interesting sources of variation—differences in religious culture and values, in family socialization—are side conditions, and their effects are assumed but not theorized in advance. Popper concluded that the real "theoretical action" is, logically, in the side conditions of the theory, which ought to be theorized in their own right, the covering law having been simply dispensed with.[24]

At the substantive level, the rational-choice specification of what counts as a religious good is heavily doctrinal, cognitive, and weighted toward specific evangelical Protestant religious beliefs (see Stark and Finke 2000). This is a problem for a theory that seeks a general explanation for the link between religious preferences and behaviors, and a more serious problem if different kinds of religious preferences predispose people to behave differently toward religious organizational participation.[25] Likewise, the theory's understanding of strictness, part of what makes a church "in tension" with society, is heavily weighted toward the kinds of demands that conservative Protestant churches make on their members—lots of time spent at church, tight social and friendship connections with fellow conservative Christians, and agreement with a conservative political and social stance on particular lifestyle issues (e.g., views on abortion, homosexuality, lipstick, and dancing).

Thus, a liberal Christian who believes there are multiple paths to salvation and that her religious calling is to exhibit Christ's love on earth does not just have different beliefs, according to this approach, but is actually less religious than a fundamentalist Protestant who believes he is on the only path to salvation. A Baptist church that views homosexuality as a sin is clearly in "tension" with mainstream middle-class values of tolerance and the increasingly widespread view that a wide range of sexual preferences ought to be tolerated. But a liberal United Methodist Church (UMC) congregation that advocates homosexual marriage and whose pastor herself conducts joining ceremonies for gay and lesbian couples is also clearly in tension with the larger society, which, although willing to protect the civil liberties of homosexual persons, draws a sharp line at endorsing same-sex marriage. In this example, a rational-choice account would define the conservative church (in a higher-commitment tradition) as being more in tension with society by definition. So it would provide no way to think about the "tension" with society in the UMC church.

In contrast, an institutional approach to culture provides a language through which to theorize the nature, causes, and effects of social and cultural embeddedness on social action.[26] The agents of institutional theory are not the rational actors of market approaches. When faced with a decision, the institutional actor may not deploy the response likely to generate the greatest benefit for the smallest cost, but may rather deploy the response that is best known, most familiar, or most likely to please powerful outsiders. An institutional approach leaves open the possibility that agents may choose to engage in value-rational action, or action to pursue ends defined as right or good for their own sake.[27] An institutional approach also makes a place for an everyday, present-rooted mode of "practical evaluative action" in which social actors may employ new ideas or new routines of practice to solve immediate problems without any attention to long-term consequences. Because of this, institutional theory does not frame a decision not to adapt as a failure of rationality. Thus, it provides a way to account for a decision by a religious leader to risk a loss of membership or money—a decline in market share—in order to preserve something deemed more valuable, such as social justice, doctrinal orthodoxy, or ritual tradition.

Institutional approaches also provide a way to think about the source of stable religious preferences and the content of preferences, another aspect of embeddedness. Institutional theories make a place for agents pursuing their interests, while explicitly theorizing the social and cultural mechanisms that lead to a nonrandom (institutionalized) pattern of preferences and interests in a society at a given time. Why are preferences organized along a liberal-conservative continuum, and why are beliefs about gender and the family so central a cultural distinction between religious traditions? These are "givens" in religious economy approaches. Institutional accounts can explain how anchoring models, such as particular models of the family, come to organize activity in a variety of institutional realms that depend on the family for resources (money and membership) and play a central role in family formation and socialization.[28]

Substantively, I will argue that an institutional framework is the best way to explain the pattern of findings in the four upstate New York communities that I studied in the course of this research. For one thing, most of the congregations in these communities are still using the "standard package" of family ministry developed in the 1950s as the basis for their weekly ministry. Most innovations take the form of one or two minor additions to this standard package. For example, single mothers will be individually encouraged to attend the "regular" mothers' group, or newly divorced members will be invited to the singles' outings. Rather than the rapid and responsive adaptation predicted by market theories, the norm in these communities is a more gradual and incremental form of adaptation based on previously institutionalized organizational routines and programming packages. An institutional approach also explains why innovations on this specific cultural dimension are organized the way they are, by pointing to two broader models of the family that have come to anchor practices across a wide range of social arenas—the family, politics, and voluntary society.

The processes and mechanisms through which innovations develop and spread are best accounted for by a cultural-institutional approach. The combination of family rhetoric, programming, and ministry practices varies according to the congregation's religious tradition—incremental adaptations come in packages, and flow along institutional channels. In addition to an evangelical family orientation, there are distinct liberal Protestant and Catholic patterns of response to change in work and family. Daycare centers are a liberal Protestant innovation; Catholics have taken the lead in ministering to blended families and the children of divorced parents; evangelical congregations do the most to be supportive of single mothers. This supports the idea that innovations do not occur in response to local market demand but are generated within and flow along institutional structures such as seminary training programs and pastors' networks.

Some adaptations are clearly undertaken and pursued regardless of market effectiveness. Some liberal Protestant pastors reject the term *family ministry* entirely and talk about "community," because they feel that the traditional congregational focus on the nuclear family can too easily be interpreted as antifeminist and antihomosexual and because it leaves out the increasing numbers of single adults and single-parent families. Most have found this a somewhat unpopular stand to take; it is a position of principle, not a marketing strategy, and it has cost some congregations members.

Some incremental adaptation is clearly organized, though, by a market logic. Quite a few pastors are employing a discourse of competition and marketing in describing their attempts to adapt to changes in work and family, especially in talking about innovations in the time and timing of ministries and programs, something that is not an ideologically sensitive issue. More than 45 percent of pastors report that their congregations have experimented with the timing of ministries in an attempt to draw in more members or to be more responsive to current members' needs. This is clearly an area where social action is organized in an entrepreneurial way and a market logic is present.

Many of the churches that have innovated in time and timing, that organize their programs in a flexible way, are conservative Protestant, although Catholic parishes have also been very flexible and adaptive on timing. These churches also tend to offer programming for divorced and single-parent members and make other innovations, such as moving programs off-site to members' homes. Relevant programming organized around members' lives and schedules brings in members. This kind of adaptability is associated with growth in a way that is directly related to members' demand for programming that is relevant, fits in with their time schedules, and supports their work-family lifestyles. Women, in particular, are highly critical of churches that making programming hard to fit with contemporary work-family lifestyles, and they often "vote with their feet" in these communities, seeking out churches that are more responsive.

In addition to churches that adapt incrementally, there are several "innovator" congregations in these four communities that have deployed multiple new forms of family ministry across issue areas. They are all very large congregations with a thriving, younger membership. In-depth interviews with pastors and leaders and fieldwork in several innovator congregations suggest that the professional staff and material resources of innovator congregations are what allowed them to innovate in the first place. Staff and money mean that someone has the time to research new ideas and that the congregation can afford to try out new ideas, see them fail, and then try something else. Professionalization and a ministry based on paid staff do not have to lead to the "out of touch" churches that Stark and Finke (2000) predict, but can allow churches to take risks and become leaders. Innovators do grow after they innovate, but they start from a resource-rich base to begin with.

Innovators tend to be large and prosperous, and most of them are either liberal or moderate mainline Protestant churches or Catholic parishes, although a few are conservative Protestant. Innovators tend to hold a strong position on family ideology, while offering lots of programs that facilitate in a practical way the various work-family lifestyles of their members. An independent Baptist innovator has programs for single parents, for divorced members, for those struggling with substance abuse. It organizes all its age-graded programming into one big "Family Night" at church, reducing weekly trips to church for busy dual-earner families. It also endorses a biblically based, neopatriarchal family as the ideal family. A United Church of Christ (UCC) innovator has daycare for members and babysitting during all its meetings and activities, and holds parenting classes for parents on Sunday while the kids are in religious education. It also endorses same-sex unions and the pastor preaches that being a family is based on the content of relationships among members (love, nurturing, support) instead of any particular family form.

This would tend to suggest that having a distinctive religious content that provides members with a meaningful expression of their own religious values, while being flexible and adaptable on practical matters—such as the timing and organization of activities—is associated with growth and vitality in these communities. Uniquely meaningful religious experiences, from this theoretical perspective, can be found in all groups, not just conservative ones. And distinctiveness may be achieved along multiple dimensions.[29] Conservative churches that demand a lot of members' time can thrive, and liberal churches that are organized around members who write checks to pay professional staff can also thrive. Each thrives if it has a strong and coherent religious rationale for its ministry that means that the congregation becomes a uniquely valued aspect of members' lives.

This argument is in some ways similar to Finke's (2004) argument that innovations that respond to contemporary contextual needs while preserving core aspects of the religious tradition lead to vitality and growth, an argument that draws on aspects of rational-choice theory while referring to insights from institutional analyses of organizations and cultural accounts of the roots of religious identity and commitment. But our arguments make different assumptions about the nature of individual commitment, the dimensions of religious authenticity, the sources of innovative ideas, and the possibilities and consequences of value-rational and pragmatic-rational action. For example, I find that features of liberal church organization that rational-choice approaches assume will be automatically bad for growth (professional staff, large size), leading to complacency or to ideological rigidity, can instead lead to innovation. These are resources that agents can harness in the service of new cultural templates for organizing ministry. Innovation can not only occur through entrepreneurs, but can also flow through standard institutional channels—seminaries, in this case, which train the highly educated pastors of liberal innovator churches and parishes.

To summarize, an institutional account allows me to designate the institutional template of family ministry—the standard package—that still organizes much of the ministry practice in these communities. It provides a language for linking the content of specific innovations in ministry to different family schemas. It allows me to identify the institutional mechanisms through which particular kinds of innovations come about, and explain why innovations tend to come in particular bundles of practices. It locates the sources of growth and vitality not in a conservative religious subculture but in a distinctive and compelling religious message, and identifies how particular features of liberal religious denominations—such as their professionalized clergy and bureaucratic structure—can serve both as sources of resistance to change and as resources to bring about change, depending upon the agency of local religious leaders. And it provides a framework that can identify which portions of the field look like a market, which ones are bureaucratic and routine-based, and which ones are organized around value-rational action, offering a more complete account of the way that social action is structured. This means that this approach provides a robust framework for examining the effects of changes in work and family life on the religious ecology of these four communities.

Substance of Change: Secularization versus Evolving Orthodoxy

Rational-choice and institutional-cultural theories speak mainly to how change comes about and do not assume an underlying trend toward secularization over time. There are many different versions of secularization theory, but they all have in common the idea that modernization undermines traditional religious authority.[30] This decline of authority can exist at all levels of analysis. Secularization may mean that political leaders and institutions are less influenced by religious groups and leaders, that religiously based prohibitions on the sale of alcohol on Sundays are lifted, or that individuals increasingly live their lives and make decisions without following the advice of religious leaders or the prescriptions of religious doctrines. It may also mean that religious leaders change what they teach over time, bringing faith traditions into line with modern or progressive attitudes and beliefs and eschewing a more orthodox view of correct religious doctrine or practice.[31]

Some have argued, however, that taking a particular historical position as "orthodox" and interpreting any change from this position to be a "decline of religious authority" imposes a teleology on historical changes that may not, in fact, be unidirectional.[32] In other words, not all religious change automatically signals a decline in religious authority. Theoretically, there can be changes that indicate a resacralization of social life. There can also be changes in which any kind of directionality (more or less secularization) is more difficult to discern.

From this perspective, those who argue that any particular change equals "modernization" and therefore "secularization" need to be able to defend their argument by demonstrating that the content of change amounts to a more "modern" outcome by some a priori criterion with which most scholars would agree. For example, a congregation changing its ministry to accommodate two-career couples is only modernization—or secularization—if a nineteenth-century understanding of appropriate gender roles is designated as "traditional" or "orthodox." Because the male-breadwinner family is itself a modern artifact of the industrial revolution, this chain of reasoning seems much less convincing.[33] So, congregations that adapt to a dual-earner lifestyle may be more *contemporary* but they are not necessarily more *modern* or more *secular*.

Drawing on Bourdieu (1977), Kurtz (1986) offers an alternative framework with which to understand changes in religious authority that avoids the teleology of decline embedded in secularization theory. Rather than positing religious orthodoxy as a "pure" or "traditional" state from which all change must be understood as secularization, religious orthodoxy is understood to be in all situations historically constructed and defined in relation to a heterodox alternative. In the political struggle between those defending an orthodox position on any given issue and their heterodox challengers, the orthodoxy is itself changed, incorporating some of the positions taken by its heterodox critics.[34] Orthodoxy, then, is best understood as an official interpretation of religious truth that is always evolving and changing as particular actors seek to influence it according to their own socially located experiences and understandings of the world.[35]

The main advantage of an "evolving orthodoxy" view is that it provides a theoretical language for talking about religious institutional change as a continuous historical process without imposing a teleology of decline and loss. The content or direction of change—what it all adds up to—is left open, and the question of secularization then becomes an empirical one. So, if religious institutions have adapted to changes in work and family, an evolving orthodoxy approach does not assume such adaptation signals accommodation to modernity or the secularization of religious authority. Rather, one would have to specify the results of the changes in order to understand if they resulted in religious institutions that exercised less authority in some area of life than was previously the case.

However, to be useful at a congregational level of analysis, the idea of evolving orthodoxy must be modified in two ways. First, a focus on religious elites and leaders must be balanced by a focus on the role of lay leadership in the dispersed authority structures typical of de facto congregationalism. Second, a focus on right doctrine (orthodoxy) must be supplemented by a focus on right practice (orthopraxy). Local congregations are practical arenas of ministry, care, education, and worship, where a kind of pragmatic "golden rule" Christianity is lived that may stand in a somewhat orthogonal relationship to official doctrine.[36] Family ideology, at the local level, is produced, reproduced, and changed as much by the practical organization of daily ministry as by rhetoric, symbol, and ritual.

I will argue that an evolving orthodoxy framework is a better explanation for the religious institutional changes that I observed in the four communities in which I conducted research for the Religion and Family Project. In the vast majority of congregations, an intact nuclear family is still not only the ideal but also the unit around which congregational ministries and practices are organized. There is little formal or informal acknowledgment of gay and lesbian members in these congregations, all of it located among a few liberal Protestant churches. Ministry to single parents exists, but is mostly being carried out through more traditional programs such as mothers' groups. In short, there is no decisive movement to a more modern understanding of "the family" in local congregational life among most congregations. And many changes—having babysitting during Sunday worship, holding parenting classes, providing referrals for substance abuse or domestic violence counseling—simply do not seem to reflect a "modernization/traditionalism" dynamic.

Regarding individual religious commitment, in chapter 4 I argue that there are two different religious involvement schemas held by individuals in these communities: a self-oriented schema and a family-oriented schema. Some have argued that self-oriented modes of commitment have become more prevalent since the 1950s and that this is evidence of ongoing secularization. But, as I argue in chapter 1, there is quite a bit of evidence that the religious attachment style of the 1950s was itself highly individualistic, driven by the desire to construct a particular kind of work-family lifestyle in the growing postwar suburbs—an achieved community to replace the ascriptive ties of kin and neighborhood left behind in older urban neighborhoods and small towns. It makes more sense to see both family-oriented and self-oriented religious involvement schemas as stemming from individual lifestyle preferences, so it makes little sense to designate a family-oriented schema as more religious and a self-oriented schema as more secular. This is especially the case when a self-oriented schema focuses on the development of the individual's own faith while a family-oriented schema focuses heavily on the secondary or nonreligious aspects of religious participation. An evolving orthodoxy approach is the best framework for understanding the transformation in individuals' religious commitment over time.

Conclusion

What is gained by a cultural and institutional approach to understanding social action and social change in the religion field? This approach highlights the
alternative frameworks that people use to interpret the relevance of religious
involvement for their own lives, changing the way we think about the effects of
marriage, children, social establishment, and gender on religious involvement.
This reintroduces the analysis of reflexive agency into a field dominated by a
structuralist perspective. The next two chapters examine the structural relationships among family formation, family disruption, work, and religious involvement and also outline how people's interpretive frameworks—what I call
religious involvement schemas—influence both the meaning of religious involvement and the relationship between structural location and patterns of
involvement.

In chapters 5 and 6, I analyze how the religious ecology in these four communities is organized around two very different models of the family, which
serve as anchoring cultural forms organizing both the discourse and the practice
of congregational life. This provides a more robust way to analyze innovation
and adaptation to social change at the congregational level than rational-choice
accounts provide. And it provides a way to analyze where and how a market
logic, a bureaucratic logic, and a value-rational logic influence the development of family ideology at the local level of religious life.

This analysis also begins to provide a language for understanding cultural
and institutional change in the field that is not locked into a teleology of
modernization, secularization, and decline. In doing so, it provides a more interesting way to think about the family ideology produced in local religious
communities. At the local level, family ideology is influenced not only by religious doctrine and elite discourse, but also by popular discourses about time
and work-family management and by assumptions about the family rooted in
middle- class professional lifestyles. The organization of social inclusion and
exclusion in local congregations does operate in part along lines of family
form and work-family lifestyle, with boundaries drawn in both rhetoric and
practice around "the good family" that reproduce taken-for-granted understandings of gender, family, and social class.

Chapter Three

RELIGION, FAMILY, AND WORK

GETTING MARRIED and having children have been strongly and consistently associated with increased religious involvement in our society.[1] But we know little about whether the *kind of family being formed* matters; for example, are there differences between male-breadwinner and dual-earner families, or first-marriage families and blended families, or middle-class and working-class families? Likewise, we know little about the religious involvement of those who do not follow the traditional life-course path—forming an early and lasting marriage that produces children and takes place in the context of secure employment and financial stability. The religious involvement of single parents, long-term singles, or those in childless couples has remained virtually unexplored.

Religious involvement, in the scholarly literature on religion and family, has been measured primarily, and often solely, by an individual's own church attendance and religious salience (the importance of religion in one's own life). As a result, we know little about other aspects of religious involvement such as participation in a broader range of congregational activities or other religious groups, or whether individuals attend church alone or with other family members. The meaning of religious involvement and the mechanisms that link family formation to involvement in a local congregation have been assumed to be relatively straightforward and shared by men and women across lines of race and social class, assumptions that seem doubtful given the voluntary and expressive nature of religious involvement in the United States. And we know little about the reciprocal question of how involvement in a local congregation shapes the way that individuals behave toward family members, how they choose to invest time in family caretaking or paid work, or feelings of commitment toward family or work.

This chapter explores three central themes. First, I examine the patterns of religious involvement for married couples with and without children, moving beyond a focus on individual church attendance to consider involvement in other church-related activities and other religious organizations for all family members. This section of the chapter draws on qualitative and quantitative data and begins to explore why involvement in a local congregation means different things to men and women and to those from different social class locations. The second part of the chapter describes the religious involvement of those who do not fit the "Ozzie and Harriet" family—single parents, the divorced, and those in blended families. The third part of the chapter explores how involvement in a local congregation changes the way that men and women participate in and feel about the activities of paid work (providing for the family) and domestic work (caring for the family).

In the conclusion, I outline the links between religion and family in these four communities. It is clear that family formation still leads to religious involvement for many individuals, and this is true for single parents as well as married parents. For many men, family formation is linked to religious involvement in the straightforward way predicted by the structural location theories described in the last chapter. However, for many women, most of the effects of family formation on involvement are dependent on their own attitudes toward and beliefs about religious institutions. Structural location theories work less well to explain women's religious involvement because women have a more expressive orientation toward religious institutions.[2] There are also gender differences in the impact that religious involvement has on family life, including men's and women's willingness to engage in helping and caring behaviors and in their decisions about managing work and family. Finally, the links between family formation and religious involvement seem to be attenuated for those who are not middle-class, those with a high school education or less who have trouble finding stable employment or who work in low-wage, low-benefit farming or service-sector jobs. These findings help us to understand how religious involvement fits into the lives of those in a variety of work and family contexts after a period of remarkable social change.

Family Formation and Religious Involvement

In many ways, what I found in these upstate New York communities supports the conventional wisdom that forming a family leads to increased religious involvement. Men and women who are part of nuclear families that consist of a wife, husband, and children are the most likely to attend church, to be involved in congregational ministries, and to be involved in other religious groups. However, several patterns exist in these communities that illuminate the relationship between family formation and religious involvement in new ways. First, *family formation* is too broad a term to capture the differences in religious involvement between married couples with children and those without children. Second, a focus on individual church attendance has masked the fact that marriage and children tend to lead to the involvement of all family members—both spouses and children if they are present—in a local congregation. Third, men and women tell different stories about the meaning of religious involvement in their own lives and think and talk differently about the relationship between their religious involvement and their family commitments. And fourth, the link between family formation and religious involvement is weaker and more tenuous for those who are not middle-class managers and professionals.

TABLE 3.1
Religious Involvement by Family Household Type (Percentages)

	Singles	Single Parents, Children at Home	Married, No Children at Home	Married, Children Less than 6 Years Old[a] at Home	Married, Children 6–18 Years Old at Home
Attends church *monthly or more*	36	35	50	65	63
Attends church *weekly or more*	26	22	39	41	43
Involved in at least one organized congregational ministry/activity	18	42	34	60	53
Respondent involved in at least one organized congregational activity and so is at least one of respondent's children	7	26	8	26	32
Involved in other religious organization[b]	13	14	12	33	27
Religion "very important"	46	41	53	45	52
High involvement— religion "very important" and attends church monthly or more	27	24	38	42	45

Source: Religion and Family Project, Resident Survey (N = 1,006, weighted N = 1,082), Penny Edgell Becker, PI, 1998

Notes: [a] The age of the child in this table refers to the youngest child; a household with both preschool and school-age children is assigned to the "married, children less than 6 years old" category.

[b] Actively involved in or volunteers for a religious group or organization besides a local congregation; examples include Promise Keepers, Knights of Labor, Loaves and Fishes or some other local food pantry, and prayer groups or Bible studies not through one's own church.

Drawing on data from a telephone survey of community residents, table 3.1 compares how single adults, single parents, married couples with no children, and married couples with children are involved in local congregations. Notably, the percentage of community residents who say that religion is "very important" to them is high across the board, with something of an exception for single parents. This suggests that much of the variation in religious involvement is

TABLE 3.2
Family Church Attendance (Percentages)

	Singles	Single Parent, Children Live at Home	Married, No Children	Married, Children Less than 6 Years Old at Home	Married, Children 6–18 Years Old at Home
Church Attenders (N = 544)					
Attends alone	52[a]	12	14	11	4
Attends with spouse/partner only	—	—	70	1	13
Attends with children only	—	64	—	22	16
Attend with spouse and children	—	—	—	67	67
Those who do not attend church (N=353)					
Spouse attends alone	—	—	14	—	2
Spouse attends with children	—	—	—	4	6
Children attend church without parents	—	32	—	2	11

Source: Religion and Family Project, Resident Survey (N = 1,006, weighted N = 1,082), Penny Edgell Becker, PI, 1998

Note: [a] Many adult singles attend with friends and some attend with their own parents.

due not to differences in subjective religious commitment, but rather to differences in patterns of investment of time and energy in organized religious activities.

People who are part of a married couple with children in the household are the most involved in organized religion. They attend religious services and are involved in the other organized activities associated with congregations, such as Bible studies, parenting classes, men's and women's fellowships, or service and outreach activities. They are also the most likely to report involvement in other religious groups or activities such as in-home Bible studies, Promise Keepers meetings, or volunteering for the food pantry.

For married couples with children, religious involvement tends to encompass the whole family. Table 3.2 shows that two-thirds (67 percent) of respondents who attend church and have a spouse and children report that everyone—parents and children—attends together. And more than nine out of ten people in married couples with children attend with at least one other family member; very few attend church alone.[3] The children in these families are also involved, not only going to church services but attending Sunday School, Youth Group, or Scout troops sponsored by the congregation.

Next to married parents, married people without children[4] are the most likely to attend church. However, they are less likely than those with children to be involved in other congregational activities or to be involved in another religious group in the community. Half (50 percent) of those who are married but do not have children at home told us that they attend church monthly or more; 39 percent attend weekly or more. The large majority (70 percent) of these married church attenders without children report that they attend regularly with their spouse or partner.

For the married, religious involvement is a couple-level phenomenon, a decision made jointly that assumes mutual commitment, cooperation, and planning.[5] This is borne out by a question that we asked of those respondents who do not attend church regularly. In a series of items exploring people's reasons for not attending church, we included one that said, "I would attend more often, but my wife (husband) is not enthusiastic about it, and that makes it harder." Especially when there are children present, the cooperation of both spouses in getting the family to church seems to make a difference, as shown in box 3.1

Gender, Family Formation, and Religious Involvement

For both men and women, marriage and parenting motivate greater involvement in a local church. But the mechanisms that link family formation to religious involvement are different for men and women, and their involvement means different things.[6] For women, marriage and children increase the subjective importance of religion, and this is what motivates their increased church attendance. As Tracey, a forty-five-year-old mother of two, explained during her interview, having children made her "realize that life was such a miracle. . . . Having children increases your awareness of that." Her feelings of

Box 3.1 Spouse's Attitude about Church	
"I would attend church more often, but my wife (husband) is not enthusiastic about it, and that makes it harder."	
	Percentage Who Agree
Married, no children	17
Married parents	28

awe and transcendence made her return to church after years of absence. Statistical analyses of the survey data from community residents show that Tracey's experience is typical. In multivariate models that control for the effects of multiple predictors of church attendance, use of other ministries, and involvement in other religious organizations, the effects of marriage and children on women's religious involvement disappear when a variable for the importance of religion is included.[7]

Not every woman, of course, finds that marriage or the birth of a child has led to an increased sense of religion's importance. However, once they have children, regardless of the salience or importance of religion in their own lives, mothers tend to seek out congregational ministries for their children. This is especially true for mothers of school-age children. For some women, this is motivated by the desire to pass on the faith tradition in which they themselves were raised; many women told us, "I want my children to grow up Catholic" (or Methodist, or Lutheran) or "I want my children to know the Lord" (in evangelical churches.)

If some mothers care about passing on a religious tradition, the in-depth interviews suggest that other mothers are differently motivated when they involve their children in religious organizations, and particularly in religious education. These women want to equip children to make their own informed decisions about the meaning of religion in their lives. They want to prepare them to choose whether to join a religious community when they become adults. As Cheryl, a married mother of two in her thirties, told us, "I want my children to know about religion, because when they get older, they may want to have that in their lives. Our church has a great religious education program, and they learn about other religions, too. So they'll be ready, when they're older, to know what they want, to choose what they want."

For men in these communities, becoming a husband or a father increases the likelihood of joining a congregation, attending a local Bible Study, or volunteering for a religious organization. And this is especially true for fathering. But this is not because marriage and parenting make religion more important to men. Our telephone survey shows that men report no increase in religious salience once they are married, and multivariate models that predict religious salience find no effects of marriage and fathering for men. Compared with women, men's religious involvement is less dependent on subjective feelings of religious importance or religious salience.

Our in-depth interviews suggest that, for men, religious involvement flows out of an understanding of what is an appropriate expression of the social roles of "husband" and "father." Men told us that going to church is a way to become established in the community, something that mattered more to them after they got married and started to "settle down." They said that congregations provide opportunities for them to spend time with their families and especially their children, opportunities that are familiar, comfortable, and wholesome.

They told us about the importance of their parenting group or men's group or individual male friends at church in providing support and encouragement for their desire to construct a life centered around marriage and parenting instead of putting so much emphasis on getting ahead at work. Many of them said that their congregations were the only places they found such support or where they could talk with sympathetic male friends about what it means to be a husband or a father.[8]

Social Class and Religious Involvement

Two of the communities I studied—Liverpool and Tompkins County—contain high proportions of middle-class managers and professionals. But Seneca County and Northside are communities filled with working-class and working-poor residents, those who have trouble finding stable employment, who are in low-paying service-sector or agricultural jobs, or who piece together two or three jobs to make ends meet.[9] In multivariate analyses, social class proves to be an independent predictor of religious involvement in these communities; those who have a college degree or more are more likely to attend religious services, and women with at least a college degree are also more likely to be involved in other church ministries and other religious organizations in the community.[10]

Not only does church attendance vary by social class in these communities, but social class mediates the effect of family formation on involvement; the effect of being married or having a child on church attendance depends in part on how much education a person has. Among married men with children, those who have at least a college degree are 25 percent more likely to attend church regularly than are those with a high school degree or less. Among married women with children, those with a college degree or more are 15 percent more likely to attend than are married mothers with a high school degree or less (see box 3.2). These differences in religious involvement associated with social class are not due to differences in religious salience, age, or religious identity.

In-depth interviews suggest that there are at least two barriers associated with social class that keep those with a high school degree or less from becoming more involved in local religious communities. The first is a time-bind effect. This is not the kind of time bind associated with a high-powered dual-career lifestyle that has received so much attention in the popular press and academic literature. Rather, this is the time bind of families with one or both parents working two or more low-paying jobs with inadequate benefits, often with a substantial commute. In such families, Sunday morning may be spent in a paid job or on household tasks or errands that cannot be completed any other time, or it may be the only true time of rest in any given week.

The second kind of barrier has more to do with the middle-class culture that many working-class and working-poor residents associate with local churches,

	Box 3.2 Education and Church Attendance (Monthly or More)	
	Percentage with High School Degree or Less Who Attend Church	*Percentage with College Degree or More Who Attend Church*
Married men with children	43	68
Married women with children	57	72

and perceptions of churches as therefore being irrelevant, unwelcoming, or a poor fit. In our in-depth interviews with those who do not attend church, we asked this question: "Think for a moment about the typical churchgoer. What image does that bring up for you? What kind of person do you associate with church membership?" Those with a high school degree or less were far more likely to tell us that churchgoers were "stuck up," "hypocrites," or "think they're better than everybody else." They associated churches with conformity ("I don't want anybody telling me what to think") and with traditional stands on women's roles—which they tend to see as discrimination.

John, a man in early sixties who is retired and living largely on Social Security disability payments, was fairly typical of this group. I asked John to give me his impression of "a typical churchgoer," and he replied: "There are two people. One is just your average person, he believes what he believes and keeps it to himself. Then there are these people, they think they are better than everyone else and if you do not believe what they believe you are wrong." He went on to say that churches were not particularly open-minded or welcoming, and that: "I have my own beliefs on women which may be different from what churches believe. The Catholic Church wants women to lie back and not try and take control, the Mormons too. And other groups, too. . . . That's why I don't like them. And it is not just churches. Women are discriminated against everywhere. But the churches do discriminate."

These negative perceptions of church and churchgoers persist even among those who told us that religion is important to them, that they still care about and identify with the religion they were raised in, and that they pray and read the Bible on a regular basis. This relationship between family formation, education, and religious involvement suggests that religious institutions foster a particular kind of middle-class family-oriented lifestyle, something that sociologists at the time pointed out about the post–World War II religious expansion.[11]

To answer a question raised at the beginning of this chapter, what kind of family one forms does matter for understanding patterns of religious involvement. As chapter 5 will show, the rhetoric about family life and what a "good family" looks like in local congregations in these four communities takes many features of a middle-class way of life for granted, including the time demands of a professional or managerial job and the tradeoffs faced by well-off dual-earner families.[12] Even church leaders who are aware that many local families worry about how to put food on the table instead of whether to enroll their child in soccer or band told us that they were at a loss for practical ideas of how to welcome and meet the needs of the poorer and less economically stable residents of their communities. As a result, most of the families involved in the communities' congregations are middle-class families.

NOT OZZIE AND HARRIET: ALTERNATIVE FAMILIES AND COMPLICATED LIFE COURSES

Rising rates of divorce mean that for more and more Americans, families form, are disrupted, and form again. Many couples cohabit either as a precursor to marriage or in lieu of marriage. How do these patterns affect contemporary religious involvement? Table 3.3 suggests that the type of long-term committed relationship one is in matters for religious involvement. Those who are cohabiting[13] are markedly less involved than those who are married and, on several measures, less involved than those who live alone and have never married.

One of the biggest changes in family life over the last forty years is the increasing number of Americans who experience family disruption and formation periodically over the course of their adult lives. The survey of community residents along with in-depth interviews suggests that family disruption leads people to a renewed sense of the importance of religion in their lives. This is underscored by the high rates of religious salience reported by both men and women who are divorced, separated, or in second (or higher) marriages (table 3.3). The process of undergoing a divorce or separation may have become more routine in our society, but it is still a time of heightened emotion and, as our interviews suggest, raises a wide range of questions about the meaning, purpose, and direction of people's lives, questions that religion is uniquely suited to address.[14]

Women, more than men, are likely to couple this increased religious salience with involvement in local religious communities. Among women, 52 percent of the divorced and 62 percent of the separated report regular church attendance; among men, the figures are 46 percent and 42 percent. These gender differences are even more striking for use of other congregational ministries and involvement in other religious groups or organizations; for men, divorce and separation lead to a marked attenuation of these other forms of religious

TABLE 3.3

Family Disruption, Recombination, and Religious Involvement (Percentages)

Women	Never Married	First Marriage	Married, Not First Marriage	Cohabiting	Divorced	Separated	Widowed
Attends church monthly or more	38	59	51	20	52	62	28
Attends church weekly or more	24	43	41	18	32	44	17
Religion "very important"	35	51	70	26	52	56	72
High involvement—religion "very important" and attends church monthly or more	27	42	49	21	38	53	21
Involved in at least one organized congregational ministry/activity	18	50	42	20	46	63	16
Involved in other religious group/organization	10	24	9	4	14	53	32

Men	Never Married	First Marriage	Married, Not First Marriage	Cohabiting	Divorced	Separated	Widowed
Attends church monthly or more	29	61	43	29	46	42	8
Attends church weekly or more	24	40	33	18	23	25	8
Religion "very important"	40	44	56	53	52	46	69
High involvement—religion "very important" and attends church monthly or more	27	40	33	29	32	17	8
Involved in at least one organized congregational ministry/activity	19	44	30	29	20	18	8
Involved in other religious group/organization	14	23	15	24	8	—	—

Source: Religion and Family Project, Resident Survey (N = 1,006, weighted N = 1,082), Penny Edgell Becker, PI, 1998.

involvement, whereas for women, these forms of religious involvement increase. For women, family transitions—whether getting married, having a child, or undergoing a divorce—make religion more important, and this leads them to seek out religious community. For men, the transition into a nuclear family leads to religious involvement understood as appropriate to their family roles; when those roles end, more men leave religious communities, regardless of the increased importance religion may have taken on for them subjectively.

High rates of divorce and remarriage mean that many find themselves living in a "blended" family, with children from a previous marriage in the household. In our survey of community residents, 18 percent of those who are married and have children younger than eighteen at home reported that the children are from a previous marriage. Among these blended families, 51 percent attend church monthly or more, and 47 percent report that they participate in some congregational activity in addition to weekly worship. These figures are somewhat lower than they are for nonblended families. However, 58 percent of those in blended families report that religion is "very important" to them, and 40 percent report "high involvement" (saying that religion is very salient and attending monthly or more).

As with divorce, being in a second marriage has more effects on religious salience—and church attendance—for women than for men. Women who are in a second marriage (or higher) report very high levels of religious salience and high rates of weekly attendance, and are more likely to report that they both attend church regularly and find religion to be "very important" in their lives. The religious involvement they seek is not simply for themselves, but for the family as a whole. They may even switch to a different church in a different religious tradition to achieve all-the-family-together involvement, as did this woman: "I married a non-Catholic, but it meant a lot to me to go to church together. He wasn't comfortable going to a Catholic church. So we looked around, looked at several area churches" (Deb, second marriage/blended family, regular church attender, mid-thirties). The loss of a spouse is also a form of family disruption and a serious life event. Particularly interesting is the disjunction between the importance of religion among the widowed and the levels of involvement in congregations and other organizations. This is likely due to health and mobility issues; the average age of those who are widowed in this sample is sixty-three years. Widows have slightly higher rates of involvement than widowers; whether this is due to women enjoying better health later in life or to their ability to draw on networks of friends and family for transportation and other help is unclear.

The story of single parents' religious involvement is complicated and different than that of other parents. Single parents are no more likely to attend church than are single nonparents. If they do attend church, however, they are as likely as are married people to use the other ministries of the church for themselves, and as likely as other parents to involve their children in church-related

+---+
| Box 3.3 |
| Perceptions of Fit |
+---+
| "If you're not part of a married couple with children, you |
| don't fit in most churches or synagogues" |
| |
| *Percentage Who Agree* |
| |
| Singles   22 |
| |
| Single parents   20 |
| |
| Married, no children   10 |
| |
| Married parents   12 |
+---+

activities. Most of the single parents we interviewed, and those who responded to our telephone survey, were women. The single mothers we spoke to want to involve their children in a congregation so that their children can learn a religious tradition or explore their own beliefs. But this is not something that they can always manage to do.

What keeps single parents out of churches? The survey data suggest that part of the story is that some single parents believe that churches are geared to married parents with children and that they feel uncomfortable as a result. In our survey of community residents, single parents—along with other singles—were twice as likely as married respondents to report feeling that they did not "fit" into most churches or synagogues (see box 3.3).

The constraints of a single-parent lifestyle also influence religious involvement. On our survey, we asked people who do not attend church regularly[15] to tell us if they agreed or disagreed with this statement: "I would attend religious services more often, but it interferes with time I spend with my family." Thirty-eight percent of single parents agreed with this statement, compared with 21 percent of married parents. Even those who do attend worship services often find that participating in other congregational programs or ministries is more difficult. Below is an excerpt from my field notes on my conversation with Diane, a single mother in rural Tompkins County, which gives some details about these kinds of church-family conflicts.[16] Diane and I found it impossible to schedule a face-to-face meeting, given the demands of her schedule, and so we spoke for more than an hour on the telephone one afternoon. Diane mentioned themes that emerged repeatedly in interviews with single parents:

P.E.: Have you ever felt like it was difficult for you to be a part of the parish or participate in the activities because you're a single parent?

D: She gave an immediate and heartfelt "yes." Mostly, for her, it's a matter of time. She works full-time to support herself and the kids, and is going back to school part-time. She would have liked to do more things, she would have liked to sing in the choir, for example . . . but it was just awkward in terms of getting to any kind of regular meeting or practice; maybe she could go one week, but not every week. Her evenings were devoted to the kids, to sports and after-school activities, or to studying. It is hard to fit in evening activities. Working full-time plus overtime plus the kids—it was just hard . . . mostly the scheduling of things, fitting in activities on a regular basis. Life seems chaotic, hit-and-miss, at her house and it's hard to make a regular commitment.

In addition to facing the time bind, single parents also have disputes with their ex-husbands or ex-wives about the children's religious participation. In the survey of community residents, more than 30 percent of single parents agreed with the statement, "I would attend church more often, but my wife (husband) is not enthusiastic about it, and that makes it harder." Although this may at first glance seem odd, the in-depth interviews help to make sense of this statement. Single parents who attend church want to take their children with them and often have no practical choice except to take younger children along. But religious education and church attendance for children are things that many single parents feel they must negotiate with their ex-spouses, and in a relationship that may already be contentious, that negotiation is sometimes difficult and strained.

When these barriers to participation are overcome, single parents tend to use congregations as venues in which to spend time with their children and as places where they can renew their own faith and sense of spiritual connection. Moreover, single parents are likely to find in their congregations networks of support that function in ways that are similar to extended family networks. In our interviews, single parents listed many and various kinds of help that they received from church friends or their pastors. Church-based networks provided father figures for sons whose fathers were not very involved in their lives, were sources of financial help in times of crisis, helped out with sick children or transportation needs, and gave friendship and social support in a life centered largely around children and work.

These findings suggest that the experiences of family disruption and recombination lead, for many people in these communities, to a renewed sense of the importance of religion. Parents in blended families, and especially mothers, are likely to seek out churches that can provide the family with a sense of togetherness, belonging, and moral community. If family disruption does lead to reduced religious involvement, for many this is due to a set of practical difficulties rather than any sense of reduced religious salience. Finding a new church home must be negotiated between two spouses who often have widely divergent religious backgrounds. For single parents, the problem is often a matter of time in a family situation in which one parent carries the roles of two. Men who undergo divorce sometimes feel that they should be the one to leave a particular congregation so their ex-wives can stay, and they are less likely to look for a new religious community than are women.

This suggests that religious communities that provide a welcoming atmosphere and practical support may be able to attract and retain families whose life-course paths are complex and feature episodes of family formation, disruption, and re-formation. The exception to this seems to be those in cohabiting relationships; cohabiting, although a form of long-term commitment, is culturally and institutionally different than marriage and does not provide the same impetus to religious participation.

How Religious Involvement Shapes Family Life

If family transitions affect people's religious involvement, it is also true that religious involvement shapes family life. Religion and family are intertwined and influence one another in multiple ways. How does one fulfill the role of wife or husband, mother or father? How do people make choices about investing time in caring for the family or in a job or a career? Family life requires a great deal of work, and figuring out who is responsible for housework, raising children, taking children to and from activities, paying bills, maintaining a home, and providing for financial needs is more complicated in an era when traditional gender roles have come to be questioned and new forms of family life have displaced a single family ideal.

Most scholars have emphasized the functional nature of religious participation for family relationships and have focused on how such participation increases feelings of satisfaction and happiness in marital and parent-child relationships, influences child-rearing practices, or leads to marital stability.[17] There has been a particular focus on how evangelical women embrace traditionally gendered roles in the family, reducing their participation in the paid labor force to concentrate on the roles of wife and mother.[18]

The in-depth interviews conducted in these upstate New York communities give additional insight into *why* religious involvement influences satisfaction with family life and family relationships. Many of those we spoke with told us that their faith had led them to a more family-oriented lifestyle and influenced their choice to spend less time at work and more time with their children and spouses. They talked about the importance of investing one's time and self in making family relationships better, about becoming better and more involved parents, and about taking more time for both caretaking activities and leisure time spent with family members. Contrary to recent studies that have focused on evangelical Protestants, interviews with residents in these communities reveal that these effects on family life are common across religious faith traditions, especially for men, regardless of what kind of church they attend.

The survey of community residents also provides support for the argument that religious involvement changes the way that people invest their time and themselves in family life. We asked people questions about their involvement in their family's daily lives. These included questions about household tasks such as cleaning, doing laundry, and running errands. We also asked about some caretaking activities—time spent caring for an elderly or sick relative and helping others out with errands or housework or yard work. And we asked about how people manage work and family and whether they have scaled back at work to spend more time with their families. The survey data support the insights from the in-depth interviews. Religious involvement shapes the way people make choices about helping and caring behavior and about work-family management, and these patterns are different for men and women.

Religion and Men's Involvement with Family and Work

The telephone survey contained several measures of caring and helping behavior: caring regularly for an elderly or sick relative, giving informal help to family and neighbors with household tasks or yard work, and time spent on household tasks in one's own home. For men, church attendance increases the likelihood of engaging in some forms of caring and helping behavior. Among men who do not attend church regularly, about 10 percent regularly care for an elderly or sick relative, whereas 22 percent of men who attend church engage in such care.[19] Multivariate statistical analysis shows that this relationship between church attendance and willingness to be a regular caretaker holds across life stage and social status.[20] For men, church attendance also increases the likelihood of giving informal help to family and neighbors with household tasks such as yard work or running errands.[21] However, this is not true for all religious traditions—conservative Protestant men are less likely to spend time on regular caretaking and informal helping behaviors than are other men who attend church.

Managing a home is a lot of work—making meals and doing dishes, doing housework, mowing the lawn, making home repairs, taking the car in for service, running errands. Using items from the community resident survey, I investigated how religious involvement is related to the time one spends in various kinds of household tasks—"female" tasks (laundry, cooking, dishes, cleaning), "male" tasks (yard work, house repair, car repair), and "other" tasks (bill paying, shopping, driving people around). Married men who attend church spend less time on all these tasks compared with married men who are not church attenders. These findings are based on statistical models that control for education, age, marital status, and the presence of children.[22] They are true of all male church attenders regardless of religious tradition. Interestingly, there are no differences between conservative Protestant men and other men in the amount of time spent on housework in general or on "male" versus "female" household tasks.

TABLE 3.4
Men—Average Hours per Week on Household Tasks by Church Attendance

	Less than Once a Month	One to Several Times a Month	Weekly or More
"Female" tasks (cleaning, cooking, dishes, laundry)	11.72	12.21	9.53
"Male" tasks (home/car repair, yard work)	7.64	9.5	6.46
"Other" tasks (shopping, paying bills, driving, errands)	5.88	5.19	4.96

A growing sociological literature argues that the conservative Protestant subculture makes men more involved in their family's lives, and that this is one of the reasons that women find this subculture attractive.[23] The argument goes that despite the traditional gender-role ideology of these churches, the informal subculture counteracts the official ideology by encouraging men to have a nurturing, involved way of interacting with their wives and children. These data suggest, however, that this does not extend to conservative Protestant men spending more time on helping and caretaking behaviors, including household tasks. For men in other religious traditions, however, religious involvement does motivate some forms of helping and caring behavior.

Being involved in a local church also changes the way that men feel about family life. In the survey of community residents, we asked a question that explores satisfaction with family life from a slightly different perspective. Does family life seem draining, tiring, or stressful? Those responding to the survey were asked to listen to five statements and to say how strongly they agreed or disagreed with each one. Responses to the five items were combined into a scale that measures how draining or stressful family life is perceived to be.[24] In these communities, married men were more likely than others to report that their family life is draining. This is less true for men who are regular church attenders than it is for others, but church attendance does not eliminate this "marriage effect" for men. Moreover, for married fathers, church attendance *increases* the likelihood that family life is perceived as draining. Perhaps the increased responsibility for fathering associated with religious involvement is stressful for men, who may have had less experience in these behaviors or encouragement from other sources to undertake them.

What about making choices about how to divide one's time between work and family? The traditional division of labor in a marriage leaves the majority of the family caretaking to the wife and assigns the husband the role of provider. But one of the most fundamental changes in family life has been the rise of the dual-earner couple. Most women, even mothers of young children, work for pay. Old routines of work-family management no longer work, but couples, workplaces, and the community institutions have been slow to react.[25] Although work-family management is often thought of as a "woman's issue," increasing numbers of men are facing choices about how much to invest in paid work and how to carve out more time to spend with their families. Religious communities provide a moral framework for these choices, one that privileges the centrality of the family and provides a critique of careerism and consumerism, and one that has, for most of this century, endorsed a relatively traditional division of labor between men and women.[26]

In these four communities, work, family, and religion fit together well in men's lives, supporting one another and not leading to feelings of conflict or stress. For example, men who work full-time are more likely to go to church and be involved in other congregational ministries. This is also true of men who work overtime; men who work long hours (41–49 hours a week) or very long hours (50+ hours a week) are the most likely to report that they make sure that their children take part in church programs and ministries such as religious education or recreational activities. Often, these men participate with their children, using these ministries as opportunities for "family time." Twenty-six percent of men who work 35–40 hours a week have children who are involved in at least one church ministry on a regular basis, while 41 percent of men who work 41–49 hours a week have children involved in a church ministry. Our in-depth interviews include many stories from men for whom church-related youth activities—Scouting, Youth Group, Sunday School, service projects, choirs, and other activities—have provided a very important and stable context in which they spent time with their children.

Men who attend church are also less likely to report that they feel caught up in the "time bind." Married men who do not attend church are more likely than other men to report that their work is keeping them from spending enough time on other things—family, community, and time to themselves. However, married men who attend church are less likely to report that their work interferes with the time they spend on themselves, in community involvement, or with their families; these effects are even larger for conservative Protestant men.[27] This may be partly due to the fact that married men who attend church, particularly fathers, have another venue for family-oriented activity.

It may also be that men report less work-family conflict when they are regular church attenders because church attendance makes men more likely to reduce or restructure the time they spend at work to increase their time with the family. In our community resident survey, we asked the following question about scaling back: "Over the last two years, have family considerations prompted you to scale down on your work, for example, turn down a promotion, turn down a job with more travel, cut back on your work hours, scale back expectations for advancement or promotion at work, or use flextime, family leave, or some other 'family friendly' policy?" This is a broad measure that captures most of the scaling back activities studied by family researchers.

In statistical models that control for age, education, marital status, and the presence of children in the home, church attendance is a strong and stable predictor of men's scaling back behavior.[28] Men's scaling back is also strongly influenced by the presence of children in the home; men with preschool children have odds of scaling back that are five times higher than those for other men. Church attendance and high religious salience also increase the odds of men scaling back at work. And the effects of having children and of religious involvement on men's scaling back are not independent. *Men with preschool children who also attend church exhibit a more than twelvefold increase in the odds of scaling back at work to spend more time with their families. For school-age children (6–18), there is almost an eightfold increase in the odds of men scaling back.* Twenty-four percent of men who attend church infrequently (less than once a month) reported scaling back on our survey, whereas 42 percent of those attending monthly and 47 percent of those attending weekly or more reported scaling back.

Overall, these findings suggest that for men, involvement in a local church influences the way they feel about work and family and some of their decisions about investing time with their families. Male church attenders are less likely to report that work keeps them from their families. In general, men who attend church regularly engage in more caretaking behaviors, although this is not true for conservative Protestant men. Religious involvement seems to have a particular impact on fathering—fathers who go to church are more likely to scale back at work to spend more time with family, and they are more likely to have their children involved in church-related activities and to be involved with them, helping out with the Youth Group, Youth Choir, Scouting, or similar activities. However, men who go to church do not increase the amount of time they spend on housework, yard work, and running errands as much as other married men do.

It may be that male church attenders view the time they spend in church, and particularly the time they spend with their children in church-related activities, as part of their contribution to "family time." In general, it seems that for men, work and family and religion fit together well and reinforce each other, instead of being a source of strain or stress. The exception to this pattern, as discussed above, is related to social class; those with a high school degree or less are less involved in religious organizations regardless of family status, and tend to feel a kind of time pressure that cannot be managed by "scaling back" at work because they are in economic conditions that do not make scaling back feasible or in jobs where they do not have that kind of autonomy.

Religion and Women's Involvement in Family and Work

Caring for loved ones has traditionally been the heart of "women's work" in the family. In contrast to the findings for men, for women religious involvement is not as related to measures of caring and helping behavior. For example,

TABLE 3.5
Women—Average Hours per Week on Household Tasks by Church Attendance

	Less than Once a Month	One to Several Times a Month	Weekly or More
"Female" tasks (cleaning, cooking, dishes, laundry)	20.55	20.47	23.19
"Male" tasks (home/car repair, yard work)	5.96	5.53	7.18
"Other" tasks (shopping, paying bills, driving, errands)	4.82	3.33	4.64

church attendance is completely unrelated to women caring for an elderly or sick relative. However, religious identity does matter; Catholic women are more likely to be regular caretakers than are other women in these communities.[29] Church attendance is related to women giving informal help to family and neighbors with household tasks—60 percent of women who attend church regularly do this, compared with 49 percent of those who do not attend church regularly.[30]

Church attendance is also related to women's time spent on tasks within their own households (see table 3.5). Multivariate statistical models show the impact of religious involvement on women's household tasks.[31] For "female" tasks, the church attendance effect disappears in models that include religious identity; Catholic women spend more time on these tasks than other women. For "male" tasks, married women spend less time than unmarried women; however, married women who attend church spend more time on these tasks than do other married women. For "other" tasks, such as shopping, paying bills, and running errands, married women tend to do more than unmarried women; however, church attendance reduces the amount of time married women spend on these tasks. Considering that women who attend church do more housework while men who attend church do less, and that most married couples attend church together, it is interesting that women who attend church are *more* likely to report that household tasks are fairly divided (48 percent of women who attend weekly or more report household tasks are divided up "very fairly" compared with 36 percent of nonattenders).

In contrast with men, the amount of time women spend on all domestic tasks is responsive to their work environment; women who work longer hours for pay spend less time on "female" tasks and less time on "other" tasks such as shopping and running errands. Women who are managers and professionals spend less time on both "female" and "male" tasks than other women, possibly because they are also more likely to report that they hire help with household tasks than other women (40 percent do, versus 31 percent of women employed in other occupations). Using the same family drain scale described above in the discussion for men, women who have children are more likely to report that they find their family life "draining," and so are women who attend church. Interestingly, the longer hours women work outside the home, the less likely they are to report that they find family life draining.

Church attendance is unrelated to whether or not women report a time conflict between work and family unless they have children. In contrast to the findings for men, women with children who attend church are more likely to report that work leaves them too little time to spend with their families, on themselves, and in community involvement. Women who work longer hours also report more time conflict between work and family.[32]

Work can also generate emotional conflicts—feelings of being tired, anxious, or depressed—or emotional benefits such as feeling valued and supported. For women, marriage and having a child increase feelings that work is emotionally draining; however, church attendance reduces these effects. For women who are not married, church attendance is associated with higher levels of emotional "work drain"—it may be that women who find work emotionally draining and have no immediate family support seek such support in church.[33] Conservative Protestant women are also less likely to report that they find work to be emotionally draining.

For women, there is some reduction in church attendance among those working long hours (50+ a week). Women who work full-time are also less likely to attend church than those who work part-time.[34] The number of hours women work outside the home is unrelated to their involvement in other church ministries. The participation of children in church ministries directed to them is also unrelated to the number of hours their mothers work.[35] For women, working longer hours is associated with less frequent attendance at religious services, but it is unrelated to women's commitment to their children's religious participation or to their own participation in more intermittent church-related activities.

Women who go to church are less likely than other women to agree with the statement, "Having a meaningful career is one of the most important things in life." However, church attendance is unrelated to women's choice to scale back at work and spend more time with family. Among women, 42 percent of weekly church attenders scale back, and 39 percent of nonattenders scale back; multivariate statistical models controlling for age and education confirm this. The exception to this pattern is for single mothers: single mothers who attend church are more likely to scale back than single mothers who do not.

Religious involvement does have some effects on how women choose to invest time in work and family life. Women who attend church are more likely to work part-time and, inversely, working longer hours in the paid labor force reduces women's own church attendance. Women who try to balance work and family and still be involved in a local church are more likely to report that both their work and their family lives are draining; fitting together all three activities may not be as easy for women as for men, perhaps because of the longer hours that women put into housework of all kinds. Religious involvement is less related to women's helping and caring behaviors, perhaps because women find encouragement for these behaviors from a wide range of sources, whereas for men, their church community may be the primary place where they find encouragement and support for these kinds of behaviors or are expected to take on them on.

Work, Family, and Religion: Patterns of Interconnection

This study points to the need to ask new questions and look at new patterns to understand the religion-family link in contemporary life. In these communities, those in nontraditional family arrangements—including single parents and those in blended families—and women who have experienced family disruption all report high levels of religious salience. The barriers to religious participation for those in newer family arrangements come not from a decrease in the importance of religion, but from the problems of coordinating family time schedules and negotiating religious involvement in blended families where parents have different religious backgrounds and children may be older and already have an established routine that does not take into account religious participation. Chapter 6 will consider what kinds of arrangements local churches are making to facilitate the participation of those in nontraditional families and what kinds of innovations work and what kinds do not.

For both men and women, the relationship between family and religion is influenced by social class location. The social class barriers to religious participation are real and enduring in these communities, and for those at the bottom of the socioeconomic ladder, these barriers interfere with the family-formation effects on religious involvement. Work, family life, and religion are too much to juggle in many single-parent households or in homes where both parents are working two stressful and low-paying jobs to make ends meet. And the perception that churches are largely organized around middle-class lives and concerns keeps many from turning to religious institutions for support.

It is also clear that religious participation has effects on family life that go beyond increasing feelings of satisfaction. Religious involvement increases many helping and caring behaviors directed toward one's extended and nuclear family. This is true for both men and women. However, there are gendered patterns in the particular relationships among work, family, and religion. For men, religious involvement increases their willingness to engage in crisis care (caring for an elderly or ill relative) or to help out with occasional informal needs that extended family (and neighbors) may have. Religious involvement also increases the likelihood that men will scale back at work and spend more time with their families. However, this time is not spent on helping around the house with domestic tasks and home maintenance. Rather, male church attenders who scale back at work spend more time on church-related activities for themselves and their children, using the congregation as a venue for family time.

For women, religious involvement is associated with two different profiles. Some women who attend church regularly also work part-time and spend more time on housework, a relatively traditional pattern for women. Other women who attend church do not scale back at work (and still spend more time on housework), which may explain their reports that they find that their work interferes with other areas of their lives and that their family lives are draining. The next chapter explores the relationships among work, family, and religion in a different way. Using measures that also incorporate people's beliefs about the meaning of religion and how religion fits into other aspects of their lives, chapter 4 explores the two different religious involvement styles in these communities, one of which is organized around family life and one of which is organized around expressing one's own religious values and identity.

Chapter Four

STYLES OF RELIGIOUS INVOLVEMENT

THE LAST CHAPTER showed that in the communities studied in the Religion and Family Project, marriage and parenting make men and women more likely to become involved in a local congregation, a finding that is consistent with a great deal of research about the links between family formation and church attendance in the United States. But this relationship between family formation and religious participation is not natural or automatic. It depends on the existence of interpretive frameworks that make joining a religious community seem an appropriate and meaningful expression of a family-oriented life and that make parents feel responsible for providing a religious identity and moral socialization for their children. In the United States, religious involvement has always been voluntary and expressive; people choose to participate because going to church (or synagogue, or mosque, or a Wicca group) makes a statement about their identity, values, and beliefs.

One of the characteristic features of the 1950s was the development of a particular kind of familism that depended on a cultural framework that associated church attendance with a suburban, family-oriented, male-breadwinner lifestyle. This familism became a powerful ideal, despite the fact that it did not fit the reality of many Americans' lives. In this context, when Mom and Dad and the children went to church or to mass or to temple together, it made a statement about their values and commitments. Others understood this statement because the cultural framework that interpreted this religious activity as an expression of a middle-class family-oriented way of life was broadly shared and reproduced in religious discourse and popular culture. But the Ozzie and Harriet family at the heart of the 1950s religious familism has all but disappeared. And studies of religious commitment have shown an increased emphasis on spirituality and religious self-expression that might either undermine the cultural legitimacy of family-oriented religious involvement or provide an alternative model that elevates the importance of one's own religious faith or spiritual journey over family commitments in making decisions about whether and how to participate in local religious communities.[1]

This chapter explores the meaning of religious involvement in the lives of the men and women in these upstate New York communities. What values and identities are expressed by religious participation, and how do people understand the fit between family and religion? Drawing on the survey of community residents and follow-up in-depth interviews, I found two different rhetorics of religious involvement, or ways of talking about what religion means, what role it plays in people's lives, and how it fits or does not fit with family life. The first is a *family-oriented rhetoric*, which draws on a schema that interprets religious involvement as an appropriate expression of a family- and community-oriented lifestyle. The second is a *self-oriented rhetoric* that is based in a different schema that interprets religious involvement as an expression of a person's own spirituality, faith, and religious identity, apart from family life and commitments.

Rhetorics assign meaning to a realm of activity by categorizing the activity and by linking it to symbols and stories that help people imagine the role a particular activity plays in their daily lives. A phone call means something different when it's "networking" or "business" than it does when it's "keeping in touch with a friend," even if the person on the other end of the line is the same. Church attendance means something different to the woman who is sitting in the pew because she feels as though she "ought to be there for her family" than it does to the woman who believes that, even if her family happens to be with her, she is in church to "express her own faith in God," or "renew her spirit." The first part of this chapter explores how self-oriented and family-oriented rhetorics frame the meaning of religious involvement.

Rhetorics also orient people's behavior by assigning moral weight to particular kinds of behaviors and particular motivations for behavior. A man who believes that "the family ought to attend church together" is more likely to attend church with his wife and children than a man who believes "you should go to church if it meets your own needs." Below, I outline how and why a family-oriented rhetoric is associated with higher levels of religious involvement particularly after marriage and the birth of children, whereas a self-oriented rhetoric is associated with lower levels of religious involvement regardless of one's own family context. I explore why some people with a self-oriented understanding of religious involvement do seek out a local congregation, and what they find there that keeps them coming back.

I also examine how these rhetorics of religious involvement are socially embedded. What kinds of people draw on each rhetoric, singly or in combination, and why? I argue that these rhetorics spring from and make sense of different life experiences that vary according to gender, social class, and community involvement. They are expressions of different ways of life and different understandings of the family and religion, or different schemas that organize the relationships between family and religion differently. These differences include divergent views on the appropriate roles of men and women in society, how to raise children, the public or private nature of family and religion, and the relevance or irrelevance of religious institutions in creating an atmosphere in which one's own life and values can be expressed and lived.

RHETORICS OF RELIGIOUS INVOLVEMENT

Religion and family life are still deeply intertwined in these communities. Getting married and having children both lead to greater religious involvement. For women, it is the increased importance that religion takes on in their own lives once they marry and have children that motivates increased involvement in religious institutions. For men, family formation triggers greater involvement in religious institutions in a direct way, not through an increase in religious salience but as a practical way to enact family-oriented behaviors in a world that provides men little support for such choices.[2]

However, further analysis of the data from the survey of community residents indicates that although many people interpret religious involvement as an appropriate expression of a family-oriented lifestyle, others do not. Moreover, these differences in interpretation—in attitudes and beliefs about whether religious involvement is or ought to be an expression of familism—are linked to variations in the choices that individuals make about their own and their children's religious participation.

In the survey I asked people a series of questions that capture their attitudes and beliefs about their own religious involvement. I included seven items that were designed to explore two different orientations to religious commitment.[3] The first is the kind of commitment that is assumed in structural location accounts of religious involvement. In this understanding, religious commitment results from social establishment, including the taking on of the adult responsibilities of marriage and parenting and a concern with providing religious community and moral socialization for one's children. This commitment is often associated with what Robert Wuthnow, in *After Heaven,* has called a "spirituality of dwelling" that includes a sense of the importance of caring for local communities of place and sees strong community institutions as an important locus of family life and a venue for living out and expressing religiously based values, including service to others.[4]

The second orientation toward religious commitment is akin to what Wuthnow and others have called a "spirituality of seeking." In this understanding, religious commitment should be motivated by one's own religious identity and religious beliefs. This understanding promotes a critical view toward religious authority and a sense that religious institutions should be embraced if they are a good fit with one's own religious values and identity.

In a principal components analysis, five of the original seven items cohered into two distinct components that capture different attitudes about religious commitment through identifying two different understandings of appropriate motivations for church attendance. Box 4.1 shows the items that loaded onto each component.[5] These are an indicator of differences in rhetoric, differences

---

Box 4.1
Rhetorics of Religious Involvement—From Survey Items

Family-Oriented Rhetoric:

Being a church member is an important way to become established in a community.

People should attend religious services together as a family.

Churches and synagogues play an important role in the moral education of children.

Self-Oriented Rhetoric:

Going to religious services is something you should do if it meets your needs.

An individual should arrive at his or her own religious beliefs independently of any church or synagogue.

---

that also appear in a more elaborate form in the in-depth interviews and that manifest two different interpretive frameworks, or schemas, for understanding the meaning and purpose of religious involvement.

The first is a *family-oriented rhetoric*. People with a family-oriented rhetoric understand their religious commitments as expressing their desire to put family first, as a way to be anchored in a local community, and as a way to achieve the moral instruction of children. They see their local congregation as a venue for spending time together as a family, and this "whole family together" aspect of church attendance is part of what makes the activity meaningful for them.

George is typical of those with a family-oriented religious involvement rhetoric. George scored well above the mean on the "family-oriented" scale described in box 4.1, and in our in-depth interview, he had quite a bit to say about the connections between his congregation and his family life. When we interviewed him in 1999, he was fifty-four years old and had been attending his United Church of Christ congregation for twenty-four years, and he told us that he regularly attends with his wife and their children. Involved in a church through his teen years, he dropped out and did not attend church during college. He "went back to church" soon after he got married and he and his wife decided to have their first child, events that followed in quick succession. Religion became more important to him as he started his own family. He told us that getting married and having children "makes you realize that that's the reason God put us on this earth—so you want to be better, be a better Christian, once you go through those experiences." The church provided most of the activities through which he spent time with their children when they were growing up—Scouts, choir, and social events for the family.

George described himself as family-centered, always being willing to take time off work when the children were sick or to help his own parents now that they are getting older. The church, he told us, gave him support in his desire to live a more family-centered life. When his children were younger, he led a small men's fellowship group where they discussed "what the Bible says about relating to your wife and kids, how to balance your job and your home life, that kind of thing." Groups like that, and parenting courses led by some of the teachers and social workers in the congregation, helped him be a better husband and a better father. Moreover, George was grateful for his church-based group of male friends who cared about family life the way that he did, because he felt awkward talking about his family commitments or his desire to "put the family first" with the men he knew through other contexts—his neighbors or his friends from the office.

George's story is different than the stories told by those with a self-oriented religious involvement rhetoric. Those with a self-oriented rhetoric will become involved in a local church if it allows them to express their faith, explore their spirituality, or experience a connection with a being—or a community—that is larger than themselves. A self-oriented rhetoric can reduce the likelihood of church attendance for those who feel no strong impetus to explore their spirituality and for those who view traditional religious institutions as a poor fit with their own spiritual needs. But self-oriented rhetoric can also lead people to involvement in local churches for those who believe they will find there some meaningful way to express their religious commitments.

Diane, a single woman in her thirties, has a self-oriented religious involvement rhetoric, scoring well above the mean on the self-oriented scale described in box 4.1. In her in-depth interview, Diane did not link her church attendance to experiences of marriage or parenting, experiences she has not undergone. Rather, she talked about the congregation she attends as a place where she can live out her core values. She had been attending a Unitarian congregation for about two years when we interviewed her in 1999. She had never attended church before in her life, and she became involved in this one when one of her friends invited her. Diane visited the church initially out of politeness, but decided to stay because, she told us: "I like their mission and I like their values. The people are very diverse in their thinking, very tolerant. I have similar values and ideas. And I like the sense of community and the emphasis on service, being involved, helping others." Diane's parents did not make her go to church when she grew up, and she was very definite that she goes to church now because she wants to and she assumes that most people in her church are the same.

Diane likes going to a church where singles, gay and lesbian couples, and families are "all mixed together." And she especially likes being part of the Caring Commission, a ministry that cares for ill church members and also identifies service and outreach opportunities in the community in which the congregation as a whole can take part. Although she embraces a self-oriented rhetoric, it should be noted that what attracted her to this congregation is the opportunity for a caring connection with others in the church and with the community as a whole, an opportunity for service that is based on a religious rationale for tolerant, progressive, and compassionate outreach.

Many of those with a self-oriented rhetoric talk about their congregations the way that Diane does—as an important community of values, a chance to be with like-minded people, or a place where they can live out their ethical commitments. But others talked more about the church filling their spiritual needs or expressing their faith. Anne, a married mother in her early forties with a self-oriented rhetoric, told us that the United Methodist church she attends fills what had been "a terrible spiritual void in her life." Anne has been involved in a local congregation almost continuously throughout her life. When she and her husband opened their own store and she had to work some Sundays, she missed church terribly. After several months, she arranged with her husband to change her schedule so she could attend church more often. Anne attends alone, and her husband and children do not attend her church or any church.

When I asked Anne whether her congregation has an impact on her family life, she told me, "It doesn't really. I pray, and I try to make good decisions, but I would do that anyway, whether I went to church or not." As our conversation about religion and family continued, Anne told me that she could not think of any specific ways that her church affected her family life, strengthened her as a wife and mother, or provided a supportive context when she faced tough family-related decisions. In fact, she said, "I've never spoken to anyone at church about family problems or family decisions."

Anne, like George, considers herself a family-centered person and told me, "My family is everything to me. Everything we [my husband and I] do is done with the family's well-being in mind." But for Anne, religious involvement is not about her family life or her roles as a wife and mother, it is about expressing her own spiritual connection to God, something that she has always needed to feel in her life since she was raised in a United Methodist church as a girl.

The in-depth interviews suggest that people's answers to the attitude items on the telephone survey are a good indicator of stable and pervasive differences in how they think and talk about the meaning of religious involvement. Whereas George has an elaborate way of talking about the links between his religious activities and his family life that includes stories about the men's breakfast and Scout troop outings and decisions to stay home with a sick child, Anne has no such stories and cannot name any specific ways that her religious commitment has shaped the decisions she has made as a wife and mother. George thinks of religion and family life as intertwined and mutually supportive; Anne thinks of both as vitally important and morally serious, but ultimately separate, commitments. Diane did not decide to stay out of a local church until she had a husband and children, but rather became involved when her friend told her about her church, a caring community that takes tolerance, service to the poor, and social justice seriously, as Diane does herself.

George was typical of the people we interviewed who have a family-oriented rhetoric, as Anne and Diane were typical of those with a self-oriented rhetoric, emphasizing either their congregation's role as a community of values or a place to express and renew their own faith and spirituality.

Social Embeddedness and the Meaning of Religious Involvement

Religious involvement rhetorics, whether measured as attitude scales constructed from survey data or revealed in stories shared in in-depth interviews, are not free-floating. They are socially embedded. To understand this social embeddedness it is necessary to identify what kinds of people use different religious involvement rhetorics and analyze how these rhetorics make sense of different lifestyles and social experiences.

These two rhetorics—family-oriented and self-oriented—express different ways of thinking about what it means to be involved in local religious organizations. However, these rhetorics are not mutually exclusive, either logically or in fact. For example, it is possible to believe that churches play an important role in teaching children about morality and ethics while also believing that it is important to find a church that meets one's needs and expresses one's core values. It is possible to believe that families should attend church together or that going to church is a way to become established in a local community while also believing that, when it comes to deciding what to believe, individuals in the final analysis bear the responsibility for making their own moral judgments.

It seemed appropriate, then, to investigate the *combinations* of rhetoric that people use in interpreting the meaning of religious involvement. In order to do this, I used the attitude scales shown in box 4.1 and developed from the survey of community residents. I divided the survey responses into four groups shown in box 4.2: those who scored above the mean on the self-oriented scale alone (29 percent), those who scored above the mean on the family-oriented scale alone (21 percent), those who scored above the mean on both scales (34 percent) and those who did not score above the mean on either (16 percent).

This cross-classification yields four groupings, but the question remains as to whether the people who fit into these four categories really comprise distinct social groups. Are they different kinds of people living different kinds of lives? To investigate this, I used the community resident survey data to analyze information about the social location of each group, including demographics, family status, and community involvement. I also investigated whether these groups differ more broadly in the way they think about family life, gender roles, and religious institutions. Several patterns emerged that suggest that understandings of religious commitment are embedded in different life experiences and shaped by differences in gender, family life, and social class. Tables 4.1 and 4.2 show the patterns that are drawn on in the discussion, below.

| Box 4.2 |
| Combinations of Rhetoric, Based on Attitude Scales from Survey Data |

		Self-Oriented Rhetoric Scale	
		Below Mean	Above Mean
Family-Oriented Rhetoric Scale	Below Mean	*Neither* *(16%)*	*Self-oriented* *(29%)*
	Above Mean	*Family-* *oriented* *(21%)*	*Both* *(34%)*

SELF-ORIENTED

Those who draw exclusively on a self-oriented rhetoric are more likely to be female and to be very well educated (having gone to graduate school). A substantial percentage of this group is married (60 percent), and 48 percent have children living at home, figures that are not significantly different than the survey sample means on these items (65 percent, 52 percent). A self-oriented understanding of religious involvement fits with and makes sense of the experiences of a particular group of middle-class, white-collar professionals and managers, especially the women in this group.

Those in this group have egalitarian views toward gender roles, believing that "more needs to be done to advance equal opportunities for women" and that "children benefit from the example of seeing both parents employed." They are unwilling to say that marriage and parenting are essential for happiness, or that working mothers and single parents cannot forge good relationships with their children. And they favor teaching children to think for themselves more than emphasizing obedience.[6] They are moderate to liberal, politically, and they would prefer to see businesses and government take more responsibility for helping people manage work and family life. But they prefer private religion, believing that religious leaders and organizations should be less involved in public debates and that religion is mainly a private affair that has little to do with public life and politics. And they are more likely than those in any other group to say that religious communities are insensitive and unresponsive to women's concerns.

FAMILY-ORIENTED

Those who draw exclusively on a family-oriented rhetoric are more likely to be male and to live in a nuclear family: 81 percent are married (compared to the sample mean of 65 percent) and 59 percent have children living at home (compared to a mean of 52 percent). There are more male-breadwinner families in this group than in any other. This group is also composed mostly of college-educated managers and professionals. However, their attitudes and beliefs about religion and family suggest that this group of middle-class community residents has chosen a different kind of lifestyle than their self-oriented counterparts.

It is striking that "the family" that people have in mind when they are responding to questions about the link between their family and religion is not the same across these groups. Those who embrace a family-oriented rhetoric believe that people who are married and have children are generally happier than the unmarried or those who go through life childless. They have doubts about the ability of single parents and working mothers to form good relationships with their children. And they are more likely to say that it is important to emphasize obedience when raising children, rather than teaching children to think for themselves.

The family-oriented rhetoric springs from a traditionalist understanding of society as divided between a public, masculine realm and a private, feminine one. This group views the family as a private institution that runs best on a traditionally gendered division of labor, believing that "it's usually better for everyone if the man earns the money and the woman takes care of the home and children." They believe that individuals are responsible for work-family management, and because they also believe that the woman is the primary caretaker of the home and children, work-family management is, for this group, a woman's responsibility. They reject the idea that the government or businesses should help to create a context that facilitates the continuation of changes in women's roles that have been ongoing for some time—more equal access to public opportunities and resources for women, and "family friendly" workplace programs that facilitate dual-earner and single-parent lifestyles. But they disagree that "religion is mainly a private affair" and they would like to see religious leaders more involved in public debates on social and political issues.

BOTH

Those who draw on both rhetorics have, on average, less education than either the self-oriented or the family-oriented; most have completed some college but many have only a high school degree. This group is the most embedded in local community life, having lived in their current neighborhood the longest, having a close and interconnected circle of friends, and engaging in both formal volunteering and informal networks of help and care. In this group, 65 percent are married and 56 percent have children, which is close to the sample

TABLE 4.1
Social Embeddedness and Rhetorics of Religious Involvement

	Self-Oriented (N = 305, 29%)	Family-Oriented (N = 220, 21%)	Both (N = 358, 34%)	Neither (N = 171, 16%)	Whole Sample (N = 1,054, 100%)
Age					
Average age (years)	42	46	49	44	46
Sex†					
Percent female	60	48	57	59	56
Percent male	40	52	42	41	44
Social class					
Percent white-collar[a]**	59	62	47	50	54
Percent blue-collar[b]**	8	9	13	20	12
Percent high school degree or less**	19	18	32	35	26
Percent college degree or more**	55	55	39	36	46
Most common (modal) level of education**	Graduate work	College degree	Some college	High school degree	Some college
Percent Household income more than $65,000**	30	31	24	15	26
Family status					
Percent married**	60	81	65	65	65
Percent with children at home*	48	59	56	48	52
Percent Living in male breadwinner couple**	9	21	7	15	15
Community involvement					
Percent who volunteer**	51	56	51	32	49
Percent who regularly give informal help and care to friends/neighbors*	52	52	62	52	55
Number of years live in neighborhood (average)**	12	12	17	13	14
Percent who say "most" or "nearly all" of their friends know one another*	42	38	52	44	45
Percent living in Tompkins County	41	40	24	40	34
Percent living in Seneca County	18	14	22	13	18
Percent living in Liverpool	17	23	26	20	22
Percent living in Northside	24	24	28	27	26

† Significant at p < .05 level   * Significant at p < .01 level   ** Significant at p < .001 level
Notes: [a] Managerial/professional
[b] Production/craft/repair labor

mean. In their attitudes about family and religion, this group is closest to those who are family-oriented. They have a slight preference for public religion and have more traditional understandings of family life. This group represents a relatively traditional community-oriented lifestyle.

NEITHER

Those who draw on neither rhetoric are much more likely to be working-class and to have completed high school but not continued on to college. In this group, 65 percent are married and 48 percent have children. Although they are less likely to engage in formal volunteering, in other ways they are as involved in their local community as those in the self- and family-oriented groups. In their understandings of family and religion, the people in this group are the most like those in the self-oriented group, having a more egalitarian and progressive understanding of the family and a preference for private, not public, religion. For this group, neither of these rhetorics, which capture well the lifestyles of their more socially established neighbors, is a good fit or an adequate expression of how they understand religious commitment.

These rhetorics are socially embedded in ways that correspond to different lifestyles and understandings of family life. In these upstate New York communities, people who understand religious involvement as an expression of a family- and community-oriented lifestyle have a particular kind of ideal family in mind, and this is true for those who draw only on a family-oriented rhetoric and for those who draw on it in combination with a more self-oriented rhetoric. This family ideal has a certain continuity with the familism of the 1950s, with women primarily responsible for home and caretaking, with work-family management being a private concern. They may favor the public involvement of religious groups and leaders in social and political debates because such involvement has been dominated, in the last decade or so, by religious conservatives who tend to share their image of the ideal family.

Those who embrace only a self-oriented religious involvement rhetoric seem to agree that local congregations are largely oriented toward facilitating not only family life but a particular kind of family life that is, to some extent, nostalgic for the idealized family of the 1950s. And this may be one of the reasons that they understand religious involvement as something that one should do if "it meets one's own needs" and why they are less enthusiastic about the public involvement of religious leaders, who have tended in the last two decades to be much more conservative than they are on gender and family issues.

Perhaps the most interesting group is the one that draws on neither rhetoric. This group, which has the highest concentration of those with only a high school education, may indicate that both of these rhetorics correspond to middle-class ways of thinking about religion and family, and leave out other dimensions of religious commitment that might be more salient in other, non-middle-class groups.

TABLE 4.2

Religious Involvement Rhetorics and Attitudes about Gender, Family, and Religion*

	Self-Oriented (N = 305, 29%)	Family-Oriented (N = 220, 21%)	Both (N = 358, 34%)	Neither (N = 171, 16%)	Whole Sample (N = 1054, 100%)
Percent agreeing to each statement					
Many churches and synagogues are insensitive and unresponsive to the concerns of women	40	22	31	32	32
Religious organizations and leaders should be more involved in public debates on important social and political issues	33	62	53	45	48
Religion is mainly a private affair, having little to do with public life and politics	58	29	39	46	33
*Traditional family form—2-item scale^*					
• Married people are generally happier than unmarried people.	Below mean (−.22261)	Above mean (.19227)	Above mean (.19775)	Below mean (−.25429)	0
• It's better for a person to have children than to go through life childless					

Scores on attitude scales—Family and gender

Gender egalitarianism—5-item scale[+]

	Above mean	Below mean	Below mean	Above mean	
• It's usually better for everyone if the man earns the money and the woman takes care of the home and children	(.32047)	(−.33558)	(−.09124)	(.05571)	0
• A working mother can establish just as good a relationship with her children as a mother who does not work					
• Children benefit from the example of seeing both parents employed					
• More needs to be done to advance equal opportunities for women					
• A single parent can bring up her child as well as a married couple can					

Public support for working families—3-item scale[^^]

	Above mean	Below mean	Below mean	Above mean	
• Businesses should provide more family-friendly programs					
• The government should step in and require businesses to be more family friendly	(.18857)	(−.14954)	(−.13701)	(.12436)	0
• It is a worker's own responsibility to balance work and family responsibilities, and people shouldn't expect special help from businesses or the government					

---

[*] All relationships significant at the p < .001 level.

[^] This factor emerged from a principal components analysis using varimax rotation with Kaiser normalization; the rotation converged in three iterations.

[+] Additive scale, alpha = .80; converted to a z-score centered on 0.

[^^] This factor emerged from a principal components analysis using varimax rotation with Kaiser normalization; the rotation converged in one iteration.

How Interpretive Frameworks Shape Religious Involvement

The interpretive frameworks that underlie these rhetorics make sense of people's behavior, but they also can orient and influence behavior and shape the ways that people choose to be involved, or uninvolved, in local religious life.[7] Table 4.3 summarizes the patterns of religious involvement for people with different rhetorics of religious involvement and shows that there is a relationship between how people interpret the meaning of religious involvement and their patterns of religious participation. Two particular patterns of religious involvement stand out. First, those with a self-oriented rhetoric alone are the least likely to be involved in any form of organized religion, report the lowest levels of religious salience, and have the least traditional beliefs. Second, those who combine a family-oriented and a self-oriented understanding of religious involvement are, in many ways, as involved as those with only a family-oriented rhetoric. This suggests that even when combined with a more self-oriented understanding of religious authority, this kind of religious familism motivates involvement in local religious communities.

Those who embrace a self-oriented rhetoric (see "Self-Oriented" column in table 4.3) are far less likely to attend church, say that religion is important to them, or participate in any kind of organized religious activity. Although 60 percent are married and 48 percent have children at home, only 20 percent attend church monthly or more (compared to a sample mean of 55 percent) and only 13 percent are involved in some organized congregational ministry (compared to a mean of 39 percent). Only 21 percent say that religion is "very important" to them, whereas the mean for the whole sample is 48 percent. More people in this group than in any other express no religious preference (22 percent, compared to a sample mean of 10 percent), and they are far less likely than any other group, and than the national average, to belong to a conservative religious group. They are more likely than others to say that the Bible is a "wise book" and not "the Word of God." They are less likely to be married to a person of the same religious faith.

Conversely, those with a family-oriented rhetoric show the highest levels of participation in organized religious activities of all kinds. In this group, 84 percent report that they attend church monthly or more, 62 percent report that they attend weekly or more (compared to a sample mean of 35 percent), and more than three-quarters (76 percent) say that religion is very important to them. About 41 percent are Catholic, which reflects well the population of these communities. About 20 percent of this group is conservative Protestant (20 percent go to a conservative Protestant church and 21 percent identify themselves as "evangelical" or "fundamentalist"). Although this is more than the community average (13 percent), it is important to note that the relatively conservative familism of this group is not driven by a rootedness in an evangelical subculture. Like all church attenders except for the self-oriented, about a quarter of

TABLE 4.3
Rhetorics and Religious Participation, Identity, and Beliefs

	Self-Oriented (N = 305, 29%)	Family-Oriented (N = 220, 21%)	Both (N = 358, 34%)	Neither (N = 171, 16%)	Whole Sample (N = 1,054, 100%)
Religious participation					
Percent who attend church monthly or more**	20	84	70	50	55
Percent who attend church weekly or more**	7	62	44	29	35
Percent who say religion is "very important" to them**	21	76	59	37	48
Percent involved in religious organization besides local congregation**	11	34	22	8	19
Percent who volunteer for a religious group/organization**	8	20	15	6	13
Percent who participate in at least one organized congregational ministry**	13	43	49	31	39
Percent of church attenders who say "most" or "nearly all" of friends attend their church+	9	25	26	19	23
Percent who report confide in pastor/rabbi**	5	20	22	12	15
Religious identity and belief					
"The Bible is God's Word, and it is true word for word" (percent who agree)**	14	28	24	20	22
"The Bible is a wise book, but God had little or nothing to do with it" (percent who agree)**	25	1	6	19	12

TABLE 4.3 (*cont.*)

	Self-Oriented (N = 305, 29%)	Family-Oriented (N = 220, 21%)	Both (N = 358, 34%)	Neither (N = 171, 16%)	Whole Sample (N = 1,054, 100%)
Husband or wife is of same religious faith**	53	82	82	67	72
Self-identified as evangelical or fundamentalist[a]**	5	20	19	7	13
Percent conservative protestant [b]**	5	21	14	15	13
Percent Catholic**	30	41	51	39	41
Percent liberal or moderate protestant[b]**	29	31	28	24	28
Percent with no religious preference**	22	2	3	12	10

[+] Significant at p < .05 level [*] Significant at p < .01 level [**] Significant at p < .001 level

Notes: [a] Based on a question that asked people to pick the term that best described their religious orientation; this does not include those who identified as religious "conservatives."

[b] Based on denomination of church currently attending or, for nonattendees, self-identified denominational preference.

them say that "most" or "nearly all" of their friends attend their church, and like those who use both rhetorics, about 20 percent report they have a close and confiding relationship with their pastor. They, along with those in the "both" category, have the highest rates of religious homogamy (marrying someone of the same religious faith).

Those who use both rhetorics have the next highest level of involvement in organized religion and also say that religion is very important to them. They are involved in organized congregational ministries and in other religious organizations in the community. Compared to the family-oriented, they are slightly more likely to be Catholic and less likely to attend a conservative Protestant congregation, but they are just as likely to self-identify as evangelical. They are as likely to have married someone of the same religious faith. Those who use neither rhetoric are more involved in organized congregational ministries than the self-oriented, but are less involved than the family-oriented or those who use both rhetorics. Half (50 percent) attend church monthly or more (compared to a sample mean of 55 percent) and 37 percent say that religion is very important to them (compared to a mean of 48 percent).

The in-depth interviews also shed light on differences in the religious involvement of those in these four groups. Those who used neither of these rhetorics had a much less elaborate way of talking about the motivations for their religious involvement. They were the most likely, if they did go to church, to understand this as a relatively straightforward expression of their religious identity, telling us, for example, that they go to church because they're Catholic (or Baptist or Methodist or Lutheran). Some in this group also talked about faith in God as their motivation, whereas others simply said that they had always gone to church. Those in this group who did not attend church were the most critical, of all our interviewees, of churches and churchgoers. Some of them told us that people generally go to church because they are stuck up or that churchgoers are hypocrites. Others simply thought that religious involvement—and religion more generally—was irrelevant to their lives and they really could not imagine or articulate any reason for choosing to be involved.

Perhaps the most interesting, in some ways, are those who embrace both rhetorics. They combine a sense of the local religious community as an important venue for the moral socialization of children with an understanding of the importance of making one's own moral judgments and engaging in religious activity because it meets one's own needs and expresses one's values and identity. Especially for mothers in this group, religious involvement is something they engage in to expose their children to a religious tradition in order to equip them to make their own choices, later in life, about the meaning and relevance of religion. Whereas those in the family-oriented group would tell us, in in-depth interviews, that they wanted to raise their children as good Catholics or they wanted them to know the Lord, those who use both rhetorics talked differently about religion and family. Debbie is an example of those who score above the mean on both the family-oriented and the self-oriented rhetoric scales. She told us, in her in-depth interview, that it is important for her children to have an opportunity to learn about religious faith and their religious tradition so that they can be well equipped later in life to make their own decisions about religious involvement. As she said to me, "How will they know if religion is something they want, something they need, if they never have a chance to learn about it?"

Debbie, in her forties, a married mother of two children, was typical of those in this group, especially the women. Involved in a church as a younger child, she dropped out in high school and did not return to church until her children were school-age. She did it because her children started to ask their parents questions about church, about God, and about what they believed. Many of her children's friends attended church and Sunday School, and her children wanted to know why their friends did this and what church was all about. She decided to find a local church with a good religious education program to give them the information they would need to decide for themselves if religion was important to them and if they wanted to be involved later in life.

Debbie's *behavior* is closer to that of those in the family-oriented group. She attends church regularly with her children, has enrolled her children in Sunday School, and participates herself in some of the congregation's social and family-oriented groups and activities. But for Debbie, her family's involvement in a local church *means something different* than it does for George, profiled in the previous section, or for others in the family-oriented group. Rachel, who was profiled in chapter 1, is another example of someone who scores above the mean on both of these attitude scales. Herself an atheist, Rachel believes in the value of religious community not only to educate her children but also to provide a particular kind of social context in which to spend time together as a family. This language of equipping children to decide for themselves what they believe, and making a distinction between the family-oriented aspects of religious involvement and one's own faith, is the way that those in the self-oriented group talk about religious involvement when they do involve their children in congregational activities.

Different ways of interpreting religious involvement, as manifest in the use of different rhetorics, are related not only to differences in gender, social class, and lifestyle, but also to different patterns of religious participation. Multivariate analyses can examine whether the links between rhetoric and religious participation still exist when controlling for differences in gender, education, and religious identity, all of which are associated with the rhetorics that people use to describe religious involvement. Tables 4.4 and 4.5 show the results of these multivariate analyses. These analyses show that the relationship between rhetorics of religious involvement and patterns of religious participation is statistically significant and remains even when other factors are accounted for.

Church attendance is the most commonly used religious involvement measure and is often a proxy for other forms of involvement. Table 4.4 reports the result of the multivariate analysis of church attendance using data from the community resident survey.[8] The comparison category is those with a self-oriented rhetoric alone. Compared to the self-oriented, those with a family-oriented rhetoric are eighteen times more likely to attend church regularly, those who use both rhetorics are more than ten times more likely to attend church, and those with neither rhetoric are four times more likely to attend church, even controlling for age, education, gender, family status (being married and having children), and religious identity and salience.[9]

This analysis of church attendance shows that the rhetorics that people use to describe the meaning of their religious involvement have a stable and predictable relationship to their behavior. But how does that stable and predictable relationship between rhetoric and practice come about? It has become common in sociological discourse to talk about causal relationships based on the kinds of statistical analyses presented here. But most of the statistical analyses available to sociologists, and virtually all of the ones that are brought to bear in analyzing survey data gathered at one point in time, do not allow for

TABLE 4.4
Religious Involvement Rhetorics and Church Attendance
(Monthly or More)

	Exp. B
Age	.980
Age squared	1.000**
Sex (1 = female)	.993
College degree	2.440**
Married	2.149**
Child at home	1.650*
Religion "very important"	5.691**
Conservative Protestant	5.519**
Catholic	2.944**
Family-oriented rhetoric (above mean)	18.408**
Both rhetorics (above mean)	10.930**
Neither rhetoric (above mean)	4.071**
Constant	0.35
Chi-square	554.897**
df	12
−2 log likelihood	860.278
Percent of cases correctly predicted	82

+ Significant at $p < .05$ level   * Significant at $p < .01$ level   ** Significant at $p < .001$ level

valid causal claims, but rather identify associations or correlations and calculate how likely those are to come about by chance alone.[10] Causal claims have to be based on theoretical frameworks or additional work that identifies the mechanisms that lead from a discrete set of independent variables (e.g., being a woman, being married, having a child at home, thinking about religious involvement in a certain way) to a particular state of a dependent variable (going to church or not going to church).

The analyses here show that there are strong and stable associations between the way that people interpret religious involvement and their patterns of actual participation—there is a link between rhetoric and behavior. But what causes what? The data from the in-depth interviews and the associations between religious involvement measures and other measures of lifestyle and belief suggest that there are different causal paths at work.

For those in the self-oriented group, and for those who use neither of these rhetorics, the best interpretation is that attitudes and interpretive frameworks drive behavior. When people do not believe that religion and family need or ought to go together, they are less likely to seek out religious communities when they form their own families, leading to low overall rates of religious involvement and an attenuation of the relationship between family formation and involvement. For those who combine a self-oriented and a family-oriented rhetoric, it is harder to sort out the causal connection between rhetoric and behavior, but it does seem clear that their interpretive framework shapes the overall meaning of their behavior. This seems especially to be the case regarding people's purpose in involving their children in religious education and what they teach their children about seeking out religious communities that meet their needs.

For those who have a family-oriented understanding of religious involvement, there are two possible causal pathways. It may be that family-oriented beliefs cause people to participate in a church once they marry and have children, or it may be that participating in a local church causes people to have a family-oriented understanding. The in-depth interviews suggest that both kinds of pathways exist. Some of the younger people we interviewed who had not yet married, and who had a family-oriented understanding of religious involvement, seemed confident that they would return to church once they married and had children, because churchgoing figures prominently in how they imagine their future family life to evolve. For these people, a family-oriented schema will most likely cause them to seek out a church (or synagogue or parish) when they form their own nuclear family. However, for people like George, profiled earlier in this chapter, the relationship between rhetoric and behavior is murkier. George may have evolved in his understanding of church as a family-oriented activity over time because of experiences he has had in his local congregation. In such a case, religious involvement would be the cause of a family-oriented schema.

Whichever pathway people take, it seems clear that church attendance and a family-oriented interpretation of it are mutually reinforcing. And whether they learn a family-oriented rhetoric in church or have a family-oriented understanding of church before they choose to attend, these analyses make it clear that one's interpretive framework—believing that churches are an important part of a family-oriented life—is a much bigger influence on involvement than actual family formation (marriage, having children).

Additional analyses can shed light on some of these questions. Table 4.5 presents the result of a different set of logistic regression analyses with the survey sample split into four groups depending on the religious involvement rhetorics people use. These analyses show that family formation effects on religious involvement are not uniform across these groups but vary depending on how people interpret the meaning of religious involvement. Marriage leads to religious involvement only for those who use both religious rhetorics. Having a child leads self- *and* family-oriented individuals to attend church, but for different reasons, as the in-depth interviews outline. Gender differences did not show up as significant in the previous model, but for the family-oriented, gender matters, perhaps because women with these beliefs find that churches are supportive environments for the more traditional gender roles they embrace.

TABLE 4.5

Religious Involvement of Those Using Different Combinations of Rhetoric—Logistic Regression, Attend Church Monthly or More

	Self-Oriented (N = 305) Exp. B	Family-Oriented (N = 220) Exp. B	Both (N = 358) Exp. B	Neither (N = 171) Exp. B
Age	1.066	1.054	.861+	1.146
Age squared	1.000	1.000	.999**	1.000
Sex (1 = female)	.682	3.223*	.711	.818
College degree	6.859**	3.002*	1.776	1.326
Married	1.090	2.189	2.235*	2.127
Child at home	3.325*	3.000*	1.908	.855
Religion "very important"	4.537**	2.407	15.779**	3.706**
Conservative Protestant	.925	11.386*	4.575*	8.644**
Catholic	4.553**	5.713**	2.215**	2.117
Constant	.016	.120	1.553	.085
Chi-square	52.611**	52.666**	138.302**	43.441**
df	9	9	9	9
−2 log likelihood	172.739	140.392	311.339	181.574
Percent of cases correctly predicted	86	84	80	70

+ Significant at p < .05 level   * Significant at p < .01 level   ** Significant at p < .001 level

For those who use both rhetorics, by far the biggest factor motivating religious involvement is religious salience, or the personal importance of religion. And for those who use neither rhetoric, religious involvement is driven by the salience of religion and a conservative Protestant identity, as reflected in the in-depth interviews.

For a long time sociologists have assumed that religious involvement naturally flows from structural location and is triggered by the kinds of events that signal the establishment of an adult life—marriage, the birth of children, and, for men, the taking on of full-time paid employment, which forms the basis of providing for a family's economic needs. This automatic relationship was only automatic, however, when there was a broad consensus that involvement in a local religious community was an appropriate and meaningful expression of a family-oriented life. This analysis of how people think and talk about their religious commitment, however, suggests that for those who live in these upstate New York communities, the automatic link between family formation, social establishment, and religious involvement is now severed for a large number of community residents, namely the 45 percent who do not have a family-oriented understanding of religious involvement.

Another implication of these findings is that "the family" associated in our culture with religious participation is not just any family, but is rather a very traditional kind of family. Put another way, those who embrace religious familism are not only embracing the idea that religious involvement is good for family life, but they are embracing a particular kind of traditional family ideology. Those who reject this religious familism—the self-oriented—have markedly lower rates of religious participation, and in-depth interviews suggest that this is in part because they associate churches with a traditional family ideology that includes a gendered division of labor and a view of the family as a private realm and work-family management as a woman's private responsibility. They find this ideology to be unresponsive to women's concerns and contemporary women's lives. Women, more than men, are likely to be in this group, especially highly educated professional women who have a preference for more public support for work-family policies that facilitate women's paid employment and who have egalitarian views of the appropriate relationship between men and women.

And it is important to note that this relatively conservative religious familism is not simply a feature of conservative Protestant subculture or Catholic subculture. Rather, it is something that characterizes the religious commitment of those across a wide range of denominations, including liberal and moderate Protestants. Some have argued that the rising number of people in our society who claim no religious identity are reacting, in part, to the public presence of politically conservative Christian Right activists and leaders, and this may be true.[11] But it may also be the case that an increasing number of those who embrace a more egalitarian understanding of gender roles are opting out of religious participation because of the traditional familism that characterizes mainstream religious institutions in the United States.

In short, whether or not family formation leads to religious involvement—and what kind of involvement results—depends on the meaning of religious involvement and people's assessment of whether religious institutions are a good fit with their own family life and their own understanding of what a good family is. And people's understanding of what a good family is and the relevance of religious involvement in their own lives is dependent on their life experiences, rooted in gender and social class. Those in the family-oriented and self-oriented groups are the most socially established middle-class managers and professionals. For them, these two rhetorics capture two different responses to the reconfiguration of family life and women's roles motivated by women's increasing levels of education and participation in the paid labor force. In particular, highly educated professional women embrace a self-oriented understanding, while well-established middle-class men living in more traditional family arrangements embrace a family-oriented rhetoric. Those who embrace neither rhetoric are more likely to be working-class, and those who embrace both rhetorics are somewhere in the middle, more socially established than those in the "neither" group but not as educated and well-off as those in either the family-oriented or self-oriented groups.

Religious Familism and Social Change

There is some indication that these different religious involvement rhetorics are not new, but have been a feature of American religious commitment for some time. Robert Wuthnow makes this argument in *After Heaven: Spirituality in America since the 1950s*. In a survey of spirituality over the course of five decades of American life, he identifies two broad spiritual orientations. In the 1950s, a spirituality of dwelling was predominant—which is similar to the family-oriented religious involvement style I discovered in upstate New York in the 1990s. Based on a "domesticated" version of the male-breadwinner family, reinforcing local community attachments, and viewing the local church as a "home," the spirituality of dwelling expressed the familism of the 1950s and the desire to create strong and stable community institutions in the rapidly changing suburbs.

Wuthnow also identifies a spirituality of "seeking," which is similar to the self-oriented religious rhetoric I found in these communities. Seekers have a critical orientation toward religious institutions and religious authority, believing that what really matters is finding a religious institution that is a good fit with one's own needs and that expresses one's values. Seekers may drop out of traditional religious organizations altogether or they may switch from one to another over the course of their lives. Seekers often combine elements of traditional religiosity with other forms of spiritual expression, including Eastern-influenced spiritual practices such as yoga or chanting, or feminist spiritual practices such as those expressed by Wiccan and other feminist religious groups. In his book *A Generation of Seekers*, Wade Clark Roof argues that this "seeker" spirituality has become much more common since the 1960s and is a quintessential feature of the religious life of the baby boom generation and their children.

This study of religious commitment in upstate New York suggests that for many people—in fact, for half of those in this sample of community residents—a spirituality of dwelling and a spirituality of seeking are at odds with one another. This is because, for these groups, both "dwelling" and "seeking" are intertwined with an understanding of religious communities as promoting a particular form of family ideology and a particular set of traditional gender roles. A small group find both the dwelling and seeking spiritualities not to be in tune with their understanding of religious commitment. And another group, those who combine these orientations, see a value in religious institutions as locations for family togetherness and a place to introduce their children to religious traditions and the morality and ethics they impart, while also wanting to encourage a more critical understanding of religious authority and to equip their children to seek out religious communities that express their own values.

The evidence suggests that there has been an increase in the number of people who embrace a religious discourse of seeking and the kind of self-oriented understanding of religious authority and commitment I identify in this chapter. And it is clear that, for those who embrace only this rhetoric, traditional forms of religious involvement become attenuated even for those who are married with children. This set of relationships has often been summed up, in the sociological literature, as a metanarrative of increasing religious individualism, which is understood as undermining religious attachment and endangering the vitality of mainstream religious institutions. Individualism, in this account, has had several effects on the American religious landscape.[12] It has reduced involvement in mainstream religious institutions and fostered new religious groups and organizations for religious seekers, groups that require less long-term commitment. Individualism is thought to undermine the authority of clergy and to lead people to view religious doctrine and teachings as less authoritative in their own lives.

However, there is a fundamental problem in summing these changes up as "increasing individualism," because *both* of these religious involvement rhetorics are individualistic. Individualism is built into the very structure of our mainstream religious institutions. Tocqueville, in *Democracy in America*, wrote about the vitality of American religious congregations as part and parcel of a much broader tendency for Americans to organize themselves together in local voluntary groups around issues, interests, and identities that mattered to them. In his 1962 book *American Life*, which hearkened back to Tocqueville's classic work in its attempt to explain the broad tenor and organization of American society, Lloyd Warner took the same view of American civic and voluntary associations. Associations let "private citizens and free individuals" be socially bound to one another. Associations mediate the private and the public, but do so in a symbolic, expressive way that corresponds to differences in lifestyle, social class, and values.

Churches were not, according to Warner, an exception to this but were rather the strongest part of American associational life. The history of American religion is characterized by vitality, pluralism, and dynamism[13] because religious institutions are individualistic and provide rich symbolic arenas in which to express—as well as practical activities that support—various lifestyles. And at the heart of differences in lifestyle are different understandings of family life and gender roles. Especially when family life "loses many of its utilitarian and instrumental aspects . . . it can emerge as an end in itself."[14] And religious institutions have been perhaps the primary arena in which Americans have expressed their symbolic preferences for particular family ideals.[15]

Sociologists in the 1950s and 1960s would not be surprised that the different religious involvement rhetorics express different lifestyles and that religious commitment in these communities is primarily an individualistic activity, symbolic and expressive of individuals' preferred values and ideals. They viewed the postwar suburban expansion, and the religious revival that accompanied it, as individualistic to the core. Analyses of the suburban expansion focused on the various lifestyles that suburban living allowed men and women to embrace—familism, consumerism, and careerism.[16] Lifestyles are expressive, chosen, and achieved—that is, they are individualistic. The increasing prosperity and geographic mobility afforded by rapid suburbanization enabled more Americans than ever before to creatively construct lifestyles regardless of their ethnic origin, their social class background, or their parents' and extended family's approval. Each of these three lifestyles sociologists identified at the time was associated with different occupational groups and entailed a different orientation toward participation in social institutions.

Likewise, historical work on the 1950s religious expansion makes it clear that the religious familism of the period was largely expressive of a middle-class, individualistic way of life that sought to construct strong communities and families in part as a bulwark against the anxiety fostered by the rapid transformation of life in postwar America.[17] Some sociologists and religious leaders had a positive view of this transformation, seeing it as a source of renewal for religious institutions and leaders who were being forced to make their religious message and organizations responsive to new ways of life, including family life.[18] They were comfortable with the idea of individualism, seeing it as the underpinning of the vitality of American associational life.

Others lamented that the religious "revival" of the 1950s was no such thing, having at its root no great religious awakening like previous waves of religious expansion, but being rather driven by suburban individualists making consumerlike demands on local churches to provide family-related ministries that had little or no real religious content.[19] Ironically, these commentators shared the view of many sociologists today, who see individualism as a dangerous force that undermines attachment to local communities of place and that weakens a host of traditional institutions. But whereas the commentators of the 1950s associated individualism with the familism of the postwar suburban expansion, today's commentators associate individualism with a spirituality of seeking and a self-oriented religious involvement rhetoric.

In short, *individualism* has always served as something of a code word to criticize those who are seen as threatening goals, ways of life, and institutions in which one has an investment. It is too easy to say that people who do not share those goals and support those institutions are being "individualistic" in the sense of "thinking only of their own good" and not concerned about the issues that social commentators see as so pressing. So the shift in where religious individualism is located, rhetorically speaking, and where the blame is placed for undermining the authority of religious institutions and the authenticity of religious commitment, is explained in large part by differences in the value commitments of those using the label.

The commentators of the 1950s who saw religious familism as undermining "real" religious commitment saw the unprecedented growth of religious institutions and the unprecedented public influence of religious leaders as an opportunity to accomplish other goals they cared about. These goals included social justice on issues of poverty and race, and they saw the concentration of religious resources in well-off suburbs as a feminization and privatization of religion. They believed that it undermined the more public—and masculine—social concern they wanted to mobilize to reach out to the poor, to improve racial relations, and to solve other pressing social problems.

Today many Americans, including many scholars, tend to look back on the 1950s with nostalgia. We idealize the era as emblematic of stable families as we analyze national surveys that show that most Americans believe that "families today are in crisis." We soften the implications for women and children of the unequal power in the male-breadwinner family by calling the 1950s version of it "domesticated." We watch movies such as *Pleasantville* and we believe that in the 1950s all our small towns were thriving and all our local communities were stable, prosperous, and crime-free. We forget just how new and how rapidly changing the postwar suburban communities were, and how widespread were the anxieties about crime and juvenile delinquency resulting from such rapid social upheaval.[20] It is this nostalgic longing for a past imagined to be more stable, more civic-minded, less hectic, and less stridently feminist that leads us to look at the changes in religious involvement and summarize them as increasing individualism.

Certainly, there are new things about the ways that individuals understand the meaning and purpose of religious involvement today, in comparison with the 1950s. One thing that is relatively new is the family schema at the heart of the self-oriented religious involvement rhetoric. This understanding of the family as an egalitarian, sharing unit, a willingness to tolerate "untraditional" family forms, and a sense that the family can be related to traditional community institutions in a variety of ways depending on members' own needs—this is not the family, or the religious familism, of the 1950s. It is a change that is driven by increasing education, by changes in the supportive networks and connections that shape the context of people's lives, and by the changing nature of women's employment. But this family is no more modern or individualistic than the male-breadwinner family of the 1950s suburbs, a phenomenon that was driven almost entirely by changes in the market and the economy, the increasing affluence of suburban life, and the demands of the organization man culture of corporate America.

At the same time, there is also a remarkable continuity between the religious familism of the 1950s and the religious familism I found in these upstate New York communities. A sizeable number of people in these communities agree that religious institutions foster a relatively traditional, neopatriarchal family life, the "domesticated" patriarchy of the 1950s. What has become contentious is whether people believe that this is a good or a bad thing. Those who find this family ideology a poor fit with their own lives and needs tend either to drop out of organized religion (the self-oriented) or they combine religious involvement with a more critical stance toward religious authority and raise their children to be familiar with a religious tradition while assuming that they will make their own choices, later in life, about the meaning and relevance of religious involvement.

Chapter Five

"THE PROBLEM WITH FAMILIES TODAY . . . "

THE PREVIOUS CHAPTERS provide a window into how people in various family situations participate in the congregations in these four communities, and how this religious involvement affects the kind of commitments they make to their families. Local congregations provide an important context for parenting and the moral socialization of children for those in "traditional" families as well as for single-parent and blended families across all four communities, although this is particularly the case for middle-class families. For some community residents, and especially for men, religious involvement is an expression of and a practical support for a family-oriented lifestyle. Others, and especially women, participate in a local congregation mostly because it meets a spiritual need, expresses important values such as inclusiveness or social justice, or provides an outlet for service to the community.

The next two chapters explore the local religious ecology of these communities. What kinds of ministries are targeted to parents, to single parents, or to gay and lesbian couples? How have congregations adapted to changing work schedules? And what messages do these religious communities send about "the good family," appropriate gender roles, and how to balance work and family life? In this chapter I begin by analyzing the way that local pastors and lay leaders talk about families and family ministry, exploring how central family ministry is in local congregational life and what "family" means to those who shape such ministry. The next chapter looks at the kinds of programs and activities congregations offer for families.

The assumption behind these two chapters is that the messages congregations send about "the good family" are an important part of what individuals are reacting to when they make decisions about the relevance of religious institutions and the meaning of religious involvement in their own lives. The messages that local religious communities send are powerful because they shape the way that religious institutions include or exclude people based on their family situations. And they are powerful because of the cultural influence that religious institutions have on the larger society and the way religious discourse can shape broader public conceptions of what kinds of families are morally legitimate. These messages are embedded in both rhetoric (the way leaders talk about the family) and practice (the profile of programs and ministries and routine ways of organizing church life).

"Families in Crisis"

Changes in family life are at the top of local religious leaders' list of priorities in these communities. My survey of area pastors asked them to respond to the following statement: "Families today are in crisis." Virtually all of the pastors (97 percent) agreed with the statement, and 50 percent said they strongly agreed. In pastor focus groups and one-on-one conversations during field-work, not only was this "crisis talk" common, but many pastors also told us that figuring out how to respond to changing families was perhaps their greatest challenge and the one into which their congregations were pouring the most time. In this sense of urgency, these local religious leaders are not atypical.[1] In a previous study of congregations in and around Oak Park, Illinois,[2] I found that many church members believed that changes in family life posed a fundamental challenge for their congregations. They talked extensively about the need to develop more relevant programming for those who were not part of "Ozzie and Harriet" families, and about the need to adapt congregational activities to changing family time schedules. A study by Hart (1986) found a similar widespread concern among pastors across the country in the 1980s.

The prevalence of "family values" debates in the media, government, courts, and other social institutions is in part responsible for the amount of "family crisis" rhetoric in local churches.[3] In addition, many pastors told us that denominational conflicts over gender and sexuality issues contribute to their sense of crisis. Denominational newsletters and national news outlets alike document conflict in the Episcopal, Presbyterian, Catholic, and United Methodist churches over the blessing of homosexual unions and the inclusion of gay and lesbian members in congregational life. The Southern Baptists put out statements endorsing male headship in the home and condemning homosexual lifestyles. And although many people think that evangelical groups have more uniformity of belief on these issues, in fact the pronouncements by Southern Baptist elites are contested and have caused some local churches, and even some regional Baptist associations, to protest or withdraw from the denomination.[4]

The perception of family crisis among pastors in upstate New York is also driven by specific historical changes in family life—rising rates of divorce and single parenting, the increasing number of dual-earner couples and mothers of young children who work full-time for pay outside the home, and competition for members' time from other community activities. Our fieldwork suggests that pastors take these changes seriously because they believe that they are having a direct impact on their congregations and on their own ability to exercise pastoral leadership. A few pastors are worried about declining membership or worship service attendance and attribute it to changes in work and family, particularly to changing gender roles.

Far more are worried that, although Sunday attendance is stable or even growing, it is increasingly hard to generate participation in other kinds of programming, such as religious education for children, fellowship programs for men and women, or committees and service work. Members are demanding that traditional programs and ways of doing things be altered to accommodate new work and family routines, and this is a source of uncertainty that makes planning effective ministry more difficult and stressful. In these concerns pastors have much in common with leaders of other kinds of voluntary institutions who are faced with a new generation of members or volunteers who have a "looser" and more intermittent style of commitment to a host of traditional institutions, and who are reshaping the nature of voluntary associational life in the United States.[5]

Christiano (2000) has suggested that a perception that families are in crisis is a recurring feature of institutions that foster familism, which he defines as the ideology that the family is precious and the central, most fundamental unit of social order in a society. So perhaps it is not surprising that pastors in these communities are so willing to affirm that the family is in crisis. It may be that this kind of talk about the family is a recurring feature of local congregational life, a means through which religious leaders and members alike keep in touch with developments in the institution to which their own fate is most centrally linked, an ongoing conversation whose primary purpose is interpretive. The centrality of family issues and the urgency with which they are discussed leads to an elaboration of rhetorics that seek to define exactly what the problem with contemporary families is and what local churches should do in response. As a result, talk about what constitutes a good family and what kinds of families are problematic is up front and available for members and potential members to hear, think about, and respond to. These rhetorics either shape congregations into inclusive communities for people in a broad range of family arrangements or make them exclusive communities where many people do not find their own family lives and choices upheld in a positive light.

Rhetorics are local styles of talk that draw upon larger cultural discourses and meld them in creative ways to provide a rationale for action within a given local context. Rhetorics that define the problem with the family—and the problems local congregations face in providing family ministry—perform three kinds of culture work in these congregations.[6] First, they work like a filter, selecting certain historical changes in family life as relevant and something the congregation must respond to and designating other changes as irrelevant. Second, the selected changes are defined as posing a particular kind of problem for the congregation to solve. Third, having defined the problem at hand, rhetorics bundle these problems with typical kinds of solutions with which the congregation is familiar, either from its members' past experience, from the expert training the pastor has in certain ministry areas, or from models found in other congregations or in denominationally sponsored programming innovations.[7] Although rhetorics are fundamentally interpretive, there are also practical implications of choosing particular interpretations of what "the problem" is with families because rhetorics provide a template for action that influences the development of programming and practices, shaping the ways that congregations innovate and change over time.

This chapter explores the interpretive frameworks that pastors and lay leaders bring to bear in understanding "the problem of the family" today. My analysis suggests that the way that local pastors and lay leaders think about family life and the family crisis they perceive is not defined by the liberal-conservative "culture war" that underlies much of the conflict in national denominational structures,[8] although there are some distinct differences between liberals and conservatives. But liberals and conservatives share to a surprising extent some common understandings of both the ideal family and the problems that contemporary families present for local churches. Many of these common understandings are similar to those found in local churches in the 1960s. This chapter explores these common interpretations of "the problem of the family" and the implications that church leaders draw for their congregations' ministry.

"The Problem with Families Today . . . "

The pastors we spoke with use two main rhetorics to interpret how changes in work and family life have affected their congregations. The discussion below draws most extensively on the focus groups conducted with pastors in each of the four communities during the summer of 2000, and on an initial, exploratory focus group conducted with pastors in 1997 at the very beginning of the project. The focus groups involved a total of forty-seven pastors. Focus groups provide a good window into the "polite social discourse" of a given arena of action, including the interpretive frameworks that structure this discourse.[9] I also draw on the survey of 125 area pastors to provide more information on some of the issues raised in the focus groups. It is important to document pastors' views because they are in the position to perform the most visible culture work in the congregation through their control of the public symbolic display of the worship service and through their monopoly over the sermon.

However, I am also interested in whether the interpretive frameworks pastors use have a larger effect on the congregation and are adopted more widely as shared understandings. To this end, I draw upon the field notes generated by fieldwork in sixteen area congregations, four in each community. Fieldwork included visits to Sunday services, fellowship activities, and various family-oriented programs run in each congregation, along with informal conversations and some formal follow-up interviews with lay leaders. We also engaged

in document review of materials for education classes, family-oriented programming, newsletters, and sermons.[10]

In the focus groups, I asked pastors to describe their congregations' ministry
for families and the effect that changes in the family have had on their
churches. The first rhetoric that pastors used—and by far the most common—
identifies the *time bind* as the major problem facing families today. Pastors believe that the time bind is caused by the long hours parents spend in paid work
and by the competition for children's time from an increasing number of organized school and community activities. But if most pastors agree that the
time bind is the problem, their understanding of the time bind is shaped by
different interpretive frameworks. One group of pastors understands the time
bind as resulting, ultimately, from members' skewed values, which leads to
poor individual choices and a decline in religious commitment. Another group
interprets the time bind as the result of structural changes, not individual values or choices, and argues that churches have an exciting opportunity to develop new and more effective ministries to meet families' new needs.

Pastors also used a rhetoric about the need *to include more people from a
wider range of family situations*. Pastors told us that the church is called to minister to people regardless of their family situation and shared an elaborate and
articulate understanding of how to go about this. There are also two different
versions of this inclusion rhetoric. One version sees contemporary changes in
the family as negative and upholds the nuclear family with children as ideal.
The other sees changes in the family as either positive or neutral and seeks, at
least symbolically, to displace the nuclear family as the central organizing ideal
of congregational ministry. Table 5.1 outlines the structure of these rhetorics,
which are discussed in detail in the two sections that follow.

The Problem Is Time

Out of all of the changes in work and family life that have occurred in the last
few decades, this rhetoric singles out two as being of particular importance
and having a particular, and sharply negative, effect on congregations. The first
is the decision by more and more wives and mothers to work full-time in the
paid labor force and the resulting predominance of the dual-earner lifestyle.
The second is the problem of coordination that arises in the era of pluralized
time schedules within the family, made more intense by demands placed on
children's time. In particular, the proliferation of organized children's activities
and the demands of alternate-weekend custody arrangements are seen as almost unmanageable and as keeping substantial numbers of children and their
parents out of congregational activities.[11]

The time bind was the dominant theme in each focus group for a good portion of our discussion, and almost 80 percent of pastors used this rhetoric.[12]
But the rhetoric is not only widespread among pastors, it also comprises a

Table 5.1

Rhetorical Structure of Pastors' Talk about Changes in the Family

	Time		Inclusion	
	Skewed Values	Meet the New Needs	Brokenness	Redefine the Family
Proximate cause(s)	Proliferation of competing children's activities Blended families and custody arrangements Rise of dual-earner couple (women working)	Proliferation of competing children's activities Blended families and custody arrangements Rise of dual-earner couple (women working)	Family disruption	Pluralism—new forms of family, new ways of defining what a family is
Individual traits	Lack of commitment Materialism Consumerist attitude toward the church	Stress Searching for authenticity, caring relationships	Brokenness, sinfulness, pain	Individuals more free to express love and form caring relationships in new ways
Effect(s) on the church	Decline in attendance (especially children's and "family" programs) Challenges to traditional ways of doing things, demands for new programs Uncertainty about what works	Challenges to traditional ways of doing things, demands for new programs	Singles, single parents, the divorced, those in blended families may feel unwelcome, church cannot carry out its full ministry	Many feel unwelcome, excluded, including those in same-sex unions

TABLE 5.1 (cont.)

	Time		Inclusion	
	Skewed Values	Meet the New Needs	Brokenness	Redefine the Family
Church's responsibility	Call on individuals to display more commitment Critique of new values Make some changes, especially in children's programs, but lament the need to	Meet the new needs—actively seek out new ideas for ministry and ways to organize, keep experimenting until you find what works	Make all feel welcome regardless of their family situation Affirm the scriptural basis for the nuclear family with children and of male "headship" Ministry to support married couples, with a focus on men's responsibilities	Make all feel welcome regardless of family situation Acknowledge oppressive and hurtful nature of neopatriarchal family models and affirm more feminist and pluralist family models as matter of justice Displace "the family" from center of congregational life

common understanding among the lay leadership and some good portion of the active membership of the congregations in which we conducted fieldwork. Talk about time was pervasive in interviews with Sunday School teachers and leaders of other family ministry programs, at informal conversations at coffee hours and potlucks, and in committee and council meetings.

The "time bind" rhetoric is secular. In the academy and the media it has become a very common frame for understanding recent changes in the structure of work and the effects of work on family life.[13] Starting with the publication of *The Overworked American* (Schor 1991), academics have agreed that Americans are stressed about time and perceive that they do not have the time for the activities and commitments they care about most. Although some scholars believe that this is just a perception and that time is increasingly "frittered away" in leisure activities such as watching television, most argue that increasing hours spent on the job are leaving less time for family, leisure, and other valued commitments.[14]

However, in some local churches, the time-bind rhetoric predates the secular preoccupation with time by as much as three decades. As part of the fieldwork for this project, I collected samples of church documents—bulletins and newsletters, annual reports, sermons, and minutes of meetings—for several congregations across faith traditions from the 1950s through the 1990s. The time bind was a relatively common theme in these publications, especially in the 1960s. For example, the Sunday bulletin from a mass at a Catholic parish in rural Tompkins County from May 1963 contains, in the priest's column, a critique of the time bind caused by working women that would strike responsive cords in some area churches today: "If the mother's outside employment is not plainly necessary, the child will feel that his own needs are being made secondary to material gain. There is an intensified likelihood of harm to the child if the mother's job allows little time for companionship with the children."

One Methodist congregation in Liverpool has in its files a pamphlet, published by the Methodist Church Board of Education, Department of the Christian Family, that was used in the adult Sunday School classes during National Family Week in 1961. The flyer describes how competition from other community activities may be keeping members from fully committing to local churches:

> The two great problems faced by the Methodist family today are a) the use of time and b) the use of money. . . . Many families are plagued by a multitude of organizations. . . . Mother belongs to the church, the Sunday school class, the Women's Society, the P.T.A., the Grange, the garden club, the sewing circle, the lodge and numerous organizations calling for her help. Then there are the community fundraising organizations, the neighborhood groups and the next door neighbors who drop in for a cup of coffee. Father belongs to the Men's Club, the Rotary Club, the Community Chest drive, the country club, the lodge, the Grange, the cooperative

organization, the official board and teaches a Sunday school class. . . . Even the children are pushed into dancing classes at an early age.

The flyer goes on to critique the materialism of contemporary lifestyles and the inattention to stewardship it implies.

The time-bind rhetoric in many congregations today is remarkably similar to these examples from the 1960s. The most articulate statement of this did not come from a pastor, but from the woman who directs family ministry programs at a rural Catholic parish. She came into Ithaca one morning for another meeting and agreed to get together with me for coffee in the bagel place in the strip mall on the north side of town. Karen and I talked for an hour and a half over bagels and coffee, and my field notes show how she started off the conversation, in response to my question of how changes in family life have affected her parish:

> The biggest change over the last fifteen years or so is the lack of time that families have now. She said that's much bigger, more important, than any other change, "more than single parents, more than divorce. It's time. The women, *all* the women, went to work. And they have no time for parish activities, to bring the kids to activities." There's been a proliferation of nonparish activities—soccer, football, baseball, all for very young kids, more things available at earlier ages. . . . Some community soccer leagues and bowling leagues meet on Sunday morning—direct competition. And it's impossible to get groups together for religious education any time except Sunday. So if they have preparation for important things (sacraments, confirmation) they do short four- or six-week sessions and require the kids to be there, or they'll run an off-Sunday preparation only at the request of a specific group of parents who all agree to the same alternate time (e.g., Monday night) and commit to getting the kids there. (11/16/98)

As we talked, Karen kept returning to the two interrelated causes of the time bind that were repeatedly mentioned in the focus groups with pastors and in our fieldwork in area churches. Her response is useful for understanding how the time-bind rhetoric in these congregations is similar to and different from the academic time-bind discourse on which it draws.

For one thing, pastors and many lay leaders are much more willing to be gender-specific in their assessment of who is spending too much time at work than are academics: although a few mentioned fathers or parents more generically, most argued that it is working *mothers* who contribute to the time bind. Second, pastors are more keenly aware of the coordination costs of juggling pluralistic family schedules—for example, in managing alternate-weekend custody arrangements. And they are very aware that they are increasingly in competition for children's time with a host of other organized school and community activities. Even "sacred" time is no longer sacred, and running Sunday afternoon or evening confirmation classes becomes increasingly difficult as soccer leagues and theater groups, bands and Scouts and sports teams are increasingly likely to have activities on Sunday.

Although almost 80 percent of pastors agree that "time is the problem," there is marked disagreement about the solution. The "time bind" rhetoric is embedded in two different interpretive frameworks in these communities, each of which links the time bind to more fundamental underlying issues and which proposes a different set of solutions for congregations to explore.

SKEWED VALUES AND POOR CHOICES

In one set of congregations, the time-bind is understood as the result of a larger historical trend in the decline of religious commitment and the rise of a more materialistic lifestyle, a trend that pastors lament. For example, the pastor of an Assemblies of God congregation told me:

> I think a lot of kids grew up in church, like I did, watched our parents struggle because they wouldn't take on extra work, they wouldn't take on extra incomes. They believed that . . . Mom belonged in the home. So we did without because Mom wasn't gonna get a job, Mom was going to stay home, raise the kids, make sure they didn't get into trouble. So that meant we did without some things. Now this choice comes up again, and . . . young couples in my church [ask] are we going to do without or are we going to work the extra hours? We're going to work the extra hours, cause we don't want to do without. We want the bigger home, we want the two cars, and you know, we want all these different things. And so I think we've become much more materialistic than we've ever been before. (Pastor Focus Group, Tompkins County, 6/9/00)

Materialism is understood as evidence of a broader problem of skewed values, which result in poor choices and a lack of commitment to the church. Pastors complain of a culture that stresses not only materialism, but also the fulfillment of individual needs over values such as duty, service, and community involvement. An Episcopal priest from Seneca County told us:

> It's the issue of cultural priorities. We still have twenty-four hours in a day and if I choose to go to soccer on Sunday mornings as opposed to church, or choose to go to soccer on Wednesday night as opposed to church that is a cultural and systemic shift in attitude and priority. (Pastor Focus Group, Seneca County, 6/6/00)

Several pastors drew a very specific contrast between their experiences today and the role of churches and of pastors in the communities in which they grew up. Pastor Davis, from an Evangelical Covenant congregation, told us: "[In] the community I came from, which was a small town in Wisconsin, the ministers got together and talked with the schools and made a deal that there was no sports activity on Wednesday night" (Pastor Focus Group, Liverpool, 6/2/00). Now, instead of other groups checking in with the pastors so as not to conflict with church programming, there is what one pastor called a "smorgasbord of choices" offered at all hours, including Wednesday night and Sunday.

More choices and more competition from new kinds of activities coincide with the emergence of a culture of individual fulfillment, these pastors believe, and churches are increasingly on "equal footing" with other activities in the competition for members' money and time. One Church of Christ pastor phrased it very succinctly: "It's a matter of the church no longer shapes the culture, the culture shapes the church" (Pastor Focus Group, Liverpool, 6/2/00).

This version of the time-bind rhetoric is pervaded by nostalgia for social forms and arrangements that were once culturally dominant and are now either lost or increasingly marginal. These social forms include the Ozzie and Harriet family and a lifestyle centered around local communities of place and dense, overlapping, long-term ties to binding local institutions.[15] There is also a nostalgic longing here for the lost status of local clergy in the new institutional configuration of community groups and activities.

In one sense, the losses that pastors and lay leaders perceive are real. In the last few decades, clergy have lost social status relative to other professions.[16] The "speedup" in organized children's activities is real, borne out by time-use studies as well as conventional wisdom. And new activities such as soccer, for which community leagues began to be organized in the 1980s and 1990s, came about long after anyone would think to ask the local pastor about whether practices would interfere with church activities.[17] What is nostalgic is how this rhetoric constructs these losses with reference to an idealized past cast in a sentimental light, focusing on a middle-class, white, privileged family model and a suburban or small-town community that was never the experience of a majority of Americans, and was not experienced in the uniformly positive way this rhetoric indicates even for those who did fit the model.

This nostalgic construction of the past makes it difficult for pastors and lay leaders to make accurate distinctions between what has changed and what has remained the same. The materials from local church files from 1960s, quoted in the introduction to this chapter, make it clear that the "time bind" is not new, but was a concern as much as forty years ago. What is different is the configuration of activities that are competing for members' time and the pluralization of family time schedules. In the 1950s and 1960s, adult men and women gave more of their time to church-related volunteer activities, making churches, parishes, and synagogues "winners" in the competition for adults'— and especially women's—time. Children were in school and perhaps dance class, but they were not as tightly (or over-) scheduled as they are today.

Perhaps more crucial, all of the activities mentioned in the Methodist flyer worked together to foster a single dominant work-family schedule and gendered division of labor, being built around the needs of the male-breadwinner family. The various activities of Mom, Dad, and the kids did not overlap and interfere with one another. Church-time was privileged time, both in individuals'

Chapter Six

THE PRACTICE OF FAMILY MINISTRY

THE LAST CHAPTER showed how pastors and lay leaders interpret changes in work and family and understand the effects of these changes on their congregations. Focus groups and fieldwork suggest that these rhetorics influence family ministry as a practical, daily activity, from formal programming to informal ways of doing things. But the relationship between rhetoric and practice is never straightforward. The practice of ministry may reinforce messages about the good family found in congregational rhetoric, rework or reinterpret the ideas about the family, or embody entirely different, alternative way of conceptualizing family life.

Some forms of culture are explicit, articulated, and on the surface of social life, and are therefore easy to observe and analyze. The rhetorics discussed in the last chapter and the survey responses of pastors are explicit culture. When a pastor says, "the problem is time," or a director of religious education says, "all the women went to work," there is an explicit meaning to the statement, readily apparent to someone who shares the same language and culture. Likewise, when a congregation runs a Sunday School, this makes an explicit statement about the importance of religious education in passing on the faith.

Other forms of culture are implicit and remain under the surface of social life. The "time-bind" rhetoric is explicit, but the family schema it embodies often remains implicit and unarticulated.[1] The presence of a Sunday School may convey an explicit meaning ("religious education is important"), but how the Sunday School is run also sends implicit messages about moral order. For example, having separate Sunday School classes for boys and girls in an evangelical church says one thing about gender roles, while the mixed-sex classes in the United Methodist Sunday School down the street send a different set of implicit messages about men's and women's natures and the appropriate relationships between men and women in the church.

As these examples suggest, the distinction between implicit and explicit culture is not exactly the difference between "talk" and "action," or between "symbol" and "practice." Both talk and practice convey explicit meanings. They also convey implicit meanings, which often anchor other, more explicit or "surface" meanings. It is the combination of explicit and implicit meanings that produce ideology as an ongoing, living system of meaning—and as an enduring feature of social life and our social institutions. The overall style of ministry in local congregations, comprising the combination of rhetoric about the family and assessments of priority and as a practical matter of scheduling. Nothing organized happened in these communities on Sunday morning except church.

In these four communities, it is mostly the pastors and lay leaders of "establishment" or "mainline" churches that perpetuate this nostalgic version of the time-bind rhetoric—Presbyterians, Episcopalians, and Catholic parishes.[18] However, some pastors of conservative and evangelical churches also engaged in this nostalgic version of the time bind, including those from smaller Assemblies of God, Evangelical Covenant, and Church of Christ congregations. Most of the pastors who use this rhetoric are men in their late forties or older, and most are pastors of congregations that were established in their local communities well before the 1950s. This understanding of the time bind is rooted in a particular social structural location and is in part a response to a displacement of cultural authority and social status on the part of pastors and lay leaders who, for years, took it for granted that families—and especially women and children—organized their schedules around the church's calendar. Demands that churches should reorganize to facilitate the participation of working women and children who have multiple other commitments are not, for this group, a welcome change.

MEET THE NEW NEEDS

Not all of the pastors who identify the time bind as the problem are looking to the past. A second version of this rhetoric is embedded in a larger interpretive framework that links the problems of time, stress, and coordinating schedules to a call for contemporary styles of evangelism and ministry that meet the new needs. A man in his forties, the head pastor at a booming independent evangelical church in Tompkins County, talked about the time bind as creating needs that churches are particularly well suited to meet:

> I think there are a number of issues that are stressing people out. With couples where both work, on weekends they are both exhausted. It's no longer the dependence on the woman to get people into church. . . . So, people are coming looking for a message of hope. So, it puts us in a delightful position but in a difficult position. We can provide that hope and encouragement. . . . There is a desire for authenticity, for relationships, for community, and a lot of them are turned off by institutions, and we foster relationships. This is a golden opportunity for the church to arise and build a community of faith, a community of persons, and it's our job to facilitate those kinds of relationships. (Pastor Focus Group, 11/20/97)

These pastors recognize that they are in direct competition for members' discretionary time. And the competition is not just with other community groups and organizations. They believe that they are also competing for time that might otherwise be spent at work, because members are working longer hours than ever before. They also are aware that they are competing for time that might be spent at home together as a family, because Sunday morning is

often one of the very few times of the week when Mom, Dad, and the children
are all free from other organized activities, school, and work.

But instead of decrying the competition, these pastors embrace it and look
to other institutional arenas for ideas about how to compete successfully, as evident in this quotation from an evangelical Methodist pastor:

> Society is changing, needs change, things change at such a pace that businesses
> that grow nowadays have several ways that they may go. . . . I think we have to do
> the same thing and say, well, God be my helper, and if things begin to unfold this
> way, and if we're smart, we'll learn from the business world. . . . We will be flexi-
> ble, we will try new things. (Pastor Focus Group, Liverpool, 6/2/00)

In sharp contrast to the more nostalgic time-bind rhetoric, there is no sense,
here, of placing any blame on church members or poor individual choices. The
root cause of the time bind is understood not as individual and moral (skewed
values, lack of commitment), but as impersonal and structural. If the nostalgic
rhetoric urges individuals to change their values and live differently, the "meet
the new needs" rhetoric views the church as responsible for adapting to structural changes in the organization of work in order to bring in members who
are living under the new time constraints.

The "meet the needs" framework is linked to a set of organizational practices. In our survey, we asked each pastor what the congregation had done re-
cently to adapt to changes in work and family, and 45 percent reported that
they had changed the time or timing of programs and ministries for families
within the last few years. This was by far the single most common response.
The focus groups and fieldwork give a good sense of what kinds of changes are
indicated by this survey response. Traditional ten- or twelve-week sacrament-
preparation classes have been replaced in many Catholic parishes by three or
four three-hour workshops. Many churches are trying "family nights," with
different programs for different age groups all meeting at the same time, to cut
down on the number of weekly trips to church. In other churches, "family
nights" are intergenerational fellowship and worship activities. Pastors and lay
leaders reported that these experiments are working. In focus groups, pastors
who used a "meet the needs" rhetoric told us that their congregations' ministries, especially those for children, are thriving. The survey of pastors supports this, indicating that churches that do experiment with the time or timing
of programs are much more likely to be growing than are other churches, and
that this relationship is statistically significant.

It is mostly pastors of evangelical congregations, especially nondenominational ones, who use this rhetoric of meeting new needs; however, some
pastors in United Methodist, Church of Christ, Catholic, and Presbyterian
congregations in the small towns, rural areas, and the less wealthy areas of
Syracuse also talk about meeting the new needs. Evangelical pastors tend to
use words such as *marketing* and *innovation*, drawing on an understanding of

marketing as a legitimate religious tool. Pastors from more liberal Protestant traditions use a religious language of social justice when they talk about meeting the new needs. For example, Pastor Karen Brown, from a small, liberal United Methodist congregation in rural Tompkins County, used a "justice" framework to argue for more openness to the new family reality; justice means that leaders need to, as she put it, "listen carefully to what people's needs are, and not expect them to fit into the mold of our preconceived ideas" (Pastor Focus Group, Tompkins County, 6/9/00). Often, the mainline Protestant pastors who employ a "meet the needs" rhetoric are younger. There are few female pastors in these communities, but most of them also used this version of the time-bind rhetoric.

The Problem Is How to Include New Kinds of Families

The other dominant rhetoric that pastors and lay leaders use when they talk about "the problem of the family," is a rhetoric of *inclusion*. In focus groups, just over half of the pastors (56 percent) said that the problem they face today is creating an atmosphere where people in a variety of family situations feel welcomed and included in the life of the congregation. As a Baptist pastor told us: "A lot of times, a family-oriented church means Mom and Dad, three kids, and the dog, and this can turn away those who don't have this type of family" (Pastor Focus Group, 11/20/97). Congregational leaders are aware that many people associate churches with nuclear families with children, and that more and more people do not live in this kind of family arrangement. Most believe that their church ought to be a welcoming place but that being welcoming has gotten harder.

Pastors who use the rhetoric of inclusion believe that the challenges they face in being more inclusive are primarily symbolic ones. How can language and rituals be changed so that all feel welcome? One strategy is to avoid terms such as *family ministry* and to avoid using names for particular ministries that are rooted in gender and life-stage imagery ("the Mothers' Group"). Sermons, programs, and newsletters use phrases such as *community night, community potluck,* or *intergenerational ministry* in an attempt to communicate that singles of all ages, single parents, and those who do not attend church with their family members are welcome. In our survey, more than 80 percent of mainline Protestant pastors, about two-thirds of Catholic priests, and just over half of evangelical pastors (54 percent) reported that they have increased the amount of intergenerational or communitywide programming in their churches in the last five years.

The prevalence of this kind of language is directly related to changes in work and family, as a Lutheran pastor explained: "*Family* indicates sort of a club, a very self-enclosed thing, and so we try to do more things that we call intergenerational, and open" (Pastor Focus Group, Northside, 6/8/00). For similar reasons, the annual Mother-Daughter Banquet has become the Women's

Banquet in many local churches, with poems, stories, speeches, and songs that celebrate women's contributions to the family, the community, the workplace, and the church.

Another strategy is to talk about the church itself as an extended family of which all are part. The "family" Thanksgiving meal at the Assemblies of God church draws together those in nuclear families and a wide range of other members. In a culture dominated by Norman Rockwell images of Thanksgiving,[19] having the church family with which to spend the holiday can be a welcome relief to those whose lives do not fit the Rockwellian image, according to one pastor:

> I'll give you an example. For Thanksgiving, well, holidays are often a very difficult time especially for those who don't have children or don't have a spouse, they're left out, they're not included. . . . And you know people often say that, "How are you, where are you spending the holiday?"—"Well we're getting together with my family." And there's the single adult or the widower or the married couple who never had kids and there's nobody left in their family and they're thinking, "Oh, great, what are we going to do?" So we have a Thanksgiving meal and we call it a family time. And we expect everybody to bring all of their family even if that family is just you . . . to be with the rest of your family at church. (Pastor Focus Group, Tompkins County, 6/9/00)

All of the pastors using an inclusion rhetoric agree about their desire to be inclusive of single persons of all ages and married couples without children. There is also agreement about the need to minister to those who have gone through episodes of family disruption and recombination. The divorced and the widowed, they argue, need a space to find healing and support. Pastors also talk about the need to support single parents and those who are newly remarried and constructing a "blended" family, during a time that is both harder and more complicated than family life was in the past.

However, pastors from different religious traditions disagree on two interrelated issues. The first is whether to be inclusive of those in gay and lesbian unions. The second point of disagreement is about whether to uphold the heterosexual nuclear family as an ideal or normative model for family life. One interpretation of being "inclusive" upholds the heterosexual nuclear family with children as a biblically endorsed ideal around which the church ought to be structured. It views divorce and single parenthood as forms of brokenness and defines gay and lesbian unions as sinful. The other version of inclusion embraces alternative family forms as positive and self-expressive, and wants to move away from endorsing the heterosexual nuclear family with children as an ideal and as the central organizing unit around which churches are built.

BROKENNESS

Evangelical and fundamentalist Protestant pastors, and some Catholic priests, talk about family disruption as a form of brokenness. Brokenness results from sinfulness, but it is not the case that these pastors single out the divorced or single parents as being especially sinful. Sin, in this theology, is a pervasive aspect of life and everyone is understood to be "broken" by it. Likewise, everyone is understood to need the healing that can be offered through Christ and His church. As the brochure for one independent fundamentalist congregation in Seneca County says in their "What We Believe" section, "We believe in . . . [t]he depravity and lost condition of all men by nature . . . [and] [t]he Holy Spirit who convicts the world of sin and regenerates, indwells, enlightens and guides believers."

Depravity is a strong word, and is found only in congregations on the most fundamentalist end of the conservative spectrum. The much larger group of evangelical pastors and members use words such as *lost, broken*, and *weighed down* to connote a similar theological stance. In this rhetoric, family disruption is contrasted directly to the ideal state described in Scripture, as a Missouri Synod Lutheran pastor explained: "[I]n Scripture, from my perspective, there are two messages. One is describing the way things are, and the other is prescribing the things that God desires. That's one aspect of Scripture, God describes a humanity that is broken and lost" (Pastor Focus Group, Tompkins County, 6/14/00). He went on to say that what is prescribed in Scripture is a heterosexual nuclear family ("Adam and Eve together . . . not two Adams, or two Eves") that has children who "honor the father and the mother."

This language not only is found among evangelical pastors, but is a feature of evangelical congregational discourse more broadly. Field notes from Family Night at one evangelical church in Seneca County, during the all-male[20] portion of the teen meeting, read as follows: One boy said, "God created Adam and Eve, not Adam and Steve," to which everyone laughed and nodded their heads. The leader said that "the world wants us to be tolerant, but God does not want us to be tolerant. He wants us to stand up for what's right" (02/18/99). The leader went on to emphasize that we should not single out homosexuals and overlook other sins, such as adultery, that are also destructive of the family and that God does not want us to tolerate. But we should open up to homosexual persons and teach them, in love, that they do not have to "give in to their sexual cravings."

What is most interesting for understanding the rhetoric of brokenness is to contrast this congregation's stance on homosexuality with its flexibility on other issues. The leadership has responded to pleas for fewer "nights of running back to the church" by having a weekly Family Night with gender-specific, age-graded programs, along with some combined social time at the end of the evening over cookies and punch. The pastor told us, and several members confirmed in informal talks and a few in longer in-depth interviews, that he has worked consistently and successfully to draw several single mothers into the various women's ministries the church provides. The church is especially supportive of biracial families and blended families. In fact, there is a great deal of tolerance here, combined with a sense of limits to that tolerance set by core doctrine.

The evangelical Protestant pastors in our focus groups were very articulate about the need to minister to the "broken" while not compromising on what they view as the biblically based family ideal. So were some of the Catholic priests, like this one from Northside: "I don't mean to exclude the other people, they should be part of your special ministry, but to strengthen the basic family I think is the duty of every religious leader. If you lose the family, where do you go? It's the last hope, as a society" (Pastor Focus Group, Northside, 6/8/00).

Strengthening the family, in this rhetoric, involves a ministry focused around preserving and strengthening marriage and the parent-child relationship, as one pastor argued: "If we say we believe in marriage, what are we doing to help marriages survive? And thrive? As well as deal with those that have gone through the very, very difficult issue of divorce" (Baptist Pastor, Liverpool Pastor Focus Group, 6/2/00). A particular focus is on ministry to married men with children, encouraging them to be better husbands and fathers,[21] as a pastor of an independent evangelical congregation told us:

> We're addressing men who are married and who for the most part have children . . . they're there [at church] every other week and they're doing projects with their wives, between the sessions, studying the Bible together, praying together . . . and I'm amazed at what it has done, in these marriages, and in their families, and what it has done for these men individually. (Pastor Focus Group, Seneca County, 6/6/00)

Our fieldwork suggests that at least some members of these congregations who have experienced family disruption respond positively to the rhetoric of brokenness because it acknowledges both the pain of the experience and their need of help—practical, spiritual, and emotional—to get through it. Elise, a single parent who attends Garnerville Baptist in rural Tompkins County, told me that, when she divorced, the pastor made sure she had money to pay the rent and got her "plugged in" to a network of women friends who she described as "my salvation through that time." Nora, a Catholic woman from Northside, told us that even though she realized that "marriage was supposed to be for life" and she "felt like a failure" after her divorce, the same church that kept "affirming marriage, especially around the holidays," was also a haven for her when her husband left. My field notes from our informal conversation describe what "being a haven" meant for her after her divorce:

> She did rely on the pastor, for counseling and help. And the staff was great, too. The director of religious education, the rectory staff, and parish housekeeper; they always made her feel welcome and they made her feel included. And they would talk with her, and it made her realize something. To her, "the divorce was just the biggest thing in the world, and every problem I had seemed huge." But she would talk to them, and they would share their stories with her, and she would realize that they had problems, too, everyone had problems. And "they didn't seem

to think that my problems were so bad, really, nothing out of the ordinary. It made me feel normal, and human," and less like she didn't fit in. (3/28/99)

In the fundamentalist and evangelical congregations in these communities, and in some Catholic parishes, the desire to redefine "family" and "family ministry" to be more inclusive means focusing on reaching out to members who have experienced divorce or the death of a spouse, trying hard to include singles of all ages in congregational activities, and organizing activities in ways that are sensitive to the scheduling constraints of dual-earner families with children. The limits of inclusivity are set by core doctrine, which upholds the ideal of the heterosexual, two-parent family with the man as the spiritual— and practical—head. This means disapproving of homosexual lifestyles and understanding family disruption as sign of brokenness in a sinful world.

REDEFINE THE FAMILY

Many mainline Protestant pastors, and some Catholic priests, are much less willing to uphold the patriarchal, heterosexual nuclear family as an ideal, and these pastors try to foster an atmosphere that sees what they call "alternative family lifestyles" as healthy and positive expressions of love. As one woman, the pastor of an American Baptist church, explained:

> A main piece of our continuing education is this broadening definition of family life. . . . We've got the single families and the biracial families . . . and gays and lesbians worshipping with us, and . . . we affirm that. And so when we use [the term] *family programming* we have to be very clear that we're not excluding alternative forms of family. (Pastor Focus Group, Tompkins County, 6/9/00)

This openness to "alternative" families goes along with an interpretation of Scripture that finds it to be a less reliable and unitary guide to what an ideal family might look like. As a Unitarian pastor, whose church has a well-known ministry for lesbian and gay community members, told us: "I think that we, we try to speak of normal families *in comparison or in contrast to the Bible*, [because] to me the Bible is just filled with a bunch of stories about dysfunctional families" (Pastor Focus Group, Tompkins County, 6/9/00). He went on to recount in colorful terms, and to the evident discomfort of some of the more conservative pastors in the focus group, the willingness of Lot, in the Old Testament, to give his daughters to his houseguests for their sexual pleasure, and the stories of Noah's children "always finding him lying around drunk in the middle of the day." If these are biblical families, he argued, then the Bible cannot be the only guide to what a good family might look like.

But this openness to alternative family arrangements is not only based in different approaches to the Scriptures. It also rests on a different understanding of the relationship between church and society. Those who use a rhetoric of brokenness explicitly reject the idea that the church is obligated to change its understanding of the family based on societal transformations, contrasting what they understand as an eternal biblical standard with society's unstable norms and ways of life. But as one Presbyterian pastor noted, many other pastors do not view keeping up with "society" as selling out: "I think it's fair to say that we have changed our thinking as to what constitutes family, in our churches, to get up to speed with society. I shudder to think what was considered a family when I was growing up in the church" (Pastor Focus Group, Seneca County, 6/6/00).

Those who interpret it as appropriate for the church to "catch up to society" have a very different style of responding to family disruption. For example, in one Episcopal church in Seneca County, an after-service conversation with four people from the adult Sunday School turned to this issue when the research assistant asked how the church had "been there" during periods of crisis. A single mother in her forties said, "The Church was a comfort during my divorce. It was a constant" (3/14/99). When the research assistant followed up by asking whether the church would run a program for divorced persons, a man in the group, also divorced, gave an emphatic "no." He explained,

> If there were a single person's group that would be kind of discriminatory in a way . . . you are stereotyping people into little slots. And that's not what [our church] is about . . . It's the Christian doctrine, really—no discrimination, everyone is a valuable human being with a potential for goodness. It's God's teaching . . . it's basic Christian teaching—everyone is good. (3/14/99)

Ultimately, it is legitimate within these religious traditions for the church to respond to changing societal understandings of the family because society and the people who comprise it are not understood to be "broken" by sin but rather redeemed by Christ's love.

None of the mainline Protestant and Catholic pastors, or lay leaders, who talked about "redefining the family" said that the two-parent heterosexual family is oppressive. There was no radical critique of patriarchy, at least in the polite social discourse of focus groups and after-church coffee hours. Rather, pastors felt that the church's job was to encourage stable, loving, healthful family contexts for its members and to figure out how to help provide and encourage these contexts in a way that acknowledged the legitimacy of homosexual unions and that did not stigmatize those having experienced divorce. For some pastors, the entire issue of family ministry was not really about providing "family programming" or talking about "the family," but rather talking about the issues of poverty and joblessness that most immediately affected the families they saw every day.

LOCAL RHETORICS AND RELIGIOUS TRADITIONS

It is the overall combination of rhetorics within a religious community that sends members and potential members a message about the ideal family—and which families are "a problem" for the local church. From the focus groups and fieldwork, it is possible to understand the typical combinations of rhetoric in different kinds of congregations. Box 5.1 outlines these combinations, and is based on the conversations in the pastor focus groups and the fieldwork in area congregations, including some follow-up additional fieldwork in Catholic parishes.[22] There are two things to keep in mind when looking at this table. First, although it is possible to identify combinations of rhetoric and which ones were most common among the pastors we spoke with, it is important to remember that the focus groups encompassed only forty-seven pastors, so it is not possible to identify precisely what percentage of pastors in the community use any given combination of rhetoric. Second, this table characterizes pastors' rhetoric, and although in the focus groups pastors were asked to talk about how their congregation as a whole deals with family issues, and although fieldwork indicated a real congruence between pastors' talk and lay members' understandings, pastors' rhetoric is not the same thing as congregational culture.

In our focus groups, the majority of mainline Protestant pastors had a *nostalgic* understanding that, having located the problem in poor choices and skewed values, calls for little in the way of congregational response except to make the kind of culture critique of the materialistic, secularized lifestyle that they perceive to be the real underlying issue. Some of these pastors refer specifically to Richard Niebuhr, placing themselves in a culture-critic tradition that has had an important place in mainline Protestant history and culture. Others refer more to their own experience, which centers around a perception of having

Box 5.1 Interpretive Frameworks: "The Problem" and Solutions		
	Rhetorics Drawn On	*Religious Tradition*
Nostalgic	Skewed values	Mainline Protestant Catholic
Progressive	Redefine the family Meet the new needs	Mainline Protestant Catholic
Patriarchal	Brokenness Skewed values	Fundamentalist Protestant
Responsive	Brokenness Meet the new needs	Evangelical Protestant Catholic
Social Justice	A focus on "family values" diverts attention from poverty as a social justice issue	Mainline Protestant Catholic

undergone a gradual decline in their own social status and religious authority and a decline of the centrality of the congregation in the local community's life. This nostalgic framework was the most common one among mainline Protestants in our focus groups.

However, some mainline Protestant pastors were more prone to use a *progressive* framework that combines the rhetoric of redefining the family with an emphasis on meeting new family needs. This group, only 12 percent of the mainline pastors we spoke with in the focus groups, comprised pastors of some of the largest and most prosperous mainline congregations, but also included many of the younger and female pastors heading up smaller churches. Many of them pastored churches in Northside, the most diverse community, or in Seneca Falls or Ithaca, both of which have a reputation for being progressive towns.

Either these pastors were very successful and secure in their status or they had entered the ministry in a time well past the 1950s Protestant heyday and did not hearken back to that as a "golden era" for the local church. They drew on a different part of their religious tradition, invoking either a language of social justice or a language of caring and community-building to develop a religious rationale for a progressive approach to family ministry that often included an openness to gay and lesbian members and a definition of "the family" that included homosexual families. Though fewer in number than those using a nostalgic rhetoric, the social visibility of their congregations and the large membership of many of them led some of them to have strong leadership roles in local ecumenical groups, and in sheer numbers they may reach as many church members as pastors with a more nostalgic view.

Conservative Protestant pastors, in these communities, could be distinguished by their willingness to either embrace or reject change in the family, and especially in women's roles. Virtually all of the fundamentalist pastors employed a *patriarchal* framework. They embraced a rhetoric of skewed values to develop a critique of poor individual choices that centered around working women, materialism, and overscheduled children, combining it with a language of brokenness that upheld not only the nuclear family but the male-breadwinner nuclear family as a biblical ideal. In contrast, almost all of the evangelical pastors combined a rhetoric of brokenness with a rhetoric of meeting the new needs to make their congregations *responsive*, within the limits of their core doctrine, to many changes in the family. They made real efforts to welcome those in single-parent and blended families, long-term singles and childless couples, and dual-earner couples with children who feel overstretched by the demands of juggling home, full-time work for two parents, and children's numerous organized activities. Yet they also upheld the two-parent nuclear family—regardless of who works outside the home—as the biblical ideal. The responsive framework was by far the most common one among conservative Protestant pastors in these four communities.

Catholic priests were the most diverse in their interpretive frameworks. The practical exigencies of offering Catholic family ministry—trying to field ten- to twelve-week confirmation classes, for example—have led most of the priests to embrace the rhetoric of meeting new family needs. Some of them combined this with a preference for a more conservative family ideal and saw many changes, including rising rates of divorce and single parenting as well as the visibility of gay and lesbian lifestyles, as a form of brokenness, leading them to a *responsive* framework. Some of them drew on feminist, liberation, and social justice frameworks within the Catholic tradition to develop a more *progressive* stance. Some priests, especially older ones with a long tenure in rural parishes, were more *nostalgic* and were unhappy with parishioners demanding changes in programming that they did not find legitimate. Ironically, in the most hierarchical denomination, the priests' views varied more than did those of pastors from other traditions; Catholic priests we spoke to were about evenly divided between these three interpretive stances. This largely reflects differences in age and training, and especially the priests' more general view of the positive or negative consequences of Vatican II reforms for the church.

Finally, it should be noted that a few pastors in our focus groups rejected these rhetorics altogether. This was particularly true in poorer communities such as Northside or rural Seneca County, where more than one pastor told us that a concentration on "family ministry" takes attention away from other issues that are more pressing—and perhaps of more immediate concern to the actual families living near their churches. These pastors believed that a focus on the family is part of a larger societal movement toward talking about "family values" as a way to avoid confronting much harder questions about *social justice* and the structural sources of poverty. As one Lutheran pastor from Northside said, inner cities are not generally bastions of two-parent-with-children families, and a focus on family ministry in this context is at best a distraction and at worse an abdication of responsibility. A Seneca County Episcopal priest declared with some passion that in his community, poverty was the real problem that families faced—a lack of good, stable jobs with health benefits being at the heart of his concerns, comments that were repeated almost verbatim by two Catholic priests from Northside. And a United Methodist pastor told us: "My concern is . . . I'm not so concerned about family life as I'm concerned about . . . my congregation is waking up and smelling the coffee and I do believe that the city . . . I think we're going to become a dumping ground of the poor. . . . And we don't know how to minister to the poor" (Pastor Focus Group, Northside, 6/8/00).

Rhetorics are local constructions, but they draw on larger discourses: the "time bind" discourse of the academy and popular media, the critique of materialism that has been part of mainline Protestantism at least since Niebuhr (1956), the discourses of marketing and innovation that evangelicals have long borrowed from the entrepreneurial world and wedded to a language of evangelism, and therapeutic discourse about functional and dysfunctional families. Local churches are part of larger religious traditions that provide authoritative discourses on what "the good family" means, and they also draw on these official discourses about the good family in forming local understandings. It is this combination of local interpretation with elements of official religious discourses and secular frameworks that tells church members and potential members what "the good family" is understood to be like in a given congregation.

In our telephone survey of area pastors, we asked them to tell us about their churches' official discourses about the family. Table 5.2 shows how these official views vary by religious tradition. What becomes clear in comparing the local rhetoric discovered in focus groups and fieldwork with the survey results is that in some congregations there is a good "fit" or resonance between local interpretive frameworks and official denominational views on gender and family roles. Conservative (evangelical and fundamentalist) Protestant traditions emphasize traditional gender roles within marriage, children's obedience to the authority of parents and pastors, and men's spiritual headship of the family. This is a good fit with both the patriarchal and responsive frameworks found in local pastors' talk.

Mainline (liberal and moderate) Protestant denominations and the Catholic church tend to promote official discourses that endorse the view that "there have been all kinds of families throughout history, and God approves of many kinds of families." Official denominational views are less likely to endorse traditional gender roles and are more likely to emphasize the importance of teaching children to think for themselves. They reject the idea that the man is the spiritual head of the family. This suggests that mainline Protestant and Catholic pastors who use a progressive framework to understand the contemporary family problems are well in line with their official religious traditions.

On the other hand, mainline Protestant and Catholic pastors who hold a nostalgic interpretation, and Catholic priests who endorse a language of brokenness, find themselves in the position of defending views that are a poor fit with official denominational teaching. For example, the rhetoric of the "time bind," so pervasive in mainline Protestant and Catholic churches, coexists with a denominational discourse that is more open to new family arrangements and much more egalitarian in its views of appropriate gender roles. What this means is that, in effect, the progressive understanding of the family in the official teachings of these traditions is undercut by a nostalgic rhetoric that hearkens fondly back to the male-breadwinner family ideal of the 1950s. It is only in the relatively few mainline Protestant and Catholic congregations that emphasize the need to redefine the family and that are attuned to issues of poverty and joblessness more than to traditional kinds of family ministry that the progressive message of the official discourse is reflected consistently in the local rhetoric. And in some Catholic parishes, the local rhetoric of the family is more conservative than the responses in table 5.2 would suggest, with pastors endorsing a rhetoric of brokenness that is distinctly patriarchal.

TABLE 5.2
Family Rhetoric—Official Views[a]

	Liberal Protestant[b]	Moderate Protestant	Conservative Protestant	Catholic
N	22	21	59	18
Progressive items—percent agreeing[c]				
Reject "family ministry" as exclusive term	46	53	13	0
Wrong to think only one kind of family is a good family	73	81	65	83
There have been all kinds of families throughout history, and God approves of many different kinds of families	86	90	0	85
Affirm congregation has gay/lesbian members[d]	55	29	10	33
Teach kids to think for themselves	68	44	0	57
Mean on Progressivism Index	*3.00*	*2.76*	*.91*	*2.33*
Traditional items[e]*—percent agreeing*				
It's better for all if man earns money, woman takes care of home/children	0	14	78	38
It's God's will that the man is the spiritual head of the family	14	0	91	14
We teach kids to trust, obey parents, teachers, the pastor	32	56	93	43
Mean on Traditionalism Index	*.50*	*.67*	*2.50*	*.78*

Notes: [a] The items "It's God's will that the man is the spiritual head of the family" and "There have been many different kinds of families throughout history, and God approves of many different kinds of families" refer to the larger faith tradition; pastors were asked to choose which one best characterizes their faith traditions' "official" stance. The items about teaching children (obey versus think for themselves) refer to what the congregation tries to teach children through its religious education activities. All other items refer to the pastors' own views.

[b] Denominations classified following Smith 1987; resulting classification is virtually identical to Steensland et al. 2000, except that "mainline Protestant" is divided, here, into "liberal" and "moderate" to better capture variation in family rhetoric and programming.

[c] When summed, the progressive items form an index with an alpha = .7, a mean of 1.86, and a standard deviation of 1.39.

[d] Pastors were asked whether or not the congregation has lesbian or gay members. This is treated as a rhetorical item because it is unlikely that this constitutes an accurate report of which congregations actually have gay and lesbian members. Rather, this item is an indicator of the willingness of lesbian and gay persons to be "out" within the congregational context and of the pastor's willingness to affirm the presence of lesbian and gay members. National data, where available, suggests that condemnation of a homosexual lifestyle is widespread. The National Congregations Study found that 59 percent of American congregations have rules or norms against homosexuality. A national study conducted at Princeton University, the Religion and Politics Survey, found that only 15 percent of congregations took any active role in "being more supportive of homosexuals."

[e] When summed, the traditionalism items form an index with an alpha = .8, a mean of 1.54, and a standard deviation of 1.24.

Defining the Ideal Family

Most studies of religious discourse around issues of the family have looked at "official" doctrine or the elite discourse of denominational leaders and activists. These studies find that there is a liberal/conservative culture war organized around pervasive and deep divisions in views of the family, gender roles, sexuality, and the authority of biblical texts to provide a guide to contemporary family relationships.[23] And there are clear liberal/conservative differences in the rhetoric of local pastors on family issues. The conservative Protestant discourse of brokenness and the fact that these pastors are unwilling to accept gay and lesbian unions as a form of family mark a distinct religious subculture that is at odds with the willingness of liberal Protestant pastors and some Catholic priests to redefine the family in ways that refuse to see family dissolution and reformulation as a moral failure and that allow their churches to welcome gay and lesbian families.

However, there are also remarkable similarities in local rhetoric that crosscut the liberal/conservative dividing line and make a culture wars framework only partially useful in understanding local religious talk about the good family.[24] The willingness of many evangelical pastors to meet new family needs results in local congregations that are as welcoming of single parents, singles, childless couples, and dual-earner families as are many of their more liberal counterparts. The nostalgia in some mainline Protestant and Catholic congregations for the male-breadwinner lifestyle results in congregations that communicate a preference for the kind of "domesticated patriarchy" that we often associate with evangelicals. And the pragmatism of many Catholic parishes means that regardless of the priest's rhetoric, the reworking of family ministry programs has made a welcoming space for dual-earner families, blended families, and single parents.

In the 1950s, a particular version of familism was institutionalized in the suburban religious expansion, anchored in a middle-class, male-breadwinner family schema—the "Ozzie and Harriet" family. The decade saw an explosion in the number and variety of programs available for children and teens, increasing numbers of women's programs during the day, committee meetings on Wednesday or Thursday evening for fathers to attend after a family dinner, and social programs for the whole family on Friday night or Saturday during the day. These ministries drew on and elaborated an already established repertoire of ministry for women and children that had been growing since the advent of the "social church" in the late nineteenth century. But in the 1950s, such ministries became more numerous and various. They were organized around reintegrating a family that spent much of the week separated by the father's long hours and long commute and teens who were more mobile and had more free time and disposable income than ever before.[25]

The rhetoric in pastor focus groups and the fieldwork in local congregations in these four communities today shows that, although many kinds of families are acceptable and even welcomed, the ideal family is still the Ozzie and Harriet family of the 1950s. Across faith traditions, the family rhetoric of local church life is firmly anchored in a particular family schema, or cultural model—that of the neopatriarchal heterosexual, middle-class, nuclear family with children. This model of the family is idealized in the nostalgic time-bind rhetoric in mainline Protestant and Catholic churches and in the rhetoric of brokenness in conservative Protestant churches.

A schema is a cultural model around which a set of resources—such as money and organizational structures and routine ways of doing things—are organized. Schema and resources, together, make up social structures, such as denominations or congregations. William Sewell argues that schemas serve to filter new information in ways that foster stability and durability in social structures over time. As he states, "Structures . . . are sets of mutually sustaining schemas and resources that empower and constrain social action and that tend to be reproduced . . . but their reproduction is never automatic" (Sewell 1992, p. 19).

Schemas are ambiguous and general enough to be open to reinterpretation, and can evolve over time because of normal processes that lead to incremental variation. And schemas can be "borrowed" from one arena (the work world, for example) and transposed to others (the church, for example). This opens up possibilities for change. So schemas provide a kind of interpretive lens that is brought to bear in understanding social facts, and although those who are embedded in particular institutions and social relationships favor certain schemas, they are also embedded in more than one institutional arena simultaneously and can draw on other schemas and transpose them to bring about change.[26]

The Ozzie and Harriet family has shown a remarkable stability as a cultural model, or schema, that organizes much of local congregational life and practice. However, this basic model has been "stretched" over time to include some new features. Harriet stayed home with the children, but many congregations today work hard to include dual-earner families. And congregations try hard to incorporate single-parent families and to provide ministry for those in blended families or facing custody arrangements that disrupt their children's regular participation in church activities. The dominant family schema in local congregations in these communities may show a nostalgia for Ozzie and Harriet, but with the exception of fundamentalist Protestant rhetoric, today's talk about the ideal family is more open to the reality of women's paid employment outside the home and to an egalitarian gender role ideology than was the family schema of mainline Protestant and Catholic churches in the 1950s.[27]

A few congregations have engaged in more radical innovation, using rhetoric that is anchored in an alternative family schema. The few pastors who say that they want to "redefine the family" have borrowed this alternative schema from secular discourses and combined it with a religious rationale that draws on a different part of their own religious tradition.[28] This alternative family schema is that of the nurturing family, the family defined by emotional bonds and caring commitments more than any particular arrangement of roles. This understanding of what a family might or should be like is borrowed from therapeutic discourse combined with religious social justice discourse and from certain strands of feminist discourse.[29]

The number of churches in these communities that are organized around an alternative family schema is small. Only about 15 percent of the pastors in the focus groups fit into either the "progressive" or the "social justice" cells in box 5.1. Data from the pastor survey, discussed in the next chapter, suggest that the number of congregations organized around a nurturing family schema may be somewhat greater than that. However, it is important to note that, although few in number, these churches all tend to be large, having 250 regular Sunday attenders or more. This means that they actually encompass a fair percentage of the churchgoing population in these communities, and this suggests that church members and potential members—especially in Unitarian, mainline Protestant, and Catholic traditions—are receptive to a more progressive family schema and seek out churches that offer it.

St. Steven's United Methodist congregation in Tompkins County is a good example of a thriving congregation organized around an alternative family schema—the nurturing family. The pastor of St. Steven's was not in our focus group, but we spoke with her during follow-up fieldwork, and her rhetoric and the congregational culture as a whole shows a progressive interpretation of the family (see box 5.1). St. Steven's is one of the few United Methodist Church (UMC) congregations in the country to have become a reconciling church, welcoming to gays and lesbians.[30] About 250 people worship there each Sunday and the pastor estimates that close to 500 people regularly participate in the congregation's ministries, programs, and fellowship activities, an estimate that seems accurate based on extensive fieldwork in this congregation.

At St. Steven's, the rhetoric of redefining the family was first developed through the use of denominational and other study materials as small groups in the congregation engaged in a two-year study to prepare for the decision to become a reconciling church. This rhetoric was also developed in the year of follow-up discussion sessions after the decision. The rhetoric is reflected in sermons and the church newsletter, in religious education classes, and is part of members' casual conversation in coffee hours and potlucks. It is reflected in the decision to use the term *community* and not *family* to describe the congregation, and in the way that single parents, divorced members, and lesbian and gay couples are incorporated into church ministry without being singled out as a "special" ministry focus.

St. Steven's pastor is aware that some people feel that the congregation is not following all of the elements of traditional Methodist doctrine. But she argues that her message, and the congregation's response to it, is being faithful to the long tradition of social justice in the Methodist church and to the core Christian tenets of love and redemption (interview 2/10/2002). Interviews and informal conversations with church members during our fieldwork suggest that it is not the progressive family message by itself that attracts them—it is the larger Christian discourse of service, justice, and social reform that they find compelling. Progressive church members can find all kinds of socially progressive groups in the larger community; they choose to give their time to churches, as opposed to secular groups, in part because they provide a religious experience and a religious grounding for their core values.[31] Churches like St. Steven's are the exception numerically, but they draw in a large number of people and have a highly visible place in the community, having a social impact beyond their proportion in the local religious ecology.

The Ideal Family as a Filter for Understanding Social Change

In most of the area congregations, the taken-for-granted Ozzie and Harriet family ideal still filters which changes in the family are acknowledged and acted on, and which ones are not. Changes that are "filtered in" are dominated by issues of relevance to middle-class, dual-earner couples—how they arrange the business of their lives, their overscheduled children, and the pluralistic nature of their family timetable. The problems of blended families are also filtered in and, to some extent, the problems of single parents and the divorced. Also filtered in are problems of emotions, feelings, the need for connection, and the desire for authenticity.

Many other changes are simply filtered out. For most congregations, the issue of homosexuality never arises as such. The general rhetoric of "inclusion" and "welcoming" is assumed to signal an openness and desire not to be hurtful, while avoidance of the specific issue of homosexuality—by far the most controversial family issue in these four communities—is also seen as avoiding unnecessary hurt that might result from an open conflict over homosexual lifestyles. There are, of course, some exceptions to this—a few large, high-profile congregations such as St. Steven's, mostly in Tompkins County and Liverpool, that have a very visible ministry to gay and lesbian members. Ironically, these congregations— Catholic, Unitarian, United Methodist, American Baptist, and United Church of Christ—provide something of a "safety valve" for other area churches. In other congregations, pastors and lay leaders sometimes feel that they can avoid the issue of homosexuality entirely as long as these visible congregations exist and draw in much of the area's religious gay and lesbian population.

Problems of abuse and family violence are also filtered out, although as the next chapter will make evident, there are some practical steps taken to meet the needs of those finding themselves in abusive situations. Perhaps most surprising, the problems of the working poor are filtered out in most area congregations. In Northside and in Seneca County, 37 percent of residents have a high school education or less. Many families live in a state of crisis, working two to four jobs between both parents for low pay and few or no benefits. As one Evangelical Lutheran Church in America (ELCA) pastor from Northside said during our focus group, these families are not worried about "what kind of table to put the food on" but rather "how to put food on the table" (6/8/00). He was one of the few mainline Protestant pastors who directly critiqued the assumptions of ease, choice, and materialism that pervaded the more nostalgic version of the time-bind rhetoric. The proportion of pastors and lay leaders who talked about the need to work actively on the issues of poverty and joblessness that confront their members was very small.

Even the issues that are "filtered in" through these rhetorics may be misunderstood or skewed because of the rhetorical framework in which they are embedded. Perhaps the most serious misunderstanding is the way in which the relationships among family, church, and work are interpreted. The time-bind rhetoric is very accurate in pointing to the rising number and variety of organized activities for children and teens. It is also accurate in its assessment that there has been a historical shift away from viewing religious involvement as an obligation and toward viewing it as something to do if it meets one's own needs, and along with this a decline in the status of churches (and pastors) among local community institutions and elites.

But the time-bind rhetoric is inaccurate in its assumption that those who work longer hours are less likely to go to church or to be involved in church programs and ministries. Our survey of community residents shows that the amount of time spent at paid work is unrelated to religious involvement except for those working more than fifty-one hours a week—23 percent of employed men, and 7 percent of employed women. And even this relationship disappears in statistical models that control for other factors, specifically education (for men) and attitudes toward religious authority and religious institutions (for women). Our survey also shows that men who work long hours are actually *more* likely to be involved in some kinds of congregational activities, especially those they can participate in with their spouses and/or children. And for men, working fewer hours may be caused by church attendance, not cause church attendance. In our sample, 71 percent of men who attend church regularly report "scaling back" at work in the last two years to spend more time with family, compared with only 49 percent of other men.

The rhetorics of local church life, and the family schema in which they are embedded, serve as a filter on pastors' understandings of the problem posed by changes in work and family for their particular congregations. They also serve as a way to bundle a particular definition of the problem with an overall style of ministry that leads to typical kinds of solutions for the problem as defined.

Catholic parishes in these communities have a kind of communal cultural style that rejects a rhetoric of individualism, but which acknowledges the need to bring in all members regardless of family status and to provide meaningful ministry and experiences of community for all. Incremental adaptation on issues of time and timing coincides with one-on-one attempts to provide support for the divorced and single parents within the congregation and referrals to supraparish programs, as well as ministry directed toward strengthening marriage and parenting. Priests direct members to Branch and Grow, a program of support groups for the separated and the divorced that draws from several parishes in a given area, but they also refer others to Marriage Encounter and weekend-long parenting workshops.

Evangelical churches embrace both individualism and a market logic, drawing examples specifically from business and entrepreneurial culture and exhibiting a comfort talking about how they "compete" for members' time with other churches, with secular voluntary organizations, and with work and family commitments. Their style of response is rooted a rhetoric of evangelism, but also in a sense of never having been an "establishment" institution. They are entrepreneurial, adaptive, flexible, and evince very little tendency to value how goals are accomplished (the means, the particular forms of ministry) as long as they are accomplished. But the limits of evangelical willingness to "sell" their programs and respond to "demand" are set by their core doctrine.

Most mainline Protestant pastors reject a "market" logic and, while recognizing that they are expected to compete for members' time, they develop a critique of the skewed values, "me first" culture, and materialism that they believe drive the competition. Their response is rooted not only in a religiously based critique of culture, but also in a particular status location. As the "establishment" churches in most communities, these congregations have a history of certain ways of doing things being valued for their own sake, of tradition, and of privilege that causes them to see current demands for change as onerous.

A few mainline Protestant pastors from more liberal traditions, along with some Unitarian pastors and pastors of independent liberal charismatic congregations, embrace alternative family forms. But this is not rooted in any generic openness to change and is not seen as adapting to market demand. In fact, these pastors have gone well beyond "demand" and offer a positive endorsement of homosexuality, single parenting, and other lifestyles that many see as controversial. The pastors who espouse this view have the same sense of being authoritative cultural critics as do the pastors who engage in a nostalgic critique of materialism. They draw on different parts of their liberal religious traditions, anchored in a different family schema, but their style of response is the same. Mainline Protestant clergy are more oriented to symbolic change than to change in program and practice, and they value talk and symbolism as forms of social action much more than do Catholic or evangelical pastors.

As the next chapter will show, these styles of response are linked to specific bundles of practice. It is possible to identify distinctly Catholic, mainline Protestant, and evangelical Protestant profiles of family ministry in these communities. As with the rhetoric of family ministry, the practice of family ministry is largely organized around reproducing a dominant nuclear-family-with-children schema. Only in a few congregations are family ministry practices anchored in an alternative family schema that emphasizes nurturing and caretaking over any particular family form.

the practice of ministry, creates the particular religious familism—the particular ideology of "the good family"—in a local religious ecology. This religious familism facilitates (or ignores, or actively forbids) certain work-family strategies and family lifestyles by anchoring the explicit meaning of discrete practices—such as daycare or a Mothers-of-Preschoolers meeting—within implicit family schema.

The Logic of Local Religious Practice

The study of social practices has received a great deal of attention in the sociology of culture within the last few decades, in a discussion that draws on several distinct theoretical traditions. Sociologists use the work of anthropologists to analyze the meanings embedded in and revealed through group practices.[2] Bourdieu's (1977) *Outline of a Theory of Practice* emphasizes the practical knowledge of the *habitus*, embedded in actions in a way that escapes articulation. He argues that practices can reproduce relationships of power in part because they convey meanings about status that cannot be voiced and therefore cannot be challenged. Symbolic interactionist accounts also emphasize the unarticulated meanings carried by face-to-face interaction.[3]

Those who study organizational behavior have often noted the power of practice without explicitly drawing on practice theory. The idea that organizations have typical routines for solving problems that tend to be tried on any problem that comes along, regardless of fit, is compatible with a practice-theoretical approach to action.[4] So is work that identifies different styles of interaction that arise in organizations with different kinds of formal structure, or in similarly structured organizations due to differences in the composition of members.[5]

Other scholars analyze the constitutive logic embedded in styles of practice. Foucault (1978) argues that the classificatory practices of medical and other modern scientific institutions not only renamed but, more fundamentally, reconstituted human sexuality according to a new set of clinical rules. The value of labor is constructed by the various practices of labor that arise within particular historical-institutional contexts; the explicit articulation or naming of labor rights, rules, and regulations comes later and is based on the value of labor as it is practiced in a given time and place.[6] Institutional approaches to organizations identify styles of practice as an object of analysis and as an explanatory mechanism for variations in organizational outcomes.[7]

Though quite diverse in theoretical language and in the main empirical problems addressed, all of this work shares an emphasis on the importance of practical action as a ground of meaning that is semiautonomous from the discursive or symbolic expression of meaning.[8] Often the emphasis is on the power of practices to reproduce relationships of status and power, in part by keeping them inarticulate—unnamed and unchallenged. In fact, one critique of practice theory is that it explains social reproduction well but has a harder time explaining, or simply neglects, social change.[9]

However, social practices, including the daily routines through which organizations make decisions and run programs, can also bring about change. Insight from anthropological studies of symbols points to one source of change. Culture is inherently multivalent, incorporating multiple and ambiguous meanings. Therefore, cultural models, or schema, can be "stretched" or reinterpreted over time. For example, evangelicals still embrace male headship of the family but have also drawn on biblical passages emphasizing mutuality and caring to build a rationale for a certain level of practical egalitarianism within marriage. The "traditional" family schema of evangelicals now quite comfortably includes dual-earner couples, a change that came about in part because of using a new rhetoric and in part because of changes in practice of ministry in local churches—women's meetings no longer held during the workday, or combined Family Night programs that reduce the number of nights a week that busy dual-earner couples have to come to the church. Practices can also incorporate new cultural models, or schema, borrowed from other realms. Running a congregation "like a business" can lead to including new family forms; reaching out to single parents or gay and lesbian couples one-on-one and involving them in a range of church ministries can change the congregation's model of the good family without any explicit rhetorical work.

At about the same time that sociologists of culture began to explore practice theory, those who study religion began to emphasize anew the importance of studying "lived religion" as a set of practices, in contrast to an approach that concentrates primarily on religious rhetoric, belief, doctrine, and symbolic culture. This coincided with a resurgence of qualitative studies of local religious groups and communities. Increasingly, the congregation, the prayer group, or the Wiccan meeting have been studied as social arenas that are influenced by larger religious traditions but also have their own distinctive local culture and routines of practice.[10]

These studies have helped to identify the underlying logic of congregational practice and to understand how that may be distinctive from denominational culture or the official rhetoric of religious elites. Congregational practice is organized around reproducing and passing on a religious tradition, building a caring community for members, and witness to the faith beyond one's own membership. Congregational leaders balance two moral imperatives embedded in these practices: to care for the individual believer and to embody authoritative moral judgments. How these imperatives are carried out is influenced by the local context and ecology, the congregation's own history and identity, by religious tradition and denominational routines.[11]

What I found in studying the family ministry practices of congregations in the four communities upstate New York is that the imperative to be caring, along with the emotional investment in interpersonal connections that characterize involvement in a small group, tends to blunt the sharp edge of ideological zeal and to make local churches, in practice, more similar in dealing with controversial issues—such as gender roles or sexuality—than religious tradition or denominational culture might lead one to suspect. Practices designed to be caring, inclusive, and responsive to members' needs move both liberal and conservative congregations away from the extreme ends of the ideological spectrum.[12] In practice, most congregations in these communities *both* organize the bulk of their ministry around nuclear families with children *and* incorporate, through informal practices, a wide variety of other members.

The Good Family In Practice

In the 1950s, churches facilitated a burgeoning family-oriented suburban lifestyle, and expanded their activities in part to replace the older urban ties of kin and neighbors that the new suburbanites had left behind, bringing about a renewed emphasis on sociability and fellowship in congregational life.[13] Congregation-based sociability in the 1950s was organized around a male-breadwinner suburban lifestyle while drawing on previous congregational routines and strengths.

Bendroth (2002) provides a good description of the practice of religious familism in postwar America. Weekly activities for the whole family, along with Sunday worship, reintegrated Dad into the family circle at the end of a long week of working and commuting, and men's roles as providers were reinforced by the weeknight vestry, council, or board meetings they attended, taking care of the business side of the congregation while their wives stayed home with the children.[14] Women, isolated in suburban homes, turned to parishes, churches, and synagogues as sites for fellowship and an outlet for volunteering.[15] The widespread fears about delinquency and purity that underlay the apparent calm of suburban life fueled an elaboration of teen-oriented programming.[16] Programs for younger children were fostered by the emphasis on nurturing and mothering that was central to the suburban, male-breadwinner lifestyle.[17] The familism of the 1950s religious expansion was expressed in the routine practice of family ministry, in the kinds of programs offered and in the way they were organized around a schedule that took for granted a male-breadwinner family.

Numerous examples from congregational archives suggest that in the daily practice of family ministry in the 1950s and 1960s, the congregations in these four upstate New York communities were typical of their time. According to its annual report for 1961, one United Church of Christ congregation in rural Seneca County was organized largely around programs for women and children and activities such as the monthly Family Nights, "family dinners that allow all members to participate with their entire family in a function that aids in getting to know other families in the church." Minutes from the meetings of the Women's Society of Christian Service at a rural United Methodist church in Tompkins County throughout the 1950s and early 1960s show that many weekday afternoons and evenings were spent over coffee and snacks discussing mothering, parenting, and preparing children for school. Sunday bulletins from St. James Catholic church from the 1950s and 1960s routinely carried a notice from the priest urging everyone in the family to have communion together at least one Sunday a month, and more often if possible, and show that the Altar Guild and other ministries in which women took part were held on Tuesday and Thursday during the daytime, so as not to interfere with family evenings together.

To find out about the contemporary practice of family ministry in these four communities, our survey of area pastors included a long section asking them to describe in detail the kinds of formal and informal programs the congregation offers and what new programs or changes in programming have come about in the recent past. This survey provides much of the data for the discussion that follows, which outlines the typical kinds of ministries offered by these churches. The data suggest that, in most area congregations, the "standard package" of family-oriented programs developed in the 1950s still provides the template for current ministry practice. It also shows that in some congregations there has been marked innovation, such that the practice of family ministry conveys a different kind of familism organized around the nurturing family model discussed in the last chapter.

The pastor survey included a long checklist of common family-oriented programs (Sunday School, Youth Group, women's ministry, etc.). In our initial focus group and survey pretest, pastors suggested other programs and services we should ask about, such as a daycare center, language classes, or counseling, and we included these, as well, in another question.[18] We also asked two open-ended questions, which allowed us to find out about other kinds of ministries and programs: (1) "Does your congregation have any kind of family ministry or program that I haven't already asked you about?" and (2) "What programs do you have that might not be called 'family ministry' that are significant in meeting the needs of families in your congregation?" For every program or service or ministry mentioned, a follow-up question asked whether it was offered formally on a regular basis or "informally, on an as-needed basis." The answers to these questions were coded and are included in the analysis that follows.

In the footnotes to the tables and in the text, more information is provided about how the programs and ministry practices are conducted, how they are organized, and what it means for a particular program to be "formal" or "informal." This information is based on the pastor focus groups, fieldwork in sixteen area congregations, and to a lesser extent on the answers to the open-ended survey questions. Together, the survey and the follow-up qualitative work provide a rich account of congregational practices and how they facilitate certain work-family strategies and family lifestyles.

"Traditional" Family Ministry

To a very large extent, family ministry in these communities is still organized around the same gender and life-stage categories as it was in the 1950s and 1960s. This is especially true for what I call formal programming, or programs that congregations run themselves, in their own facilities, on a regular basis (either weekly or monthly). Table 6.1 shows the distribution of ministries organized around age, gender roles, and life stage in these congregations. Take a moment to look at the last four lines of this table, in which the total number of congregational programs (formal and informal) are compared to the number of programs (formal and informal) organized around gender and life-stage categories. Across all traditions, more than three-quarters of formal family-oriented programming is organized according to gender and traditional life-stage categories.

The kind of family programming that proliferated in the 1950s and 1960s is still a template that most congregations follow. National data, where available, suggest that these congregations are not atypical in this regard. The Faith Communities Today (FCT) project, based on a national sample of congregations in several denominations, suggests that traditional family programming is alive and well.[19] About 50 percent of congregations in the FCT study encourage family devotions and discourage premarital sex. Almost 90 percent run a Sunday School, about 85 percent a youth or teen group, and 50 percent have groups that focus on marriage or parenting. The National Congregations Study finds about the same percentage of congregations having programs for youth and shows that about 40 percent have classes or programs to discuss parenting.[20]

There are variations in the amount of this kind of programming across religious traditions. Table 6.1 shows that moderate Protestant congregations—Presbyterian, Episcopal, Evangelical Lutheran Church in America—have the fewest of these "traditional" programs and conservative Protestants have the most. To some extent, this is related to conservative Protestant beliefs that define the neopatriarchal family with children not only as a cultural ideal but as a religious one, endorsed by the Bible and exemplifying God's will for human relationships more so than other family forms or family lifestyles. But other factors besides religious belief foster a profile of traditional family programs. Congregations with more than 250 regular attenders have more of these programs, and more of all kinds of programs; these large congregations make up about 25 percent of the total in these four communities. The relative scarcity of such programs in moderate Protestant congregations is probably owing to size; only 10 percent of these congregations have more than 250 regular attenders.

TABLE 6.1
"Standard" Gender and Life-Stage Programming[a]

	Liberal Protestant	Moderate Protestant	Conservative Protestant	Catholic
Number of congregations represented	22	21	59	18
Sunday school or equivalent	95% (95%)[b]	95% (100%)	93% (95%)	94% (100%)
Teen groups	77% (94%)	71% (93%)	88% (87%)	83% (87%)
Tutoring for children	9% (0%)	5% (100%)	20% (50%)	39%(71%)
Scouts	64% (86%)	48% (90%)	14% (88%)	35% (83%)
Total number of children's and teens' programs— mean (mode)	2.5 (2)	2.2 (2)	2.2 (2)	2.5 (3)
Parenting classes	32% (14%)	19% (25%)	36% (29%)	33% (50%)
Women's groups	86% (79%)	81% (88%)	86% (76%)	72% (69%)
Men's groups	64% (71%)	43% (78%)	83% (53%)	44% (50%)
Mothers' groups	23% (60%)	14% (33%)	39% (26%)	22% (57%)
Married-couple fellowship or marriage classes	41% (44%)	24% (20%)	59% (40%)	39% (57%)
Empty nesters' group	14% (67%)	5% (100%)	37% (32%)	22% (50%)
Seniors' group	45% (80%)	43% (89%)	49% (52%)	61% (82%)
Widow(er)s' group	23% (20%)	5% (0%)	31% (40%)	28% (39%)
Total number of programs organized by gender and life stage—mean (mode)	6.5 (5)	5.1 (5)	7.4 (6)	6.8 (5)
Total number of all family-oriented programs in congregation—mean (mode)	11.4 (10)	9.2 (9)	12 (15)	10.2 (15)
Total number of formal programs organized by gender and life stage—mean (mode)	4.6 (5)	4.1 (3)	4.2 (4)	5 (2)
Total number of all formal family-oriented programs in congregation—mean (mode)	6 (6)	5.3 (4)	5 (5)	6 (2)

Source: Religion and Family Project, Pastor Survey (N = 125), Penny Edgell Becker, PI, 1998.

Notes: [a] Denominations classified following Smith 1987; cf. Steensland et al. 2000.

[b] The main entry indicates the percentage of congregations in each category that offer the program or service at all; the number in parentheses is the percent of those offering the program that run it as a formal, regular part of the church calendar. So line one, column one, indicates that 95 percent of liberal Protestant congregations offer Sunday school or its equivalent, and of those 95 percent do so as a formal program on a regular basis. (In this case, the other 5 percent do not offer Sunday school through the summer months.) For scouting, "formal" means that the troop meets regularly at the church and a church member is a leader; "informal" means the troop occasionally does projects for or through the church or uses church facilities. A "formal" teen group meets regularly and is led by someone from the church; "informal" teen groups meet intermittently for special programs or projects and may be led by parents on a rotating volunteer basis.

Only 13 percent of conservative Protestant congregations in these communities have more than 250 members, but as a group these congregations have slightly more traditional family programs than liberal Protestant and Catholic congregations. A conservative view of the family explains part of this, as does the composition of membership in these churches. Congregations in which more than 50 percent of the membership is composed of people who are currently married and have children have more "traditional" family oriented programs. Just over half of conservative Protestant congregations fit this profile (51 percent), compared to 44 percent of Catholic parishes, 10 percent of liberal Protestant congregations, and 19 percent of moderate Protestant congregations.

Programs to educate children, to provide a wholesome environment for teen social activities, discussion and fellowship activities for parents, social activities for empty nesters and retirees—these programs proclaim in practice the congregation's commitment to facilitating the major stages of family formation, socialization of children, and transition into a time when children leave home. With every weekly calendar inserted into the church bulletin that lists the Girl Scout meeting, Youth Group pizza party, MOPs (Mothers-of-Preschoolers) meeting, Seniors' lunch, and Men's Monthly Pancake Breakfast at the firehouse, the centrality of "the traditional family" to congregational life is constituted anew, reinforcing the dominant family model as elaborated in congregational rhetoric.

Contemporary Family Needs

If the practice of congregational ministry is still organized to a large extent around the same kinds of activities that burgeoned in the 1950s, many congregations have also adapted at least some of their programming and ways of organizing their ministry to post-1950s changes in work and family. The survey of pastors indicates that virtually all congregations (93 percent) have attempted some change in programming or practice in the last five years in order to meet new family needs, and most congregations have tried three different innovations in that time period. The urgency with which pastors spoke of these issues in the focus groups is linked to a willingness to explore new practices that meet contemporary family needs. Most innovations are initiated by either the pastor or lay leaders in the congregation (see box 6.1). But some new ideas are "borrowed" from other congregations in the area, and a few are facilitated by denominational programs such as the one in the Rochester archdiocese that provides a full-time staff member to assist directors of family ministry in local parishes in developing new programs and new ways of running traditional ones, such as confirmation classes for youth.

The pastor focus groups suggest that quite a few changes are attempted for a short time and then abandoned, but others find their way into the routine of congregational life. Table 6.2 shows the distributions of "innovations that

Box 6.1	
Sources Named by Pastors of Ideas for Innovative Ministry	
Source	*Percentage of Pastors*
Members	66
Clergy/staff	64
Denominational officials/programs	31
Other congregation in the area	22
Other	8

worked," or that are part of the routine ministry of the congregation. It shows the broad range of practices through which congregations in these communities are trying to meet the needs of those who do not fit the "Ozzie and Harriet" family. Some of these involve facilitating more contemporary forms of the nuclear family—for example, ministry designed to bring in dual-earner couples or those in blended families. Other programs and practices are oriented toward acknowledging that family life is problematic or stressful in ways that tended to remain unvoiced in congregational life in the 1950s (counseling for victims of domestic violence, or programs to help members cope with stressful work environments). Yet other practices are oriented toward those living in alternative family arrangements.

In contrast to the formal programming that comprises the bulk of traditional family ministry, congregations meet contemporary family needs mostly through informal programming and other practices that would not show up in the weekly bulletin or make it onto the monthly calendar. Informal practices and the restructuring of the timing and format of formal programming are the dominant means of addressing the needs of the post-1950s family. Among the most common innovations are changes in the way formal programs are run in order to ease the time bind that pastors and lay leaders perceive to be the biggest challenge to effective family ministry. Providing child care during worship services and other congregational meetings and activities is motivated by the same kinds of concerns. Fieldwork, focus groups, and interviews suggest that these programs and practices, listed in the first two sections of table 6.2, are designed to facilitate the participation of dual-earner couples, blended families, and single parents. Other than denominational tradition, there are no factors that predict the willingness of a congregation to experiment with timing. And low-level child care (babysitting) is also fairly evenly distributed, with Catholics having less than other denominations, but no other factors really being predictive.

Daycare is another story. Daycare is offered by congregations in more liberal traditions and, more specifically, by the more liberal congregations within each tradition. (See box 6.2.) Daycare is a practice oriented toward meeting the

TABLE 6.2
Innovative Family Programming[a]

	Liberal Protestant	Moderate Protestant	Conservative Protestant	Catholic
N	22	21	59	18
Timing and flexibility				
Change time/timing of programs	23%	38%	65%	54%
Move programming off-site, closer to members' homes	9%	5%	32%	11%
Child care[b]				
Daycare for members	23%	33%	5%	33%
Babysitting during meetings/activities	86%	81%	85%	61%
Babysitting/nursery during worship	96%	76%	83%	50%
Family disruption/ nontraditional life course				
Intergenerational programming	68% (53%)	81% (59%)	68% (44%)	54% (30%)
Programs for single parents	10% (0%)	0% (0%)	33% (5%)	17% (67%)
Programs for divorced members	18% (0%)	19% (50%)	25% (20%)	22% (25%)
Counseling/therapeutic[c]				
Programs that help people cope with work-related stress	27% (50%)	14% (33%)	29% (18%)	17% (0%)
Counseling—domestic violence	23% (40%)	24% (40%)	27% (19%)	22% (67%)
Counseling—family or marital	73% (25%)	62% (15%)	83% (12%)	50% (22%)
Total number of counseling programs—mean (mode)	1.7 (2)	1.4 (0)	1.9 (1)	1.2 (0)
Other family programming				
Job training workshops	14% (33%)	5% (0%)	10% (33%)	22% (67%)
Language classes	9% (100%)	14% (100%)	20% (58%)	17% (100%)
Community center/ drop-in center	41% (67%)	10% (50%)	8% (20%)	22% (75%)

Source: Religion and Family Project, Pastor Survey (N = 125), Penny Edgell Becker, PI, 1998.

Notes: [a] Denominations classified following Smith 1987; cf. Steensland et al. 2000.

[b] All daycare programs are offered formally if offered at all. Babysitting for activities besides the Sunday worship service is almost always on an informal, as-needed basis.

[c] For counseling programs, offering a program "informally" usually means that the pastor provides short-term, one-on-one counseling him- or herself, and refers individuals to community-based counseling services for more severe or longer-term problems.

Box 6.2
Congregations Offering Daycare*

Score below the mean on the traditionalism index**

Have pastors who agree with the statement, "God approves of all kinds of families"

Have a pastor with either a Master's of Divinity or a doctorate

Are more likely to have a female pastor than are other congregations

Emphasize teaching children to think for themselves (rather than obedience)

Have many programs for children and parents, but few of the other programs organized by life stage and gender

Have more counseling programs and "other" family programs (job training/community center/language classes)

Are large (250+ regular attenders)

Are likely to be liberal or moderate Protestant or Catholic

---

* Based on pastor survey; all relationships significant at p < .01 or greater.

** This index is discussed in chapter 5.

---

needs of dual-earner and single-parent families, and it is the only innovation that through its very organization explicitly decouples the practice of parenting from a male-breadwinner family form or other expressions of traditional gender roles.

About one-third of Catholic parishes and liberal/moderate Protestant churches offer daycare for members, ranging from part-time to full-time programs. Because most congregations offering daycare are large, that means that a relatively high proportion of churchgoers experience a congregation that offers daycare. Part-time or full-time daycare, offered on the congregation's premises and available for members (either exclusively or at reduced rates), is made available only in congregations having more than 250 regular Sunday worshippers. National data suggest that this is commonly the case; the Religion and Politics Survey, conducted at Princeton University, found that 46 percent of churchgoers were in congregations that offered daycare. Box 6.2 shows that the pastor's education, gender, and beliefs about gender and family also relate to the congregation's likelihood of providing daycare.

Daycare is oriented toward parents, if not toward "traditional" nuclear families, and it takes for granted the central role of the congregation in fostering family formation and the socialization of children. In contrast, programs for divorced men and women and for single parents and intergenerational activities are designed to include long-term single adults or those who have experienced family disruption. These programs are a different kind of innovation, because they are motivated by the desire to change the perception that "If you're not part of a married couple with children, you don't 'fit' in most churches," as discussed in chapter 3. Focus groups, in addition to the survey, suggest that these kinds of programs are fostered by a desire to be more welcoming to those who are in alternative family arrangements or who do not attend church with their family members. Small moderate Protestant congregations have the most intergenerational programming.

Ministry for gay and lesbian members is also a form of innovation in family ministry that challenges traditional ideals of "the good family." However, although a quarter (26 percent) of pastors told us on the survey that their congregations have gay or lesbian members, only two or three congregations offer fellowship or support programs for gay or lesbian members; these congregations are discussed in chapter 5. In these communities, congregations having a formal ministry for gay or lesbian members are liberal Protestant or Unitarian.

Whether a congregation has ministries for divorced members or single parents is related to both its size and its religious tradition. Large conservative Protestant congregations with a high percentage of members in nuclear families with children provide the most ministry for those experiencing family disruption. (See box 6.3.) Focus groups and fieldwork indicate that this kind of ministry does not undermine the traditional family schema within these congregations. Rather, family disruption is framed as a form of brokenness for which the congregation provides healing and support while affirming the two-parent family with children as an ideal and as the family model based in Scripture.

Therapeutic programs often exemplify a post-1950s understanding of the family as a nurturing unit as well as the more general post-1950s therapeutic turn in religious discourse. Such programs are included in Table 6.2 as an example of "innovative" ministry responding to post-1950s changes in family life. This is particularly true if a congregation runs these programs formally and on a regular basis—for example, bringing in community-based professionals to run workshops on domestic violence or how to cope with stressful work and family contexts, having a pastor trained in counseling in addition to ministry, facilitating members' participation in denominationally run counseling programs, or organizing a support group within the congregation for members with a trained facilitator. Box 6.3 shows the other characteristics that tend to go along with having some kind of formal therapeutic ministry in the congregation.

Perhaps the most innovative are programs that are designed to help families but are not organized around family life per se. The fieldwork and focus groups with pastors suggest that community centers, language classes, and job training workshops are all designed to help families cope with needs related to poverty (see table 6.2). In Northside and Liverpool, a "community center" can mean that the parish or church runs a multiservice space open much of the day, every day, to meet a variety of needs of members and nonmembers. Sometimes this includes a drop-in center where caregivers can leave elderly or ill relatives for a time in order to run errands or go shopping, an essential service for

---

Box 6.3
Family Disruption, Therapeutic Programs[+]

Family Disruption*
    Size (both membership and attendance)
    More than 50 percent of members in intact nuclear families with children
    Larger budget
    Having more gender/life-stage programs, total
    Having more counseling programs, formal
    Religious tradition (conservative Protestant)

Therapeutic Programs**
    Daycare center
    Ministry for divorced/single-parent members
    "Other" family programs (community center, job training, language classes)
    Having more formal gender/life-stage programs
    Scoring below the mean on traditionalism index
    Scoring above the mean on progressivism index

  [+] All correlations significant at p < .01 or greater
  * Measure = having a ministry (formal or informal) for single parents OR divorced members
  ** Measure = total number of formal counseling programs provided through congregation, denomination, or formal arrangement with a community organization

---

those who cannot afford the cost of a practical nurse or other in-home care. Congregations with such programs tend to be larger and better-off financially and have more family ministries of all kinds, both traditional and innovative. As discussed in chapter 5, focus groups suggest that at least a few pastors of these congregations link the practice of such programs to a larger critique of the way that "family values" rhetoric displaces concern about—and derails activism to correct—the long-term structural inequality driving much family disruption and instability.

Overall Profiles of Family Ministry

The distribution of specific ministry practices across different types of congregations—large and small, evangelical and mainline Protestant and Catholic—says something about the factors that influence a congregation to, for example, run a daycare center or have a large number of programs for youth. And it is possible, using such measures, to identify styles of ministry distinctive to particular kinds of congregations. Large congregations have more innovative *and* traditional family ministry; evangelical Protestant congregations have traditional family programming but also innovate in the timing, location, and organization of ministry and draw in those experiencing family disruption.

But even given these variations and the presence of some forms of innovative ministry, it is clear that the majority of all programming is organized around parenting and the large majority of formal programming is organized around the traditional gender and life-stage categories targeted to the needs of two-parent families with children. This family ideal still serves as a kind of anchoring schema for local congregational practice within the mainstream religious institutions that embraced the familism of the postwar suburbs in the 1950s.

This pattern becomes even more clear if, instead of looking at the distribution of discrete programs and practices across congregational types, we use a measure that looks at how congregations *combine* formal programs and informal practices into an overall profile of ministry. Discrete programs and practices tend to come in "bundles," and the bundles confront members and potential members with a set of choices and trade-offs in looking for a congregation that has relevant programs.

There are three overall profiles or bundles of family ministry in the congregations of these four communities. Most congregations have what I call a "standard package" of programs organized around the two-parent family with children: a mother's group, Sunday School for children, and a teen or youth group. A few congregations have *only* this standard package—and a few of the very smallest ones have only a women's group and children's Sunday School and no teen program. The largest group of congregations have the "standard package" plus one or two innovative ministries. And a few large congregations innovate along multiple dimensions in a way that genuinely challenges the centrality of the traditional family schema to congregational life.

"STANDARD PACKAGE"

In these communities, 12 percent of congregations either have only a women's group and a Sunday School for children or these two plus a teen program. A few congregations have these programs only on a informal basis or for part of the year. These congregations with the "standard package" are mostly small churches in Seneca County or rural parts of Tompkins County, although there are a few in Ithaca (the central town in Tompkins County) and in Liverpool.

"STANDARD PACKAGE PLUS"

This is the largest group, comprising about three-quarters of the congregations (74 percent), and it is made up of congregations that have multiple programs within the "standard package" of family ministry, with one or two innovative ministry practices as well. A conservative Protestant congregation might have the standard package plus a single parents' group or a program for divorced people, and a liberal Protestant congregation might have the "standard package" plus a daycare center and a work-stress program.[21] A Catholic congregation might have the "standard package" but have an innovative way of organizing its sacrament preparation classes for youth, or offer babysitting and counseling.

"innovators"

This is a small group of congregations, about 14 percent, which have the "standard package" plus multiple other programs, offered both formally and on an informal, as-needed basis. Most innovators are liberal or moderate Protestant congregations, but there are a few conservative Protestant and Catholic innovators, too. These congregations are almost all large, with more than 250 members and very good financial resources. They have all hired pastors committed to activism and change, and they are all congregations with a history of innovation in other areas as well—for example, being active in forming cross-racial alliances with other congregations, in community development and anti-poverty activism, or in outreach to those with AIDS.

Fieldwork and focus groups suggest that innovator congregations have a large effect on the local religious ecology. Pastors and lay leaders, in focus groups and in fieldwork, repeatedly pointed to innovator congregations as models from which they drew ideas for their own congregation's more incremental moves toward innovative programming. Innovators provide a kind of social laboratory where many innovations are attempted and from which successful ones spread to other congregations. Innovator churches, then, tend to foster more incremental adaptation in the congregations in their surrounding area.

However, as was discussed in the previous chapter, this tends not to be true regarding ministry for gay and lesbian members. Innovator congregations that explicitly welcome gay and lesbian members seem to provide a kind of "safety valve" for other congregations in the area. Other pastors refer gay and lesbian members or potential members to these congregations. And other pastors and lay leaders use the presence of these other congregations as a reason to avoid discussing whether and how to welcome gay and lesbian persons into their own churches, because they know how controversial and divisive such discussions have proven to be in many local churches across the United States. In a local religious ecology, innovators have their own specialized niche as well as being models from which other churches borrow ideas.[22]

Innovative Ministry and a New Model of the Family

Understanding which congregations offer innovative programming is a good way to assess the degree to which the local religious ecology makes a place for those who do not fit the traditional "Ozzie and Harriet" family ideal. But as the last chapter shows, innovations that seem in practice to endorse alternative family forms and lifestyles can be framed rhetorically in a way that reinforces a more traditional family schema. Pilgrim Baptist, in Tompkins County, is a good example of an evangelical congregation that is highly innovative in its ministry practices but rhetorically emphasizes the male-breadwinner family as the best family, the biblically based ideal for family life. Pilgrim Baptist has changed the timing of ministries to facilitate the participation of dual-earner couples and the children of blended families and moved many programs off-site to members' homes to reduce commuting time for members. Pilgrim has programs for single parents and divorced members, an intergenerational ministry, and an active adult singles group. It offers informal family counseling through its own pastoral staff, runs marriage counseling workshops with a trained outside facilitator, and provides referrals to community programs for domestic violence counseling and practical help.

And yet the leaders of Pilgrim Baptist church view divorce and single parenthood as forms of brokenness. They understand their singles' ministry as preparation for finding a Christian spouse, and conversations with the singles who participate in that ministry show that they share this view. The pastoral staff and the lay leaders we spoke with believe that homosexuality is sinful and draw a sharp line at including any congregational programming that might suggest otherwise. This church is an example of a congregation in which innovative ministry that includes a wide range of people who are not part of traditional nuclear families nevertheless builds around and supports a traditional family schema. One of the larger and more innovative Catholic parishes in this sample, in Liverpool, has a similar profile of ministry practices and endorses a similar family rhetoric that views the nuclear, male-breadwinner family as the only really appropriate and biblically based model for family life.

However, in some congregations, innovative programming and ministry practices coincide with a rhetoric that is more progressive, resulting in a congregation that is organized around a fundamentally different model of the family. A reliability analysis of survey items that include both pastors' rhetoric and congregational practices helps to identify such congregations. Box 6.4 shows the items included in the Alternative Family Index, a simple additive scale with each variable weighted equally. In these communities, 42 percent of congregations score a 0 on this index, and just under 17 percent of congregations score one standard deviation above the mean (3 or 4). In other words, out of 125 congregations participating in the survey, 21 (17 percent) couple innovative ministry practices with a progressive family rhetoric.

Having a high score in this index is strongly related to a combination of the congregation's religious tradition, material resources, and the gender of the pastor. Box 6.5 shows the congregational characteristics that are associated with a higher score on the Alternative Family Index, and those characteristics associated with being more than one standard deviation above the mean on this index. Not surprisingly, larger and more well-off congregations with a more highly educated pastor or a female pastor are more likely to have a progressive family schema, as are congregations from more liberal religious traditions.

Sociologists who study organizations have made a distinction between two kinds of innovation. *Incremental innovation* involves adopting new programs,

---

Box 6.4
Alternative Family Index

"We teach children to learn as early as possible how to make their own moral judgments, even if it means sometimes disagreeing with their parents, teachers, or pastor."

"There have been all kinds of families throughout history, and God approves of many different kinds of families."

Congregation has a daycare program.

Pastor affirms that the congregation has gay and/or lesbian members.

Index characteristics: Additive scale, alpha = .73, mean = 1.15, std. dev. = 1.2

---

routines, or organizational structures that are compatible with the existing cultural model, or schema, around which the organization is built. *Radical innovation* involves organizational changes that fundamentally alter the cultural understanding of what the organization is about, or the underlying cultural schema.[23] The previous discussion makes clear that many congregations in this community are involved in a process of incremental innovation, adding programs for single adults, single parents, divorced members, or blended families in congregations that remain organized around a relatively traditional model of the good family. The official beliefs about male headship in evangelical

---

Box 6.5
Alternative Family Index, Significant Correlates

Significant Correlates—Positive Score on Alternative Family Index (p < .01)
    Size (especially having more than 250 regular attendees)
    Budget (especially having annual budget > 200,000 a year)
    Pastor's education (pastor has master's or doctorate)
    Pastor's gender (female pastors associated with higher score)

Liberal Protestant congregations have the highest score of all traditions, followed by moderate Protestant congregations and then Catholic parishes; conservative Protestant congregations have the lowest score of all traditions.

Significant Correlates (p < .01) of Congregations Scoring One Standard Deviation above the Mean on Alternative Family Index
    Pastor's education (Master of Divinity or doctorate)
    Budget (> $200,000 a year)
    Liberal Protestant (positive relationship)
    Conservative Protestant (negative relationship)

Protestant churches and the local time-bind rhetoric of many mainline Protestant and Catholic churches make it clear that although ministry is provided for other kinds of families, the good family, ideally, is an intact, nuclear, heterosexual, male-breadwinner family.

In contrast, the twenty-one congregations that score at least one standard deviation above the mean on the Alternative Family Index can be understood as radical innovators. These congregations are organized around the nurturing family schema, which is open to multiple family forms and arrangements. The pastors of these churches explicitly critique the more conservative family rhetorics in other area congregations, using a variety of feminist and social justice discourses drawn from both secular and religious sources. Where does such radical innovation come from?

Box 6.5 suggests that this kind of radical innovation stems from three primary sources. The first is the congregation's religious tradition—almost all of these congregations are United Methodist, United Church of Christ, Evangelical Lutheran Church in America, American Baptist, or Unitarian. These denominations all ordain women and have a history of openness to feminism. They all either have official policies that are welcoming to gay and lesbian members or have within the denomination high-profile activist groups working for such policies. In focus groups, pastors from these denominations all drew on religious social justice rhetoric—as opposed to a language of marketing or evangelism—in explaining why it is important for congregations to redefine what a "family" means in today's society. The few Catholic priests who lead radically innovative parishes all draw on an explicit liberation theology in their rationale for their parishes' progressive stance toward the family.

Resources also matter. The second source of radical innovation is the pastor's own background and education: more highly educated pastors are more likely to be favorable to the alternative family schema. And the third source of a more radically innovative stance is the congregation's level of financial resources. Large congregations—and especially those with a budget of $200,000 a year or more—are the most likely to be radically innovative. Why are resources so important to radical innovation?

In the spring of 2002, a project research assistant and I conducted follow-up interviews with pastors from seven innovator congregations.[24] These interviews suggest that resources provide two kinds of impetus for radical innovation. The first is the presence of more paid clergy and administrative staff, who take responsibility for running innovative programming and also run discussion and education forums for members such as those conducted at St. Steven's United Methodist Church during and after the decision to become a reconciling church (see chapter 5). Perhaps more important, the financial resources of these larger congregations provide a "cushion" that allows pastors and lay leaders to feel that they can take risks, try new programs, and bring up controversial issues. Aware that a more progressive family orientation may not appeal to all church members, pastors who undertake initiatives to move their congregations in this direction need to feel that the congregation's finances are stable so that if some key contributors decide to leave, the church can still thrive.

My field notes from my interview with the pastor of St. Steven's, a radical innovator, show that pastors think through the financial implications of radical innovations in some detail. I asked her how she had come to the decision that it was an appropriate time to put the issue of whether to becoming a reconciling church to the congregation for a formal vote. She indicated that she had considered carefully the financial implications, and that the results of the vote bore out her own assessment: There was a 90 percent positive vote to become a reconciling church, and that vote represented 95 percent of the congregation's financial resources or more—so it was viable to go forward (Interview 2/19/2002).

The relative rareness of innovative congregations—around 17 percent of the local religious ecology—would seem to indicate a low supply of congregations for those seeking an alternative to the traditional approach to family ministry. Or it may indicate a relative lack of demand for such programming. Since members are a major source of the ideas for innovation, perhaps many congregations do not innovate because members do not wish them to do so. However, the large size of innovative congregations suggests that, in fact, the demand for progressive or alternative family ministry may be larger than the figures thus far would leave one to believe.

Nationally, the typical congregation has fewer than 75 regular, active participants according to data from the National Congregations Study.[25] But the average person participates in a congregation of 400 or more members. Put another way, the fewer than 10 percent of congregations that have 400 regular participants nevertheless contain half of those persons going to church regularly in the United States. In these four communities, the 25 percent of congregations that have more than 250 regular participants encompass more than half of the churchgoers, even by the most conservative estimate. And the twenty-one congregations that are radical innovators comprise just over 40 percent of the average churchgoing population on any given Sunday. Innovation is in demand, and the congregations that provide it are large and well-supported by their members. Women, single parents, gay and lesbian members, and long-term adult singles are particularly motivated to seek out congregations that are sensitive to new family forms and work-family arrangements and they "vote with their feet" to find one that is compatible (see chapter 3).

FAMILISM AND THE PRACTICE OF MINISTRY

There are different forms of religious familism in these upstate New York communities, some more like the religious familism of the 1950s religious expansion, and some quite different. Conservative Protestant congregations have a great deal of programming for mothers, children, and teens. They also innovate in ways that facilitate the participation of dual-earners and single parents, being flexible about timing and location of ministries. And they do a great deal, much of it informal, to facilitate the participation of those who have experienced family disruption. Their practice is consonant with their rhetoric, which upholds a neopatriarchal family ideal but is also welcoming and affirming of those who have experienced the "brokenness" that keeps them from this ideal.

Overall, there is a discernible mainline Protestant familism, as well, but there are some differences between those from more liberal traditions and those from more moderate traditions. Congregations from more liberal traditions (Unitarian, United Methodist) have a more progressive rhetoric while those from more moderate traditions (Episcopal, Lutheran, Presbyterian) are more likely to endorse at least some more traditional views, especially of gender roles in the family. Larger congregations and especially those in liberal Protestant traditions are the sources of a much more radical innovation in religious familism, playing a distinct role in the local religious ecology.

In smaller mainline congregations, and especially those in moderate Protestant traditions, there is an unwillingness on the part of pastors and lay leaders to innovate to meet family needs because they see those needs as resulting from skewed values and from a consumerist orientation to religion of which they are highly critical. These congregations are the least likely to have changed the time or timing of their programs to meet the needs of dual-earner couples or those facing alternate-weekend custody arrangements, and the least likely to minister to single parents, either through programs for these groups or through the kind of one-on-one visitation to bring such members into other congregational programming that Catholic and evangelical pastors report doing on a routine basis. Focus groups suggest that, by and large, the organization of ministry in these congregations exhibits a kind of nostalgia for the male-breadwinner family of the past, and many mainline pastors still lament the loss of volunteer labor that occurred in the 1970s when large numbers of their female members went to work in the paid labor force.

Catholic congregations incorporate elements from both ends of the ideological spectrum in their rhetoric about the "ideal" family. While being genuinely open to those in single-parent families, blended families, and gay and lesbian unions, Catholic parishes also embrace more traditional gender roles than do mainline Protestants. And Catholic pastors are the most likely, in these four communities, to develop an explicit critique of the dual-earner lifestyle, especially for middle-class members, and to argue explicitly that mothers who do not need the money should stay home with their young children. In practice, Catholics are the most likely to report changing the time and timing of their family programs. Focus groups and fieldwork suggest that this is because the proliferation of organized activities for children, along with alternate-weekend custody arrangement, have had the most severe impact on Catholic religious education, especially the tradition of having ten to twelve weeks of sacrament preparation classes on successive weekends. And a few Catholic pastors call on their denomination's discourses of social justice and liberation theology to join their liberal Protestant counterparts in developing a progressive ministry organized around an alternative family schema.

There is diversity in family rhetoric and, among Protestants, this is organized along a left/right "culture wars" dynamic. The "left" here is confined mostly to large, resource-rich liberal Protestant churches, and the "right" to fundamentalist churches. In the practice of family ministry, however, there is also a vast middle of congregations that in rhetoric endorse the male-breadwinner family of the past while in practice they incorporate as many incremental innovations as their size allows and their members suggest. Particularly common are innovations that support new forms of parenting and that seek to integrate those experiencing family disruption—single parents, those in blended families, the divorced, the widowed, and empty nesters can all choose from a range of congregations that attempt in some formal or informal way to meet their needs and integrate them into congregational life.

Lakoff (1996) argues that cultural models of the family provide a kind of anchoring schema; they organize many other social and political divisions throughout our society and structure many of our institutions.[26] For the religious institutions that expanded so rapidly in the postwar era by organizing ministry around the nuclear, male-breadwinner family, that model remains a kind anchoring schema for congregational rhetoric. Most congregations that have adapted to changes in work and family have done so in a partial, incremental way, and most innovations revolve around facilitating new nuclear family arrangements. In the vast majority of congregations, the nuclear family, and in particular the socialization of children, is at the very center of congregational life.

The exception to this general pattern are large, liberal Protestant (and a few Catholic) congregations that innovate in multiple ways and combine innovative programs such as daycare with progressive family rhetoric. Though relatively rare in number, these large congregations comprise a good percentage of the weekly churchgoing population in these communities, and they serve as models for other congregations that innovate in more incremental ways. These congregations suggest that, particularly in informal programs and practices, but through some formal programs as well, a new family schema is being embodied in daily congregational practice.

This new, alternative family schema is still largely organized around parenting, but parenting as divorced from either a nuclear family structure or a traditionally gendered division of labor. This schema is also open to gay and lesbian families. It corresponds most closely to what Lakoff (1996) called "the nurturing family." Specific roles and duties are less important than the nurturing and mutual caretaking of members. Congregations, which already privilege practices organized around caretaking, have found caring practices to be a natural way to extend and adapt their model of the family. In the caring practices (daycare, affirming lesbian and gay members) and in the rhetoric of inclusion used by some pastors (God approves of all kinds of families), a few congregations are beginning to embody a daily practice that undercuts the Ozzie and Harriet ideal.

Chapter Seven

RELIGIOUS FAMILISM AND SOCIAL CHANGE

THIS STUDY set out to answer two core questions: How do individuals in a variety of family contexts think about and participate in local religious communities? And how have a particular set of religious institutions that were organized explicitly around the "Ozzie and Harriet" family responded to changes in work and family life? In the next section, I argue that the answers to these questions are important in part because of the cultural power that religious communities exert in our society to shape our understandings of the family and moral evaluations of changes in family life. In the following section, I outline the religious familism in these four communities today and address why a culture wars thesis is not adequate to understand religious understandings of the good family at the local level. The third section of the chapter summarizes the changes in individual commitment and in religious institutions in these communities and addresses how these findings can help us to rethink some of the core theoretical issues raised at the beginning of the book. The chapter concludes with an exploration of the implications of this local community-based study for larger questions about the changing interconnection between religion and family in our society.

RELIGION AND CULTURAL POWER

Religious institutions are powerful social actors. In a society like ours, which has a high degree of religious pluralism and a formal separation between church and state, the power of religious institutions is largely cultural. The exercise of cultural power involves the establishment of cultural models that define ideal social arrangements and the establishment of accompanying scripts of appropriate behavior that orient action.[1] Religious family schemas—or cultural models of "the good family"—can be found within official religious discourse and practice, within religious social movements or parachurch organizations, within local congregations, and at the level of what individual religious persons believe about the family and the family-oriented behaviors they engage in. Religious involvement styles draw on interpretive frameworks that link religion and family life in different ways, and are found in individual discourse and behavior and reflected in the types of ministry offered in local congregations and in how such ministry is organized. Taken together, these schemas and religious involvement styles have the power to shape ideals of the good family, define appropriate family- and work-oriented behaviors for men and women, influence understandings of the family as public or private, create boundaries within and between religious communities based on family form, lifestyle, and gender, and affect the tenor and organization of local religious life.

Discussions of culture and power often make a distinction between culture as taken for granted and culture as something to which people explicitly and intentionally orient their behavior. This is sometimes conflated with a distinction between culture as practice and culture as rhetoric, but these two dimensions are not the same and should not be conflated. Religious family schemas—or models of "the good family"—are found in many of the routine institutional practices of local religious life, and as such are reproduced without what Jepperson (1991) calls "action" or Sewell (1992) calls "agency"—without anyone consciously orienting their behavior to these models and intending to reproduce them. They are taken for granted. But they are also taken for granted in much of the rhetoric of congregational life, for example in the prominence of the time-bind rhetoric or in nostalgic references to the Ozzie and Harriet families of the past. Taken-for-granted culture is powerful because it is taken for granted—what is not named cannot be challenged or critiqued, and institutional routines of practice and nostalgic family rhetorics organize material resources in ways that reproduce cultural models automatically. Religious involvement styles generally operate in this taken-for-granted way.

Religious culture is also powerful, however, because sometimes it becomes explicit and social agents put a great deal of time and other resources into persuading others to believe in it and into attempting to institutionalize it in laws and in formal organizations. If many local churches are powerful because they foster the taken-for-grantedness of certain family forms and behaviors, others are powerful when their leaders consciously promote a more inclusive model of the family and justify it based on social justice commitments within their religious tradition. The exercise of explicit cultural power can be accomplished through both rhetoric and practice. The making and keeping of a pledge of chastity before marriage, as encouraged by some evangelical pastors, or the offering of joining ceremonies at St. Steven's for gay and lesbian couples are examples of practices engaged in for the explicit purpose of promoting a particular cultural model of the family in a direct way that equates with the conscious exercise of agency.

Religious culture is powerful in both of these senses. Religious culture establishes taken-for-granted understandings of the world and it also makes explicit particular models of how the world should be and motivates people to act in the service of those models. Religious family schemas are powerful to the extent that they shape broader societal understandings of what families are or should be like, to the extent that they include or exclude people from participation in religious institutions based on the kind of family they choose to form, and to the extent that they shape the behavior of individual believers or church-attenders in ways that reproduce or undermine particular forms of family life, a gendered division of labor, and specific work-family strategies. Put another way, these schemas are powerful insofar as they organize institutional routines and practices and individual behavior, and to the extent that they garner supporters who explicitly try to persuade others of their rightness or to change laws, institutions, and organizations to reflect them.

Religious culture is able to achieve both kinds of power for many reasons. For many individuals, religion is a primary, formative source of identity and socialization. For others, religious participation and living by religiously based moral codes is a source of legitimacy, a way of signaling social establishment and respectability and asserting that one is a good person as conventionally understood.[2] Williams and Demerath (1991) argue that the authority of religious leaders stems in part from a widespread perception that such leaders operate from caring and moral principles that they promote in disinterested ways. That is, religious culture may be powerful to the extent that is it understood as being about "what is right," "what is true," or "what is caring" and not about "what benefits me" or "what is expedient."[3] Rachel, quoted in chapter 1, values precisely this aspect of her religious community, which has shaped not only what she believes about family life, but also how she lives it.

Religious institutions exert cultural power in many arenas. But they are particularly powerful in establishing models of the good family and the moral frameworks that apportion responsibility for different kinds of behaviors within families. The production of familism—ideologies of family life— historically has been central to religious institutions in the United States. It is both expected and legitimate for religious leaders and institutions to promote cultural models of the good family and for local religious institutions to be largely a place for the moral socialization of children and the public sociability of families with other families. Scholars of religion take for granted that religion and family are intertwined and interdependent institutions. Religious pluralism and disestablishment, far from leading to religious decline have created the perfect environment for religion to take on expressive functions, which include the conferring of social identity and lifestyles. As discussed in the first chapter, many scholars firmly locate both the family and religion in the private realm and see the privatization of religion as being part of the reason that familism has become so central to religious cultural production in the United States.

However, many scholars have argued that religious pluralism and disestablishment lead not to a privatization of religion but to a reinvigorated public role for religious leaders and institutions. Lakoff (1996) provides an important corrective for those who believe that the family is a private institution and that family schemas have no public impact. He argues rather that cultural models of the family serve as organizing templates through which people understand where the dividing line between "private" and "public" is located and through which they orient their behavior to the state and the market as well as their attachments to neighbors, local communities, and kin. Cott (2002) argues that understandings of family life are formative of our sense of national identity. It is important, then, to understand the family schemas embedded in religious institutions because such schemas influence both "private" life as traditionally conceived—intimate relationships of family and friendship and voluntary association—and the "public" realms of the state, legal institutions, and the market.

For example, if neotraditional family arrangements take on the aura of divine ordination or become taken for granted as "natural" and "the way things are," then work-family management is women's responsibility and long-term differences in women's and men's occupational attainment that result from neotraditional gender roles in marriage are not likely to generate much concern—or policy reform. By contrast, a religiously based ideal of marriage as a loving union between equal partners may persuade people to lobby for legal changes that run the gamut from paid family leave to the legalization of same-sex marriages. The two religious involvement styles found in the communities in this study coincide with different understandings of the appropriate public role of religious leaders and institutions, and with different preferences for either public or private management of the costs of coordinating particular work-family strategies.

Gerson (2002) recognizes the importance of understanding the cultural frameworks that apportion moral responsibility in the family, especially the traditionally gendered responsibilities of direct caretaking and financial providing. She argues that this is particularly important as historical changes in work, education, and American culture have created moral dilemmas for women and men who no longer can—or in many cases, want to—embrace traditionally gendered roles within the family but who have few models or institutional supports for the more egalitarian and flexible work-family arrangements they prefer. Attention to how religious culture establishes moral frameworks of responsibility for men and women in the family helps to fill this gap, explaining contemporary patterns of behavior within families and analyzing institutional mechanisms that either foster or hinder solutions to the moral dilemmas involved in contemporary caretaking and providing.

However, much of the scholarship on the family and on work-family strategies proceeds without regard to the effects of religious identity and affiliation, and much of the work on religion and family is conducted on a narrow range of questions and without reference to the broader family and work-family literatures. This is partly the effect of subdisciplinary boundaries that lead to increasing specialization in scholarship. But it also has to do with an assumption on the part of many scholars of the family that religion is always a force for traditionalism, fostering patriarchal family arrangements and being harmful to women's independence, long-term economic attainment, and freedom to leave bad marriages. For their part, scholars of religion have focused on the functional nature of religion for marital happiness and stability and good parent-child relationships, often avoiding questions that are central to family scholars, such as how religion may promote inequality between men and women or analyzing the effects that religious belief and affiliation have on those living in nontraditional family arrangements.

The religious familism of the 1950s was manifest in a dominant family schema institutionalized in congregational rhetoric and practice. But it also shaped a culturally dominant male-breadwinner lifestyle and a family-oriented style of religious involvement. Many men and women thought of religious participation as a natural expression of a good and stable family life and used local congregations as a venue for family sociability and the moral instruction of children in ways that were organized around the male-breadwinner family's schedule. By analyzing the shape of contemporary religious familism we can understand the messages that religious institutions send about appropriate gender roles and family lifestyles today, how they promote understandings of religion and family as either public or private, and the mechanisms leading to cultural stability and cultural change in religious institutions.

FAMILY SCHEMAS AND RELIGIOUS INVOLVEMENT STYLES

The majority of congregations in these upstate New York communities contain a "stretched" version of the dominant 1950s family schema. Congregational activities are organized around two-parent families with children, although there is some attempt to be inclusive of those who are undergoing family disruption and of single-parent families. The work schedules of dual-earner couples are accommodated in the timing and organization of ministry, while in some ways the male-breadwinner lifestyle is still upheld as an ideal. In evangelical churches this takes the form of official rhetoric that stresses the man's role as the main provider and head of household and the woman's role as the nurturer. In mainline Protestant and Catholic churches this preference is expressed through a rhetoric nostalgic for the Ozzie and Harriet family of the past—and for the plentiful pool of women's volunteer time and labor that has now largely disappeared. Most congregations organized around this family model avoid the question of homosexuality as being too divisive to talk about. The few exceptions are among the more conservative evangelical Protestant churches, mostly small independent congregations in Baptist or Holiness traditions, which have pastors who are willing to explicitly critique homosexuality. The "standard package" of ministry from the 1950s and the cultural model of the family on which it is based are still influential in a broad range of congregations today.

Likewise, the family-oriented religious involvement style in these communities today is very like the dominant religious familism of the 1950s. Men, married parents, and older people have a more family-oriented style, and this is especially true for college-educated community members. They are very embedded in their local communities and in networks of neighbors and local kin. A family-oriented style is common among conservative Protestants and Catholics, although it is more common among—and more strongly held by—men than women across all religious traditions. This lifestyle is associated with more conservative attitudes about gender roles, a preference for publicly involved religious institutions, and a view that work-family management is largely a private affair—and, largely, a woman's responsibility.

There has also been significant change since the 1950s, though, among some congregations and individuals in these communities. Some mainline Protestant and a few Catholic congregations—the innovators described in chapter 6—have institutionalized the nurturing family schema drawn from religious discourses of social justice and caring and have formed local religious communities that welcome gay and lesbian families, single-parent families, long-term singles, and others who do not fit the traditional family schema. Mostly large congregations led by seminary-trained pastors with a strong social justice commitment and by lay leaders who want a local church that reflects their own experience with contemporary family forms, these innovators are not a large percentage of local churches (17 percent). But they are thriving, encompassing about 40 percent of the churchgoers in these communities on an average Sunday.

The decades since the 1950s have also seen the emergence of a self-oriented religious involvement style that displaces family life from the center of religious commitment. This religious involvement style is associated with managers and professionals, with a lifestyle that is more cosmopolitan and friendship networks that are more widely dispersed. It is practiced by people in a wider range of family situations—singles and married people without children, as well as some who are married and have children. Women are more likely to embrace this style regardless of their religious identity, education, or family status. So are mainline Protestants, while some Catholics and a few conservative Protestants embrace this style, too. A self-oriented understanding of religious involvement is rooted in a particular lifestyle and associated with egalitarian beliefs, a distrust of publicly involved religious institutions and leaders, and an understanding of work-family management as a public issue that ought to be facilitated by the state and by businesses.

In some ways, the local congregations in these upstate New York communities show the effects of the post-1950s divergence in our society between religious liberals and conservatives in understandings of core issues of morality and lifestyle, as well as religious authority. The official discourses of conservative religious leaders—both evangelical Protestant and Catholic—set the limits of the innovation in which local churches will engage to meet the new needs created by rapid changes in work and family life. It is important not to down-play the power of official religious discourse that finds biblical justification for patriarchal gender roles within marriage, promotes obedience to authority as central to the raising of children, and designates homosexuals, the divorced, and single parents as "broken" and sinful.

Likewise, it is important to emphasize that mainline Protestant elites—and some Catholic leaders, too—have provided a language of social justice that has made available to local churches a radically new way of conceptualizing family life. This has resulted in some local congregations that fully include lesbian and gay members, explicitly critique patriarchal gender relations in the family, encourage the development of children's independent moral judgment, recognize family disruption and recombination as a painful but tolerable route to stable and loving unions, and create ways of including all members that are not so dependent upon gender, life stage, and family status. Moreover, the different family schemas institutionalized in local religious life have some of the implications that Lakoff (1996) identifies, leading to different ways of thinking about the public or private nature of religion and family.

However, local religious culture, while being influenced by the ongoing "culture war" between liberal and conservative elites, is not adequately character-ized by the culture wars label. There are very few fundamentalist congregations here, and few that explicitly politicize issues such as abortion or homosexual-ity. Most local congregations *across* religious traditions have a neoconservative religious familism that nevertheless has accommodated and "stretched" the dominant male-breadwinner family schema of the 1950s into a new schema that focuses on parenting and intact families and is inclusive of various ways of managing gender roles within the family, different work-family strategies, and those experiencing family disruption and recombination. And the liberal in-novator congregations, while engaging in activism on a range of issues from poverty to racism, are not activist on hot-button family issues, rather prefer-ring the kind of "quiet" influence that comes simply from providing a model of inclusive community at the local level.[4]

Moreover, and contrary to the culture wars thesis, both versions of religious familism have important aspects in common. Both make central the role of parenting and of nurturing relationships within the family. This emphasis on parenting and nurturing, and the accompanying critique of lifestyles orga-nized around work and materialism, has a particular effect on men. Across all religious traditions, involvement in a local church makes men more likely to engage in some forms of caring and helping behavior, and more likely to scale back at work and spend more time with their families. Structural location ar-guments used to posit that women would become "more like men" in their re-ligious involvement as their structural location became more similar to men's—particularly as they took on more involving and rewarding work roles. However, it seems that religious involvement makes men, in some limited ways, more like women—more involved in their families and particularly in parenting. Wilcox (2004) has made a similar argument about religion as domesticating American men, leading them to greater involvement with their families on a wide range of measures.

But it is important to emphasize that the limits of male "domestication" by religion are real, and that both religious involvement and involvement in family life are still highly gendered in these communities. Men who go to church, and especially white-collar men who work long hours, use their congregations as venues for spending time with their children and spouses and as places to talk with other parents and give and receive support for a family-oriented lifestyle. But they also do less housework—of all kinds—than do other married men, and they are more likely to believe that, all things being equal, it is better if the man is the primary breadwinner and that work-family management is a private responsibility—which usually means, in practice, that it is a woman's responsibility.

Although first-order analyses suggest that this is more true for conservative Protestant men than for other men, additional analyses suggest that these differences are due not so much to the content of the religious subculture as to level of involvement (church attendance and salience of religion) and to the family-oriented religious involvement style that men tend to avow. Conservative Protestant men tend to attend church more, report higher religious salience, and affirm a family-oriented commitment style. However, men across religious traditions who are highly involved and who affirm a family-oriented style tend to look similar in the way they think about the links between religion and family in their own lives and in the way that religious involvement influences their involvement in their families' lives. For men, religion and work and family seem to fit together in a way that is taken for granted, and religious institutions bolster fathers' identity as *both* providers and as involved and caring parents.

Women in these communities have not become "more like men" in their religious involvement. Instead, they are likely to have a critical assessment of religious institutions and an individualistic view of religious authority and "official" religious discourse, and to make sure that their religious involvement meets their own needs and expresses their own values. This is true of women across religious tradition and social class, although it is more broadly true of mainline Protestant women. It is particularly true for women across religious traditions with at least a college degree and women who have white-collar jobs. A self-directed, critical stance toward religious institutions is fostered by educational and professional experiences that encourage autonomy, independence, and control—but this is especially the case for women. This makes sense when one considers that historically women have been outside the formal power structure and ideological production of religious institutions and that changes in women's roles have made their relationship to religious institutions problematic. The prominence of the time-bind rhetoric in local churches evidences this, as do the cultural connotations of the term *working mother*—which imply a contradiction that is entirely different from the connotations of the historically male role of "provider."

This argument is supported by other work that finds that the increasing polarization between liberal and conservative religious elites and elite discourses has a subtle and nuanced influence on religious men and women. Wilcox (2004) also finds that across religious traditions, involvement in a local congregation increases men's family involvement, particularly in parenting. And although he finds some differences between conservative Protestant men and other religiously involved men, he also finds much in common. This study helps to explain why differences in official family ideology have a subtle effect on individual belief and behavior. Most people encounter the teachings of their religious tradition in a local congregation, and local congregational life is a distinct level of analysis, with a distinct religious culture, organized around institutional imperatives that temper ideological division and lead to a great deal of similarity across religious traditions.

But if the domesticating effects of religion on men's behavior have been examined, what has remained unexplored is the marked disjuncture between women's family commitments and their religious involvement. It is clear that there are some exceptions to this pattern; for example, conservative Protestant women are more likely to work part-time and to have episodic employment organized around the birth and rearing of young children, and these patterns are influenced by the content of conservative religious beliefs about gender roles in marriage.[5] But this analysis shows that women across religious traditions are both critical of religious institutions and are involved not so much for their children and family as for themselves, meeting their own spiritual needs and expressing their own values. And most women make decisions about work-family management and caretaking in ways that are much more influenced by their education, occupation, and family demands than by religious belief or involvement.

What has also remained virtually unexplored in both the "culture wars" scholarship and in the religion and family scholarship is that religious familism is largely about expressing white middle-class lifestyles and values. Concerns about materialism and the time bind are not responsive to the needs of those in Syracuse's Northside who cannot find stable employment or to those in rural Seneca or Tompkins Counties who are piecing together three or four jobs between the husband and the wife, often with long commutes and inadequate health care and other benefits, just to pay for the basics of living such as food and rent. Nostalgic laments for a time when most churchwomen were homemakers suggest that many religious leaders have been out of touch with the needs and lives of working-class families, in which having two paid workers was the norm even in the 1950s. The inclusion of single parents does not involve reaching out across racial or economic lines. Evangelical pastors' talk about the stress of contemporary life and the need for authentic relationships brackets out concerns about economic hardships that cause stress and over-work. Of course, a few congregations do respond to the needs and concerns of non-middle-class members, with programs such as language classes and job training. Some Northside congregations advocate for economic redevelop-ment money, and in rural Seneca County, pastors help residents find the often geographically dispersed and hard to locate social services that are available for the poor and working poor. But these are very much the exceptions, not the rule.

Although it is tempting to see this state of affairs as stemming from the local demographics—the communities taken together are more than 94 percent white—this is not entirely compelling. More than a third of those in Northside and Seneca County have high school degrees or less. And both communities have seen serious economic downturns due in one case to the flight of jobs to the suburbs and a general metropolitan-area economic decline and in the other to the collapse of agriculture and the rise of a service-based economy that fosters underemployment. It seems more likely that the middle-class na-ture of religious familism in these communities stems from the middle-class familism of the 1950s that was dominant in the set of mainstream religious in-stitutions represented here, and from the middle-class values and discourses that are still dominant in these institutions in many ways.

RELIGIOUS RESPONSES TO SOCIAL CHANGE

There has been significant change in the religious familism in these communi-ties since the 1950s. In place of a single dominant model of the good family, there are two family schemas—one a transformed version of the dominant model of the 1950s, and one a substantively different, and more progressive, model. And in place of a single religious involvement style, there are two styles, including a self-oriented style that does not interpret religious involvement as primarily expressive of family status or a family-oriented life.

These changes can be understood according to Greenwood and Hining's (1996) template, which identifies two different forms of change in an institu-tional field. *Incremental innovation* leaves in place the basic cultural model around which organizations within the field are formed but stretches this model to include some new variations. Incremental change characterizes what has occurred in a large portion of the congregations in these communities, which are organized around a kind of familism similar to that of the 1950s, but with more inclusion of dual-earner and single-parent families, and it charac-terizes the family-oriented religious involvement model that sees congrega-tions as the appropriate context through which to spend time together as a family and to socialize children. *Radical innovation* changes the basic cultural model around which organizations in a field are constituted, and characterizes the familism of innovator congregations and those with a self-oriented religious involvement style.

These changes have been motivated by changes in the environment. The fundamental reorganization of gender, family, and work since the 1970s and the rise of the dual-earner couple as the dominant family type have challenged not only the content of church-based ministry programs but also the timing and organization of programs. Changing patterns of family formation, dissolution, and recombination, including rising rates of divorce, increasing numbers of single-parent families, and more "blended" families, have challenged churches to strike a balance between promoting stable marriages, nurturing relationships, and good parenting and providing a welcoming atmosphere for those for whom first marriages do not lead to lifelong unions. The feminist and gay rights movements have challenged traditional assumptions about what families might and should be like.

Coupled with a theology of social justice, local churches in mainline Protestant traditions now confront not only a cultural pluralism in family models in the larger society but also a substantial portion of their own leadership that embraces a fundamentally new conception of what constitutes a family. Leaders of Catholic and conservative Protestant congregations also accommodate cultural, as well as practical, challenges and emphasize the importance of nurturing and good parenting, the importance of a family-centered as opposed to a materialistic life, and the need to accommodate both working women and those experiencing family disruption. A few Catholic parishes and conservative Protestant congregations have engaged in a high degree of this incremental innovation, and their innovations have broadened the kinds of people who feel welcome and included in the life of these churches and have influenced other congregations in their communities to be more innovative, too.

How do we understand these cultural changes? At the level of the local congregation, it makes sense to understand the dynamics of cultural change as a process of changing orthopraxy, not orthodoxy.[6] Whether engaging in incremental or radical innovation, local churches maintain an ongoing and largely pragmatic balance between instituting the moral imperatives of their religious tradition (doing "what is right") and the desire to include and be responsive to those in a variety of family contexts (doing "what is caring"). It is through the endogenous tension between these two core moral imperatives of local religious life that local religious familism changes over time.

Defining the good family in local congregational life and interpreting the appropriate relationship between one's own family life and participation in a local church are practical matters accomplished in a routine way. Individuals make decisions about placing their children in Sunday School or leading the church's Scout troop. Men choose a congregation where they can find other men to talk with about parenting and family life, and women choose congregations where they are not defined by their status as "wife" or "mother" and can express their spirituality and their values. Women's ministries are expanded to include single mothers and moved to weeknights instead of weekdays because most women in the congregation work outside the home during the day. Pastors reach out to those undergoing divorce. The Mother-Daughter Banquet in the Baptist church is renamed the Women's Spring Banquet and women's achievements at work and community service are celebrated along with the celebration of motherhood. Catholic parishes no longer run a three-month-long series of confirmation classes on successive Sunday nights, but explore other ways to bring in more children of blended families and busy dual-earner couples. The practical wisdom expressed in informal rhetorics—the centrality of the time bind, the imperative to "meet the new needs"—filters and selects which changes in family life are attended to.

Official orthodoxies that come from religious elites and denominational leaders have an influence, because they shape some—although not all—of the frameworks to which local religious leaders refer in determining "what is right." They set the limits of incremental changes for conservative congregations that draw the line at affirming gay and lesbian lifestyles. But within that limit, some evangelical churches and a few Catholic parishes in these communities have engaged in such a broad range of incremental innovation that they are in fact more welcoming of those in a variety of family contexts than are some of the mainline Protestant churches in the area. Official orthodoxy provides models that motivate some mainline Protestant churches to engage in a form of more radical innovation organized around a fundamentally different conception of what families are and how family ministry fits into local church ministry—although only after the result of an exhaustive process that seeks to include all points of view and to emphasize continuity with older models (see Becker 1999). It took years at St. Steven's United Methodist Church for members to decide to become a reconciling congregation, and the pastor continually emphasizes the continuity of their present emphasis on caring families—of all types—with the congregation's past, and the centrality of common moral concerns (promoting good parenting and stable, loving families) that bridge the remaining divisions between more progressive, newer members and older, more conservative ones.

Local congregations should be understood as a source of moral frameworks that are not straightforward expressions of larger religious traditions. They are embedded in religious traditions and denominational structures that local leaders draw on for both routine practices and official discourses, doctrines, and rituals. But agents in local congregations—as with those in any organization in a large and complex field—are situated at an intersection of social structures. Their members can draw on a wide range of other organizations and institutions for discourses and routine practices, and for cultural schemas that seem appropriate for solving practical problems of action as they are confronted. The time-bind rhetoric, originating in popular cultural media and academic discourse, serves as the most common interpretive framework for understanding family life in the congregations of these communities. Feminist understandings shape women's religious involvement styles and inform their critical stance toward local religious organizations. The schema of the male-breadwinner family—not a biblical model, but a product of the industrial revolution, idealized by secular elites—formed a template for family ministry in a period of religious expansion in the 1950s, and because of institutional inertia this model has a formative influence on how much innovation can occur long after family life has been fundamentally reconfigured.

The mechanisms through which local religious culture changes are best understood using an institutional framework. Incremental changes come about partly through demand—particularly changes in the time and timing of programs to accommodate dual-earner couples, and changes in rhetoric and practice that reflect women's changing expectations. But demand is filtered through institutionalized mechanisms. The dominant family schema institutionalized in the 1950s still provides the organizing template for ministry in most area congregations. The rhetoric of the time bind filters which changes congregations notice and respond to. Institutional routines shape the particular decisions congregations make, leading to distinct profiles of ministry in mainline Protestant, Catholic, and evangelical churches, respectively. The balancing of a moral imperative to be caring and inclusive with the moral imperative to do what is right shapes the dynamic of all congregations' changes in how "the good family" is talked about and in the kinds of ministries provided.

Radical innovations come about because of the value-rational action of committed leaders, and take place in congregations with the most educated clergy and the most resources. These factors, which according to market accounts should insulate leaders from demand and make them less innovative, provide the resources for innovation based not on concerns about marketing but on core value commitments. And value-based innovation is rewarded, resulting in thriving congregations with committed members, despite not being found in the "high tension" churches for which market accounts predict success.

It is not that market accounts are wrong about the sources and dynamics of innovation; rather, they are partial, and they take the resulting cultural divisions—the content of religious culture—as a given. In these communities, there have been some changes in both rhetoric and programming that respond to changing member demands. Some religious entrepreneurs in evangelical churches do put effort into meeting new needs—and thus constructing demand and building market share. But this is only one set of dynamics leading to change. Other changes are driven not by instrumental rationality but by value rationality. And institutional forces not only constitute inertia and resistance to innovation—a form of irrationality in market-based accounts—but

also enable innovation in two ways. They enable incremental innovation by
providing schemas and routine ways of doing things that can be stretched to
form new responses to new situations. And they enable more radical innovation through providing some religious leaders with the training and resources
to propose changes based on their own professional commitments and religious values.

Institutional accounts provide a way to analyze the content of religious
culture—how it emerges and changes over time, why the field of American religion is structured around particular cultural models, the interplay of official
culture and local culture, and why the particular cultural content of religious
beliefs matters. Institutional analysis provides a language for talking about
agency and self-interest while also providing specific ways to analyze how cultural schemas both constrain and enable action and providing a vocabulary of
agency that can encompass both instrumental and value rationality.

If market approaches do not provide the most robust framework for understanding the mechanisms and the consequences of religious cultural change,
they are correct in their critique of theories that link religious change to an underlying teleology of secularization and modernization. A nostalgia for the perceived stability of the 1950s makes it hard to recognize the expressive, privatized
role that religion played in that decade, and the fact that local religious life was
organized largely around facilitating a particular—and secular—work-family
lifestyle with its accompanying status concerns and interests. But scholars writing in that time period recognized the link between religious familism and a
middle-class, male-breadwinner lifestyle and the expressive nature of volun-
taristic religious commitment.

It makes no sense to characterize the post-1950s changes in religious commitment and religious familism as resulting in increased privatization or secularization of religion. The male-breadwinner suburban lifestyle of the 1950s
was a product of secular trends in the economy and education. The style of religious commitment that accompanied it may have transmitted religiosity to
the young, but it is that generation of young people who avidly participated in
the social movements of the 1960s and 1970s that so transformed the fabric of
our social institutions, particularly regarding gender and family. And the self-
oriented style of religious commitment held by many residents of these communities today is in some ways less privatized than is a family-oriented style; it
places the expression of spirituality and of religious belief and values at the
heart of religious participation and displaces the secondary functions of family
socialization and sociability.

The argument about the privatization of religion has been pervasive in part
because of the assumption built into most sociological theory that modernization is an ongoing, uniform process that erodes all forms of traditional authority and identity, and is especially damaging to religion. For example, Wilcox
(2004) argues that the dynamics of religious familism are driven by ongoing

modernization and the choices that religious leaders face either to resist this modernization or to accommodate it; in this, he draws on a chief argument of culture war scholars. Wilcox views the religious familism of conservative Protestants as more successful than those of mainline Protestants because they have innovated in ways that preserve the core of their religious belief and tradition and maintain a distinctive moral voice that resists the modernization of family life. And it is true that over the decades since the 1950s, evangelical churches have boomed and mainline Protestant churches have declined. (Catholicism has grown largely through the immigration of predominately Catholic Latino populations.) Resisting the modernization of the family has been seen as central in the growth of conservative Protestant groups since the 1950s.

But this study strongly suggests that mainline Protestant innovation can lead to thriving congregations and strongly committed members when it also is organized around core values of the religious tradition and when it is offered affirmatively as a moral vision. This is an important corrective to views based in modernization and secularization theories, because such theories assume that all liberal/progressive innovation is accommodating to modernity and will therefore weaken religious authority and religious identity. Religious organizations do not thrive by resisting or being in tension with modernity. They thrive when they offer religiously based visions of a moral good that are framed as a coherent expression of a religious tradition, when they offer people meaningful frameworks that are different from the more interest- or expediency-based frameworks they encounter in other institutions, and when they express important social identities.[7]

The congregations in these communities provide these frameworks for members. These frameworks are rooted in and express two different ways of constructing a middle-class life. These differences include choices about the gendering of work and family obligations and assumptions about who should bear the costs of solving the moral dilemmas of caretaking and providing that Gerson (2002) outlines. Both of these familisms are firmly rooted in middle-class lives and experiences, and both are equally "modern." In the absence of reformulations of the state and the market in ways that facilitate flexible, innovative, and appropriate ways to share contemporary family caretaking and providing, men and women are forced to seek private solutions. Religious organizations, historically associated with family life, are natural venues for constructing visions of the good family, for practical programs of help and support, for conversation with like-minded men and women confronting similar dilemmas, for places to recharge and renew one's own faith, and for support in attempting to resist the encroachment of paid work on family life.

It is important to note that one of these visions involves an emphasis on egalitarian roles for men and women, openness to gay and lesbian families, and an unwillingness to stigmatize those who have gone through family disruption and reformulation. In an era of vocal family values rhetoric from religious conservatives, Hout and Fischer (2002) argue that some liberal and moderate individuals have chosen to distance themselves from organized religion, associating it with the conservative profamily agenda. This study suggests that others choose to affiliate with local churches that explicitly promote a different ideal of "the good family." Sociologists have emphasized the success of evangelical groups that endorse a "gentler" and more "domesticated" version of patriarchy and the decline of mainline churches that accommodate changes in family life—and particularly in women's roles. But the thriving liberal congregations in these communities that offer a more progressive, egalitarian family model suggest that it is not the accommodation of liberal elites on family values rhetoric that leads to decline but a nostalgic longing for the Ozzie and Harriet family in local mainline congregations that alienates a potential membership that is looking for an affirmative, religiously based vision of contemporary family life.

From Local Communities to Larger Questions

What I found in these communities suggests that in order to understand the ongoing cultural contestation over family values that some have termed the culture war, we need to pay attention to local religious communities not only as reflections of larger religious traditions but as creative arenas where a different kind of religious culture is produced through dialogue with official religious discourse in ways that may influence how religious traditions develop and change over time. Congregations are central locations for the production of religious familism, where leaders and members stake out positions on what kinds of unions are families and what kinds of families are good families. The dynamics of that contestation in these communities can shed some light on broader questions of how religion shapes the way we as a society evaluate the moral and practical dimensions of changes in family life and how religious communities provide more or less inclusive social spaces for those in a variety of family situations.

This is a study of one set of communities in upstate New York, focusing on the links between religion and family in a few very particular local religious ecologies. The particularities of these communities shape the way that the insights from this local study are applicable to broader questions about the interrelationships between religion and family in our society. Some of the things I found in these communities one might expect to find in other kinds of communities across America, while some things would only likely be found in similar communities—communities without a great deal of ethnic diversity or high rates of immigration, where the dominant form of religious expression is organized around mainstream religious institutions.

For example, in these communities both congregational culture and individual religious commitment are very much influenced by the white middle-class culture that reflects the lifestyles and preferences of the most involved and vocal lay members, resonates with the life experiences and professional training of most of the pastors, and is institutionalized in the culture of the denominational structures represented here.[8] The nostalgia for the Ozzie and Harriet family is shaped by both the history of the religious institutions that dominate this religious ecology and the history of white middle-class women's rapid movement into paid employment from the 1970s onward. The understanding that religious institutions should be responsive to contemporary needs, the critical stance toward religious authority, and the more reflexive orientation to institutions more generally that characterize the self-oriented religious involvement style may have become more widespread throughout our society over the last forty years, but this self-oriented religious involvement style is also expressed here in a way that is influenced by the preferences for autonomy and flexibility that characterize the professional middle-class culture of many church members and leaders.[9]

One would expect that in other communities, the particular rhetorics and practices of family ministry would reflect different concerns. For example, congregations may concentrate more on bolstering fatherhood in African American communities, and feature an unabashed endorsement of the ideal of the man as the family provider and protector.[10] Even in these four communities it is evident that social context influences both the content of congregational rhetoric and the kinds of programming offered, with pastors in some poorer communities arguing that a focus on family values distracts from the real issues of poverty and joblessness, and pastors in Northside reporting that their congregations' family ministry includes job training and language classes. And in many ethnic and immigrant communities, Ozzie and Harriet are irrelevant; the dominant cultural ideal is the extended family that is both emotionally and financially interdependent across generations.[11] Very likely these differences are expressed in congregational rhetoric about the family.

On the other hand, many of the tensions and contradictions that these particular congregations in upstate New York negotiate in constructing family ministry are ones that may well be common across many kinds of communities. These include a nostalgia for past family forms and a resistance to changing "how we do things here" in tension with a desire to meet new needs and provide relevant ministry, a desire to preserve core tenets of faith that may lead to the exclusion of some people from congregational life in tension with the mandate to be a loving and inclusive Christian community, and a desire to acknowledge the painful effects of family disruption without creating an atmosphere of judgment and censure of those who find themselves undergoing divorce or confronting the difficulties of single parenthood.

By and large, the congregations in these communities provide useful examples for how religious communities can meet the needs of those undergoing family disruption and reformulation. The ability to negotiate practical and emotional crises in the first two years after a divorce is the key to setting a long-term trajectory of success (high levels of autonomy and satisfaction for adults, flexibility and stability for children) or failure (low levels of autonomy and satisfaction for adults, behavioral and emotional problems for children).[12] These congregations provide the kind of social and practical support that may be crucial in ameliorating some of the damaging effects of family disruption on both children's and adults' lives, and they are especially likely to play this role immediately during and after episodes of family disruption, when the trajectory of success or failure is set. This may be especially true for women, for whom family disruption and reformation lead to high levels of religious salience, who report that it is mostly practical barriers that keep them from religious participation as they undergo these major life transitions, and who make extensive use of congregational support when these practical barriers are overcome. Likewise, congregations may help blended families negotiate the crucial formative period when new family routines are being established.

Of course, in different kinds of communities family disruption may occur at higher rates or lead to very different social and economic consequences than what occurs in upstate New York. But what can be learned from these communities is the importance of overcoming the specific practical barriers to religious participation for those undergoing episodes of family disruption in a given social context. When these practical barriers are overcome, congregations can provide a context for the social support that contributes to long-term happiness and stability of adults and children after divorce and that may ameliorate the challenges blended families face. This is important because the best research to date shows that although family disruption is painful in the short term, it does not automatically lead to long-term harm for either adults or children given the availability of sufficient economic resources and the practical and emotional support received from strong social connections.[13]

The fact that religious involvement means different things to women and men is likely to be the case across all kinds of communities. Although models of the ideal family differ and economic conditions shape different lifestyles and provide different opportunities and constraints, virtually all understandings of the ideal family and virtually all of the practical routines of managing family life in our society assume some (greater or lesser) degree of gender difference and gender-role specialization. As long as the production of familism is central to what religious communities are and do, congregations will be central locations for maintaining or challenging our ideas about gender—socially constructed ideals of male and female qualities and responsibilities and practical ways to enact these ideals.

Both women and men seek out local congregations that affirm the particular gender role ideology that is consonant with their own family lives, both growing up and in the families they form as adults, and this may be particularly true for women. Moreover, men and women seek out congregations that interweave rhetoric about the good family and the provision of family ministry in a way that draws on the core tenets of the religious tradition and makes them relevant to family life today. The nostalgia in many mainline Protestant and Catholic churches for the Ozzie and Harriet family is not a problem because it is traditional per se, but because the traditionalism it implies is out of line with the progressive, social-justice-oriented, inclusive theology that church members in these traditions recognize as authentic. Likewise, the traditionalism of fundamentalist churches is not a problem because it is too traditional, but because it does not combine a traditional ideal of the family—which *is* authentic within this religious tradition—with a focus on the practical meeting of members' needs as part of building a caring and responsive Christian community.

Congregations thrive when they balance an authoritative voice that speaks to "what is right" and provide a strong moral vision of the good family while also acting authoritatively to achieve "what is caring" and inclusive.[14] They thrive when they adapt to changes in the family while providing a distinctive moral voice that helps members assess new family realities in light of an enduring religious tradition. Ironically, congregations that do this also find themselves attracting not only "traditional" families but also single parents, single adults, childless couples, and those who attend primarily to express their own religious values and not because the congregation is intimately intertwined with their own family or the raising of children.

These insights have more than academic importance for two reasons. The first is the importance of the social support that congregations offer for establishing stable marriages and partnerships, for the moral socialization of children, and for those experiencing family disruption. Evangelical churches that welcome the divorced and single-parent families provide a supportive context that is responsive to new family realities. But it is vital that congregations in progressive liberal traditions not cede moral discourse on family life to religious conservatives by avoiding the new realities facing contemporary families or allow themselves to be trapped by a nostalgia for the Ozzie and Harriet family. The progressive innovator congregations in these communities can provide models—not so much for specific profiles of family ministry, because those work best when they are context-specific and responsive to local concerns. But more generally, these thriving innovators show that a progressive understanding of family life can be religiously authentic and can provide a strong moral vision while not excluding those whose lives do not fit an idealized version of the past.

However, it is important to keep in mind that in these communities, even innovative congregations—both liberal and conservative—have been less successful in meeting the needs of poor and working-class community members. Because this is due in part to rhetoric that is widely institutionalized in the kinds of churches represented here, and because these religious institutions still make up the majority of American congregations, this may be a very widespread barrier to developing family ministry that is truly responsive to the needs of those who are economically marginalized.

It is also important to understand the familism of local religious communities because these communities serve as an important realm of cultural contestation that may be more caring and inclusive—and more practical—than the polarizing discourse of elites who perpetuate a divisive culture war. It is appropriate that debates over the family take place within the civic sphere of life, in social spaces not controlled by the state, and in local communities that display an ideological spectrum while not being driven to ideological extremes. Men and women face truly remarkable challenges in today's society, where the continuity and stability of family life cannot be taken for granted, the costs of work-family management still fall disproportionately on women, and well-paying jobs with adequate benefits are not available to all who need them.

Religious communities are no substitute for more responsive and humane social and economic policies. And in a pluralistic society, religious voices should both reflect the pluralism of religious belief and be raised in civil conversation with secular visions of the good family. But religious communities can provide a venue where men and women can construct a moral vision that may have an impact on law and social policy as our society continues to grapple with the implications of the rapid and fundamental restructuring of family life that has taken place over the last thirty years. Such venues—religious and secular, liberal and conservative—are the foundation of the good society.

Appendix

CHOICES

WHEN THIS PROJECT was conceptualized, there were numerous individual-level studies of religious preference and affiliation based on census data and surveys, much of which is reviewed in Sherkat and Ellison (1999). There were also some ethnographic case studies of individual congregations' family ministries (Marler 1995, Airhart and Bendroth 1996, Lyon and Smith 1998, Demmitt 1992), and studies of religious leaders' discourse on the family (Browning et al. 1997, Hunter 1991, Bellah et al. 1991). The survey and census data provided a good overall depiction of the nature and scope of the changes in the relationship between religion and family in our society. The ethnographies outlined some initial organizational responses, mostly evaluated from the standpoint of practical theology.

What was missing was research that allows a systematic, comparative understanding of what effects nontraditional families are having on religious organizations and institutions and a systematic and comparative understanding of how nontraditional families are affected by their participation in religious life at various stages of the life course. The first question is a matter of institutional and organizational adaptation that sociologists are particularly suited to address. The second question addresses the impact of religious organizations on family life after a period of rapid social change.

It is appropriate to begin this research at the level of the congregation. There is no doubt that religious-institutional change comes "from above," from changes in theology, doctrine, and denominational practices. But a good part of change in religious institutions also comes "from below," from congregations that are subject to organizational and cultural constraints that operate apart from and crosscut theological factors. And while changes in family life no doubt have an impact on religious institutions at all levels, the local congregation is the most direct organizational link between family and religion, and it is the erosion of the link at this level that causes so much concern.

DATA COLLECTION—RELIGION AND FAMILY PROJECT

What is the best approach to studying the changing interrelationship between families and congregations? What should such a study emphasize? In thinking through these questions, I decided that:

- Such a study should be *comparative* across congregations to allow us to identify patterned differences in how congregations respond to nontraditional families.
- It should compare congregations *within their local context and ecology* for two reasons. First, local communities vary greatly in their family composition. Second, congregations often define themselves within a local ecology and specialize their mission vis-à-vis other congregations in their immediate area.
- The study should seek both *reliability* and *validity*. Because there is little research in this area, it would be helpful to combine *qualitative methods*, which can increase validity by revealing the mechanisms by which adaptation comes about and the meaning of that adaptation for participating individuals, with *quantitative methods* that can place particular cases within a larger population, telling how typical they are and increasing reliability.
- Such a study needs to do more than gather data within congregations; it needs to *take the congregation seriously as a distinct level of analysis*. Congregations as organizations have certain structural features that will influence process and decision making. Congregations also have cultural features, some of which flow from the larger religious tradition and some of which are unique to the congregation's own history and local culture.
- Finally, such a study should be *reciprocal*, asking not only how congregations adapt to nontraditional families but also seeking to understand what effect congregations have on the lives of families within their own four walls and in their communities. This includes understanding the effect of congregational programs and services, certainly, but also the cultural, spiritual, and ethical effects of religious belonging. This effort should be inclusive across socioeconomic diversity and across all life-course stages.

The purpose of the data collection combined exploratory and descriptive goals with explanatory ones. For example, the purpose of fieldwork in area congregations and focus groups with pastors was to hear the informal ways of talking about "the family" or "the good family" that occur in local congregational life—in pastors' own talk, in sermons, in what the speaker says at the Thursday Family Night program. On the other hand, the sociological literature is very specific about the effects of family formation on religious involvement for men and women, so the survey of community residents was designed to collect data on family formation and disruption as well as people's attitudes about how religion and family *ought* to go together. Table A.1 describes the research design and data collection in these four communities.

A census survey of all the pastors in each of the four communities was conducted in 1998 (N = 125, response rate 78 percent). It was designed to collect data unavailable through other sources on congregations' networks, including congregations considered to be peers and competitors, congregations and other organizations that are partners in ministry programs, and membership in local ecumenical groups. The survey also focused on congregations' ministries

TABLE A.1
Religion and Family Project Data (1998–2001, Penny Edgell Becker, Principal Investigator)

	Individual Level	Congregation Level
Quantitative	Survey of Community Residents (N = 1,006, response rate 60 percent). Random-digit-dial telephone survey, twenty-minute average, drawn evenly from all four communities, some oversampling of areas with high numbers of working-class respondents.	Survey of Pastors (N = 125). Telephone census survey of pastors of every congregation in each community, forty-five-minute average, response rate 78 percent. Pastor served as key informant on congregation's membership and programming.
	Data collected on: demographics and family structure (age, sex, marital status, parenting status, household structure); household division of labor; evaluation of family relationships (satisfaction/ drain/commitment) and attitudes and beliefs toward family (gender egalitarianism, marriage and children essential to happiness, etc.); education and occupation for respondent (and spouse); employment status for respondent (and spouse) including number of hours worked, commute time, work schedule; evaluation of work (satisfaction/drain/commitment); religious affiliation, salience, church attendance, use of other congregational ministries, participation in other religious organizations, views of reli- gious authority, views of religion's role in socialization of children, views of religious institutions' openness to various work/family arrangements, religious behaviors/practices of those not attending; community involvement (length of residence, local networks, volunteering).	Data collected on: membership (demographics, family status, trends over time); building and plant; denominational affiliation(s); membership in ecumenical or denominational networks/ organizations; local peers/ competitors; family ministries; recent changes/ innovations in family ministries; congregational rhetoric (gender roles, children's roles, legitimate family forms); partnerships with other organizations (congregations or secular) for specific ministries/ programs; pastor's education; congregational resources; founding date Census data married to original survey database includes community demographic and economic information by tract (and larger units).
	119 persons refusing to respond to the initial survey were administered a much-shortened version of the survey collecting basic demographic	Participant-observation of Sunday worship was used to fill in partial (demographic/programming) data for twelve congregations not

TABLE A.1 (*cont.*)

	Individual Level	*Congregation Level*
	data, religious affiliation, church attendance, and some attitude/belief items. Designed to check for systematic nonresponse bias based on religious affiliation/beliefs.	cooperating with original survey.
Qualitative	Eighty in-depth telephone interviews with respondents to initial telephone survey, lasting forty-five minutes to an hour. Covered respondent's history of religious involvement and more details on attitude/belief items.	Five focus groups with nine to twelve pastors, one in each community (two in Ithaca), presenting initial survey findings for feedback and exploring more detail about changes in family ministry and family ideology/rhetoric. (N = 47)
		Participant-observation in sixteen congregations (four in each community) cooperating with original survey. Observations of main worship service, at least one "family ministry" as designated by pastor, informal conversations with members, and follow-up interviews with pastors and lay leaders.
		Participant-observation in seven area congregations designated as "innovators," summer 2000.

and programming, on recent changes made to accommodate changes in work and family, and on pastors' own views of appropriate gender roles and family forms. Community demographic data (1990 census) was married to this file at the census tract level.

Following up on the survey, fieldwork was conducted by a small team of researchers in sixteen area congregations, and included visits to worship services, weekly ministry programs, interviews with lay leaders, and document review. Additional fieldwork was conducted in the spring and summer of 2000 on seven congregations that had a particularly innovative profile of ministry, particularly family-oriented ministry. A series of pastor focus groups, drawing on almost fifty area pastors, rounded out the data collection on the local congregations. This qualitative data serves as more than a supplement to the survey. It is the primary mode of data collection for several of the rhetorical and discursive questions that motivate this research.

These communities also have a distinctive religious ecology, one that is dominated by the kinds of mainstream religious institutions that were so prominent during the 1950s religious expansion. Table A.2 compares these communities to data from the National Congregations Study, to give a sense of the particularities of the local religious ecology.

A random-sample survey of individuals in each community (total N = 1,006, roughly 250 in each community, response rate 60 percent) allowed me to go beyond community residents' demographic characteristics to assess how their beliefs, attitudes, commitments, and work-family strategies influence their "demand for" and evaluation of local congregations' family ministries. Eighty follow-up in-depth interviews with survey respondents allowed me to understand pathways into and out of religious involvement and the meaning of religious involvement with greater richness than a survey format would allow.

Focus Communities

The four communities were chosen for a mix of pragmatic and conceptual reasons. Practically, they had to be within a reasonable commute of Cornell University—even in winter, which effectively ruled out going farther afield to communities in Rochester (northwest) or down south closer to New York City. Conceptually, it was important to capture the major dimensions of local variation in community life and individual lifestyle. In this region, rural / urban and middle-class / working-class distinctions form the major dimensions of diversity in social life. Racial and ethnic variation exist to some degree, but not in the way that they do in larger urban centers or other regions of the country. Table A.3 compares 2000 census data for the United States as a whole and each of the four focus communities. Tables containing census data for each focus community for every decade from 1950 to 2000 are available on request.

Histories of the communities show very different paths of development both economically and socially. Tompkins County history dates from the Revolutionary War and has seen a relatively steady trajectory of growth, with an economy that stabilized in the late nineteenth century with the establishment of Cornell University (1865) and the railroad lines that soon followed. The Village of Liverpool was formed in 1830 and the village and surrounding area experienced rapid expansion in the post–World War II era, increasing in population 450 percent between 1960 and 1990. The Northside of Syracuse includes several historic neighborhoods that have experienced a period of economic decline since the 1970s, and have seen recent redevelopment efforts funded by federal grants and the City of Syracuse. Seneca County has made a transition in the postwar era from a farm-based economy to one dominated by service, sales, and professional occupations.

Comparing Religion and Family Project Congregational Census to
National Congregations Study Sample

	Religion and Family Project (N = 125, response rate 78%)	National Congregations Study [a] (N = 1236, response rate 80%)
Denomination (percent)		
Catholic	14	6
Jewish	1	1
Baptist	17	30
Methodist	14	14
Lutheran	5	6
Presbyterian	7	5
Episcopal	6	3
Other Protestant	34	31
Other non-Protestant	1	3
Unknown	1	2
Religious tradition (percent)		
Catholic	14	6
Liberal/moderate		
Protestant	34	27
Conservative Protestant	47	56
Other	3	5
Black Christian [b]		5
Year founded (percent)		
pre-1945	58	53
1945–65	18	18
1966–89	18	19
post-1990	1	10
Size [c] (percent)		
1–50	16	39
51–100	22	24
101–250	37	22
251–500	14	9
501–999	5	3
1000+	7	3

Sources: Religion and Family Project, Penny Edgell Becker, PI, 2003; Mark Chaves, National Congregations Study, Data File and Codebook (Tucson, Arizona: University of Arizona, Department of Sociology, 1998).

Notes: [a] All NCS percentages are based on weighted data to compensate for the disproportionate representation of larger congregations in the original sample.

[b] I included "black Christian" congregations in the "moderate Protestant" category. However, there were few of these in the communities I studied and this difference in coding does not account for the different percentages of liberal/moderate Protestants in comparing my sample with the National Congregations Study.

[c] Total number of regular participants, adults and children.

TABLE A.3
Census Data 2000, United States and Four Focus Communities

	United States	Tompkins	Seneca	Northside*	Liverpool**
Population	281,421,906	96,501	33,342	29,540	53,073
Urban/Rural (percent)					
Urban	79	58.4	42.5	100	99.5
Rural	21	41.6	57.5	0	0.5
Sex (percent)					
Male	49.1	49.4	50	47.5	48
Female	50.9	50.6	50	52.5	52
Age (percent)					
Under 18	26.7	19	24.8	24.6	25.5
15–24	13.9	29.6	11.9	13.6	11.9
25–34	14.2	13.4	12.9	16.4	15.3
35–44	16	12.8	15.8	14.8	16.8
45–54	13.4	12.5	14.2	11.2	14.8
55–64	8.6	6.8	9.6	6.9	8.5
65 and over	12.4	9.6	15.1	15.6	11.2
Family type (percent)					
Married with kids under 18	23.5	18.3	22.4	22.5	37.2
Married without kids under 18	28.2	22.9	31.2	30.4	42
Male householder, no wife present	4.2	5.8	6.5	10.7	5.2
with kids under 18	2.1	3.6	4.1	5.7	2.9
without kids under 18	2.1	2.2	2.4	5	2.3
Female householder, no husband	12.2	8.2	10.3	36.2	15.4
with kids under 18	7.2	5.6	6.6	24.9	9.7
without kids under 18	5	2.6	3.7	11.3	5.7
Employment (percent)					
All parents in household work, with children age 0–5	57.6	64.4	65.5	57.1	53.8
Race (percent)					
White	75.1	85.5	95	75.77	91.6
Black	12.9	3.6	2.3	11.14	3.5
Persons of Hispanic origin	12.5	3.1	2	3.8	1.4

TABLE A.3 (*cont.*)

	United States	Tompkins	Seneca	Northside*	Liverpool**
Occupation (percent)					
Manager/professional	33.6	50.2	30.4	23.4	40.5
Education (persons 25 and over, percent)					
Less than high school graduation	19.6	8.6	20.9	30.8	9.7
High school graduation	28.6	22.3	35.7	33	28.5
Some college or more	51.7	69.1	43.5	36.2	61.5
Bachelor's degree or more	24.4	47.5	17.5	13.5	29.8
Income (dollars)					
Median household	41,994	37,272	37,140	23,374	48,036
Median family	50,046	53,041	45,445	29,231	55,298

*Census tracts for Northside: 36.067.0002.00, 36.067.0003.00, 36.067.0004.00, 36.067.0005.00, 36.067.0006.00, 36.067.0007.00, 36.067.0008.00, 36.067.0013.00, 36.067.0014.00, 36.067.0015.00, 36.067.0016.00, 36.067.0023.00, 36.067.0024.00
**ZIP codes for Liverpool: 13088, 13090

Web-based resources for these communities are generally well developed and can provide additional information. Tompkins County has an excellent Web site that includes a history by the official county historian (http://www.co. tompkins.ny.us/guide/history.html). The City of Syracuse maintains a link to neighborhood information and a good description of Northside (http:// www. syracuse.ny.us/nhood2.asp). A history and current description of Seneca County, including a history of women's rights activism in the community, can be found on the official county Web page (http://www.co.seneca.ny.us/). The Web page for the Village of Liverpool (http://www.villageofliverpool.org/) includes information about the village itself and the surrounding area.

NOTES

1. There are several good reviews of these changes, among them Spain and Bianchi's *Balancing Act* (1996). Jacobs and Gerson 2004 reviews the time bind literature in detail; cf. Hochschild 1989, 1997. Wilcox 2004 reviews the literature on changes in fathering and men's identity; see also Nock 1998 on the changing meaning of marriage in men's lives. Riley et al. 1994 discusses how institutions have been slow to adapt to these changes and have created costs that are mostly borne privately by individuals and families.

2. The "culture wars" literature is vast. For two summaries that include chapters on family-related issues, see Hunter 1991 and Bellah et al. 1991. For research that focuses specifically on the role that religious institutions play in the culture wars and especially on the rise of a conservative evangelical subculture and discourse on women and family, see Woodberry and Smith 1998, Bartkowski 1997a, and Bendroth 1993, 2002. For a review of the controversy over gay marriage, see Hull 2001, 2003. For two well-balanced and extensive reviews of the research on divorce and well-being, see Hetherington and Kelly 2002 and Amato 2000. For a discussion of changing life course patterns of family formation and dissolution, see Furstenberg 1999 and Treas 1999.

3. For a discussion of this increasing pluralism, see Skolnick 1991. See also Stacey 1991.

4. For a discussion that links the state of the family to views of "the good society," see Bellah et al. 1991, Christiano 2000, and Cott 2002.

5. See DiMaggio et al. 1996 for a discussion of why the "culture wars" between liberal and conservative elites do not adequately represent the views of most Americans on a wide range of policy issues. See Williams 1997 for a critique of the culture wars thesis.

6. See Christiano 2000 and Ammerman and Roof 1995 for reviews.

7. The following discussion draws on several good recent reviews of the religion and family literature, including Ammerman and Roof 1995, Bahr and Chadwick 1985, Booth et al. 1995, Christiano 2000, D'Antonio 1980 and 1983, Hart 1986, Houseknecht and Pankhurst 2000, Jenkins 1991, Sherkat and Ellison 1999, and Thornton 1985.

8. For discussions of the 1950s religious expansion and its link to the growth of family-oriented suburban communities, see Hudnut-Buemler 1994, May 1999, Bendroth 2002, Dobriner 1958a and 1958b, Berger 1967, Nash and Berger 1962, Warner 1961 and 1962, Whyte 1956, Ellwood 1997, Seidler and Meyer 1989, Fairchild and Wynn 1961, and Glock and Stark 1965.

9. See Coontz 1992 and May 1999 for histories of the development of this cultural ideal. For a history of the role that mainstream religious institutions played in fostering this family ideal, see Bendroth 2002.

10. These newer forms include exurban megachurches and post-denominational churches. In addition, the number of new religious groups and movements and the ethnic and racial diversity of American religion are increasing. For a study of exurbs and

megachurches, see Eiesland 2000. For an in-depth profile of a megachurch and a review of the origins and implications of the emerging megachurch movement, see Thumma 1996. For a study of the newer "post-denominational" forms of churches, see Miller 1997. For increasing ethnic and racial diversity in American religious life, see Eck 2001.

11. For a discussion of how religious leaders exert cultural power, see Williams 1995, 1996b, and 1999.

12. For a history of mainline Protestant views on homosexuality and the kinds of discussion forums that these churches provide their members regarding this issue, see Cadge 2002. For a comparison of two congregations grappling with this issue, see Moon 2004.

13. For an example, see Bartkowski 2004.

14. For a discussion of local congregations as moral arenas that operate in ways that are distinctive from both denominational dynamics and the discourse and activism of religious elites, see Becker 1997, 1998a, and 1999. See also Bass 1994 and Anderson 1999. See Halle 1997 for a lengthy treatment of the study of lived religion.

15. For all quotations, plain text indicates a paraphrase excerpted directly from field notes, quotation marks indicate a direct quotation from the speaker, ellipses indicate excluded material, and brackets [] indicate words added for clarity/grammar. All names are pseudonyms.

16. In-depth interview, April 22, 2002.

17. In-depth interview, March 28, 1999.

18. See Houseknecht and Pankhurst 2000 for a description of religion-family interdependency. The following discussion draws from this book and in particular the chapter by Kevin Christiano on the history of American religious familism. See also Sherkat and Ellison 1999.

19. Of course, there are large variations in the degree to which different groups have emphasized paternal versus maternal religious responsibility in American history. On religion and family in colonial times, see Moran 1992 and Morgan 1966. Becker 1998b reviews the literature on the nineteenth-century culture that emphasized the link between women, domesticity, and religious instruction; for much more extensive treatments, see McDannell 1986 and Hackett 1995. Bloch 1978a and 1978b review the differences between eighteenth- and nineteenth-century American ideals of domesticity, parenting styles, and religious instruction. Holifield 1994 reviews the history of the emergence of children's religious instruction programs in local congregations and parishes.

20. Holifield 1994 and Bendroth 2002.

21. McDannell 1995 writes extensively about the tug-of-war between elites and laywomen in the twentieth-century Catholic church; see Becker 1998b for a study of women's roles in nineteenth-century Catholicism. For discussions of nineteenth-century Protestantism and the controversy over the feminization of religion, see Douglas 1998, Welter 1976, and Porterfield 1980.

22. See Fishburn 1991 for a contemporary statement, from the point of view of a mainstream Protestant theologian, of the consequences of the 1950s "idolatry" of the family. For a statement from the period by a liberal Protestant religious leader, see Berger 1959 or Winter 1962. For a sociological study, see Warner 1962; see also Bendroth 2002 and Wuthnow 1998a. Warner 1999 also notes a devaluation of "the private" and "the feminine" in this time period.

23. Bahr and Chadwick 1985, Booth et al. 1995, D'Antonio 1983, D'Antonio and Aldous 1983, Pearce and Axinn 1998, Sherkat and Ellison 1999.

24. I use the term *ideology* to refer to highly articulated and explicit meaning systems that construct and regulate patterns of conduct.

25. For an excellent and comprehensive history of the public and political nature of family ideology in the United States, see Cott 2002. See Bellah et al. 1991, Bendroth 2002, Christiano 2000, Kimmel 1996, Lakoff 1996, and McDannell 1986 for works that link family ideology to notions of citizenship over American history.

26. For a review of familistic religious ideologies in the United States, see Christiano 2000, D'Antonio 1983, Fishburn 1991, and Sherkat and Ellison 1999.

27. For a review of the "separate spheres" ideology, see Becker 1998b. For a much broader historical review of the idea of "gender polarization," see Bem 1993; and for historical perspectives on the family in the United States, see Hareven 1991. Woodberry and Smith 1998 reviews research on the family ideology of evangelical Protestants. See also Bendroth 1993. The religious communities of the new (post-1965) immigrants are particularly likely to promote a traditionally gendered division of labor in both the home and the church (Ebaugh and Chafetz 2000, Warner and Wittner 1998).

28. See Lincoln and Mamiya 1990 for general history and background on African American Christianity; see Gilkes 1995 for how some contemporary African American churches conduct family ministry; and for a case study of an African American congregation, see Freedman 1993. Bendroth 2002 contains a brief description of African American familism since the 1950s.

29. D'Antonio and Aldous (1983) argue that Catholic/Protestant variation in family norms was always driven in large part by ethnic and socioeconomic differences. And Bendroth (2002) sees a great similarity between the familistic ideology of mainline Protestant churches and the Catholic Christian Family Movement in postwar America.

30. See Alwin 1986.

31. Bendroth (1993, 2002) provides an excellent history of the divergence of fundamentalist and evangelical institutions and culture in post–World War II America as well as the historical antecedents of this divergence. Woodberry and Smith 1998 and Smith 1998 contain good reviews of the literature on evangelical Protestant approaches to child rearing and gender roles; see also Christiano 2000 and Sherkat and Ellison 1999. Smith 1998 provides a good overview of the distinctions between evangelical and fundamentalist Protestants in the United States.

32. See Hunter 1991 and Bellah et al. 1991 for statements of this position; for critiques, see Williams 1997, and Becker 1998a and 1997.

33. Lakoff 1996 elaborates this argument that different models of the family underlie the liberal/conservative "culture wars" in American society.

34. Perhaps the most famous is Peter Berger's elaboration in *The Sacred Canopy* (1967). The following discussion draws heavily on Becker 2000 and Christiano 2000. See also Warner 1999.

35. See Greenwald's (1989) study of comparable worth activism in Seattle or Cott's (2002) history of marriage laws in the United States.

36. See Helly and Reverby 1992 for a review of the historical literature; see Epstein 1988 for a review of the sociological literature. See Becker 2000 for a discussion of how this has influenced scholarship in the sociology of religion.

37. See Hull 2001, 2003 for discussions of legal battles over same-sex marriage and the meanings that gay and lesbian couples understand to be embedded within church-conducted joining or marriage ceremonies.

38. For a review of the history of the family-as-haven ideology, see Hareven 1991. See Wuthnow 1998a for a description of the "spirituality of dwelling" that characterized this time period. On the 1950s religious expansion and its link to family life, see Hudnut-Buemler 1994, May 1999, Bendroth 2002, Dobriner 1958b, Berger 1967, Nash and Berger 1962, Warner 1961 and 1962, Whyte 1956, Ellwood 1997, Seidler and Meyer 1989, Fairchild and Wynn 1961, and Glock and Stark 1965. The 1950s expansion was a time of institution building for all mainstream religious groups—Protestant, Catholic, and Jewish denominations thrived (Herberg 1960), Catholic schools exploded in numbers and enrollments, and suburban Sunday schools were filled with hundreds of children each week. Bendroth 2002 and Fishburn 1991 have excellent discussions of the middle-class, white, and Protestant origin of the period's religious familism and the development of a particular family ideal that was widely institutionalized in other religious and social contexts.

39. Bendroth 2002 contains an excellent description of the elaboration of a particular kind of family programming in mainline Protestant and Catholic churches in this time period; cf. Nash and Berger 1962.

40. For a discussion of the development of this cultural ideal and its relationship to the actual lives of most American families, see Coontz 1992 or May 1999. For a treatment of working-class women's lives in this era, see Meyerowitz 1994.

41. For an excellent discussion in this time period, see Fairchild and Wynn 1961.

42. Wuthnow 1998a also discusses the domesticated patriarchy of mainstream religious institutions in the 1950s. His particular focus is on the tension within these institutions between two forms of spirituality—a spirituality of dwelling and a spirituality of seeking.

43. The following discussion draws on Furstenberg 1999 and Treas 1999.

44. See Spain and Bianchi 1996 for a recent review.

45. See Figart and Golden 1998 or Jacobs and Gerson 1998.

46. See Becker and Moen 1999 for a brief review of this literature.

47. Nonetheless, Schor 1991 points out that there is an increasing gap between those who have benefited from the increased income that results from higher education and longer work hours and the rest of the workforce. A substantial portion of Americans, and in particular working-class men, have experienced durable under- and unemployment as skilled blue-collar jobs have disappeared or relocated, leading to substantial family disruption.

48. Spain and Bianchi 1996 argue that work-family management is still largely perceived by individual Americans, by academics, and by policy makers as a "woman's issue."

49. There is a huge literature on increasing individualism in American society, which is far too large to recap here. Veroff et al. 1981 and Glenn 1987 provide good reviews of changes in individual-level attitudes and beliefs, and Bellah et al. 1991 provides a good review of changes in cultural discourses about the individual and commitment to a variety of institutions. Furstenberg 1999 has a good discussion of the effects of individualism on changing gender roles and family forms. See Wuthnow 1988 and Roof 1993 for different takes on the causes and consequences of individualism in American religious

institutions, and Becker 1999 for a limited discussion and critique. Ammerman and Roof 1995 provides a good discussion of how individualism has changed the relationships between work, family, and religion (see introduction) along with a good bibliography. But see Sherkat 1998 for a critique of the thesis that increasing individualism has fundamentally restructured religious commitment.

50. See Fishburn 1991 for a description of the mainline Protestant trajectory post-1960. See Browning et al. 1997 for a summary and call to action by a group of academic and religious leaders concerned about family decline and about the relative silence of liberal and mainstream religious groups on these issues. See also Airhart and Bendroth 1996 for a review of familism across faith traditions.

51. For a review, see Woodberry and Smith 1998. See also Demmitt 1992 for a study of an evangelical Protestant congregation's adjustment to the dual-career lifestyle.

52. See Demmitt 1992 and Bartkowski 1997b for case studies of evangelical congregations, and Becker 1999 for local pastors' discussions of family ministry in a set of congregations in and around Oak Park, IL.

53. See Ecklund 2003, Becker 1999, and Neitz 1987.

54. This literature is reviewed in the introduction to Ammerman and Roof 1995.

55. For an exception, see Becker and Hofmeister 2001.

56. See Sherkat 2000.

57. For example, see the January 5, 2000, article by Don Lattin in the *San Francisco Chronicle* titled "Methodists Divided on Gay Rights: Church Leaders Anguish over Same-Sex Unions." It profiles the efforts of a "Methodist church panel trying to decide whether to hold church trials for 67 Northern California clergy who defied their denomination's ban on 'holy union' ceremonies for same-sex couples." Or look at the article in the *Houston Chronicle* from November 10, 1999, by Richard Vara, "Texas Baptists Vote to Reject Call for Wives to Submit." The article states, "Texas Baptists voted overwhelmingly Tuesday to ignore a 1998 amendment to the Southern Baptist Convention's confessional statement asking wives to submit to their husbands' leadership. The action came as the moderate-controlled Baptist General Convention of Texas, which has 2.7 million members in more than 5,000 churches, concluded its annual two-day meeting at the El Paso Civic Center." Articles like these have appeared with increasing frequency over the last ten years as battles have increased, both within denominations and between denominational offices and local pastors, over homosexual unions, the ordination of homosexual clergy, and the role of women in churches that have historically restricted women's liturgical roles.

58. Roof 1993, Wuthnow 1994b and 1998b.

59. Ammerman 1997, McPherson and Rotolo 1996.

60. For studies of religious ecologies, see Becker 1999, Eiesland 2000, and Ellingson et al. 2001. For a general overview of ecological influences on change and "borrowing and niching" within a field, see Strang and Soule 1998.

61. This is a census survey and not a sample. However, 22 percent of the congregations in these communities did not cooperate with our survey, and these tend to be smaller churches. With this taken into account, the actual distribution of congregations by size in these communities is close to the NCS distribution.

62. See Hout and Fischer 2002.

63. See Hetherington and Kelly 2002, Amato 2000.

CHAPTER TWO
RELIGIOUS INVOLVEMENT AND RELIGIOUS INSTITUTIONAL CHANGE

1. See Weber 1978, 1998. For accounts of social action that emphasize the determining nature of social structures, see Durkheim 1951. Coleman 1990 provides an influential sociological statement of the actor as a utility-maximizing agent and embeds this within a larger theoretical account of social action that emphasizes methodological individualism.

2. Emirbayer and Mische 1998, Alexander 1988, Swidler 1986 and 2001a, Ortner 1996. This mode of pragmatic, daily action is different than both value-rational and instrumental-rational action in its temporal focus (rooted in the present, not focused long-term goals). In the creative pragmatism of present-focused action, typical means-ends relationships can be either reproduced or changed by social actors, regardless of long-term goals (see Emirbayer and Mische 1998 and Swidler 1986 for discussion).

3. This body of work draws on both Giddens's 1979 reflexive sociology and on other traditions that emphasize the embeddedness of culture within social structure and the resulting cultural influence on routine forms of practice as a way to balance older cultural accounts that focused on discourse, symbols, and individual meaning-making (e.g., Bourdieu 1977, Ortner 1996; also see Wuthnow 1987). The "rules" that constitute the cultural element of social structure have been conceived of variously as schema (Sewell 1992), as institutional rules (Stryker 1994), or as "constitutive rules" (Swidler 2001a, Swidler and Jepperson 1994).

4. Swidler 2001a and 2001b, Swidler and Jepperson 1994.

5. Becker 1999.

6. Johnston and Klandermans 1995, Becker 1999. Sewell (1992) outlines how this happens when he writes about cultural schema as being both subject to reinterpretation when new situations arise and transposable across arenas of social action (cf. Friedland and Alford 1991).

7. Booth et al. 1995, Christiano 2000, D'Antonio 1980 and 1983, Gesch 1995, Lehrer 1996, Myers 1996, Sherkat 1998, Sherkat and Ellison 1999, and Thornton 1985.

8. Structural location explanations were developed in large part as a critique of other explanations for women's higher rates of religious involvement. These other explanations focus either on psychological factors (women as "naturally" more religious than men) or on socialization (women are said to be socialized into values such as nurturance and gentleness that are "congruent" with religion). See de Vaus and McAllister 1987 for a review.

9. Argue et al. 1999; Firebaugh and Harley 1991; Marler 1995; Stolzenberg et al. 1995. But as Stolzenberg et al. note, the effects of family formation may vary by gender because men and women play different roles within the family, even in families embracing a more egalitarian gender ideology (cf. Wilson and Sherkat 1994). See Hout and Greeley 1998 for a review of church attendance measures more generally.

10. Cf. Sherkat 1998, pp. 1093–94; Luckmann 1967.

11. See Hertel 1995, Gesch 1995, and Stolzenberg et al. 1995.

12. Becker 1999, Becker and Hofmeister 2001, Bellah et al. 1985, Wuthnow 1998a and 1998b, Hammond 1988, 1992; but see Sherkat 1998 for an alternative interpretation. This is consistent with Veroff et al.'s (1981) description of the rise of a more generalized

"individualistic" orientation toward social institutions, which they describe as an increased emphasis on self-expression and self-direction in social life and a waning valuation of organizational integration (cf. Glenn 1987; Luckmann 1967).

13. Cf. Hammond 1992.

14. See Sherkat 1998, 2001.

15. Johnston 1995 discusses these methodological difficulties in some detail.

16. Measured through attitude scales, and also shown in in-depth interview responses. See Becker and Hofmeister 2001.

17. The following discussion draws extensively on Stark and Finke 2000, and on several good reviews of rational-choice approaches to the study of religion in the United States, especially Young 1997, Sherkat and Ellison 1999, and a special symposium issue on rational choice in the *Journal for the Scientific Study of Religion* in March 1995. For a review of the "rational systems" approach to organizations, see Scott 1998 or Hage 1999. The approach outlined and critiqued in this chapter is a rational-choice approach to religious markets. It is important to remember the distinction between rational-choice approaches, which use a very specific economic paradigm, and those of scholars who use the term *market* metaphorically to emphasize the pluralism, vitality, and choice they see as characteristic of American religion either historically (Warner 1993) or in the postwar era (Roof 1999).

18. For a good theoretical discussion, see Sherkat 1998; for a literature review, see Sherkat and Ellison 1999.

19. Sherkat 1997; cf. Stark and Finke 2000.

20. Sherkat 1998, 2000.

21. However, the empirical claims about the relationship between religious pluralism and religious vitality have been challenged in recent work; for a review and critique of the religious economy argument, see Chaves and Gorski 2001. See also the work of Steve Bruce (1996), who argues that although modernization may, under certain national circumstances, lead to increased religious participation by individuals, it does nevertheless also lead to secularization, understood as a decline in religious authority and in religion's public influence. For a counterargument, see Finke and Stark 1992 or Casanova 1994.

22. Stark and Finke 2000 use the term *church* interchangeably with *religious organization*, denoting non-Christian groups as well (cf. Durkheim 1965).

23. Cf. Sherkat 1998. Similarly, Finke (2004) draws on institutional analyses of organizations and cultural accounts of religious identity and commitment to explain why innovations that preserve core religious tenets lead to growth (increased market share); he finds these useful additions to a rational-choice framework.

24. Popper 1959. See also an excellent discussion of Popper's views on covering laws and their application to this question in Abbott 1992, p. 67. Other critics of the rational-choice approach make a similar argument; several chapters in Cook and Levi 1990 take this approach, particularly the one by Elster.

25. This discussion draws from a presentation given by Nancy Ammerman at a conference on vital liberal congregations, Louisville Institute, December 2002. Many thanks to Nancy for sharing her presentation notes with me and talking with me about rational-choice accounts.

26. For good overviews of institutional theory, see Powell and DiMaggio 1991, Stinchcombe 1997, Greenwood and Hinings 1996, and Ingram and Clay 2000.

27. See Cook and Levi 1990 for specifications of the limits of rational-choice approaches, especially the chapter by Elster, which outlines differences between "strict" rational-choice approaches and other approaches.

28. See Lakoff 1996 for an account of how family models (or schema) anchor other institutions in our society.

29. Smith 2003, Ammerman 2003, Marty 1976. See Becker and Dhingra 2001 for a view of why members themselves link uniquely religious experiences to religious commitment (both subjective and behavioral).

30. See note 21. Chaves 1994 reviews versions of secularization theory and develops the idea that secularization means a decline of religious authority, at any level of analysis.

31. See Hunter 1991 for a discussion of "progressive" versus "orthodox" approaches to religious truth. Seidler and Meyer 1989 notes that this process is seldom smooth or even and develops the idea of "contested accommodation" of religious institutions to modernity.

32. See Warner 1993 for this argument.

33. Furstenberg (1999, pp. 154ff.) makes a similar argument.

34. Note that this is different than Seidler and Meyer's (1989) idea of religious institutions changing over time through a process of *contested accommodation*. They retain the idea that modernization is an ongoing and unidirectional process that religious institutions resist at first and gradually accommodate. In the short term, sometimes religious institutions can "win" and maintain a sphere of authority and influence in the face of societal change, but in the long run religious authority is reduced and the scope of influence of religious institutions is limited.

35. This is different than Hunter's (1991) definition of the "orthodox" as an unchanging approach to religious truth (which he contrasts with a "progressive" or evolving understanding of the truth).

36. Ammerman 1997, Becker 1999.

Chapter Three
Religion, Family, and Work

1. See Sherkat and Ellison 1999 or Christiano 2000 for recent reviews.

2. See Tolbert and Moen 1998 and Ammerman and Roof 1995 for the differences in men's and women's orientations toward a host of "traditional" institutions; cf. Veroff et al. 1981.

3. To some extent, the ages of the children who are at home influences the religious involvement of parents. Those with preschool children who attend church attend as a whole family, attend alone, or take their children to church with them while their spouses stay home. Those with older children are less likely to attend alone and more likely to attend with their spouse while the older children stay home. And those with older children are more likely to send the children to church even if they do not attend themselves, either with a spouse or alone (17 percent, compared with 6 percent of parents of younger children; see table 3.2).

4. "Without children" here indicates that the respondent has no children living at home. Some of this group are part of long-term childless couples, some have been

divorced and remarried and do not have custody of children from a previous marriage, and a few are older people who were parents but whose children have left home.

5. For a discussion of church attendance as a couple-level activity using other data from a different upstate New York sample, see Hofmeister and Edgell 2003.

6. The following discussion, for both women and men, draws extensively on a paper based on the Religion and Family Project data by this author and a colleague who also worked on the research project. For details of the statistical analyses, see Becker and Hofmeister 2001.

7. See Becker and Hofmeister 2001.

8. See Wilcox 2004 for a treatment of the changing role of marriage and parenting in men's lives and the role that religious communities play in fostering a lifestyle for men that is more centered around family and less around paid work, and that incorporates an emphasis on caretaking as well as financial provision.

9. There are multiple ways to measure differences in social class, including combinations of education, occupation, and income. This discussion is based on differences in education because, in these communities, education is a good way to capture differences in income, occupation, and lifestyle. Those with a high school degree or less are much more likely to be unemployed, underemployed, or working two or more jobs that have low pay and poor benefits in order to make ends meet. They often commute long distances to work, especially those living in rural Tompkins County or in Seneca County. Education, then, is a proxy for different socioeconomic locations and lifestyles in these communities; in particular, having a high school degree or less is a proxy for being working poor or working class.

10. See Becker and Hofmeister 2001.

11. See Mowrer 1958, Bell 1958, Fairchild and Wynn 1961.

12. See Becker 1999 for a discussion of the white middle-class culture that pervades mainstream religious institutions in the United States.

13. Our measure is the answer to this question: "Are you currently living with someone in a long-term committed relationship?" This measure captures both heterosexual and gay/lesbian couples.

14. For an elaboration of the questions of meaning and purpose for which religion typically provides answers, see Geertz 1973. Davidman's (1991) study of Orthodox Jewish women suggests that major life transitions and particularly experiences of family disruption lead women to rethink their religious beliefs and identity and to seek out religious communities that provide familylike attachments.

15. This refers to those who said that they never attend church or attend only at the holidays.

16. Most of the interview data included in this book are in the form of direct quotations. This interview had to be completed by telephone because finding a time to meet in person proved impossible for Diane's schedule. The interview was not taped; I took notes during the conversation and typed up field notes immediately following the conversation.

17. See Sherkat and Ellison 1999 for a review; see also Wilcox 2004.

18. Lehrer 1995 and 1996, Sherkat 2000, Woodberry and Smith 1998.

19. The question was designed to elicit information about long-term care arrangements, not about caring for a child who is occasionally sick.

20. Based on a logistic regression of the variable *eldcare*, coded 1 = yes, 0 = no, based on the following survey question: "Do you regularly spend time caring for an elderly or

sick relative (not a child who is occasionally sick)?" Models controlled for age, education, marital status, and presence of children—controls for hours spent at work and occupation were entered but were not significant and therefore were deleted from final models.

21. Based on a logistic regression on the variable *givehelp*, coded 1 = yes 0 = no, based on the following question: "Do you regularly give anyone informal help with these household tasks (yard work, laundry, accounting, child care, elder care, housecleaning, or shopping)?" Models controlled for age, education, marital status, and presence of children—controls for hours spent at work and occupation were entered but were not significant and therefore were deleted from final models.

22. Based on ordinary least squares (OLS) regression on three items: *time_ft* sums the hours and minutes spent each week on meal preparation, dishes, laundry, and cleaning; *time_mt* sums the hours spent weekly on yard work, home repair, and car repair; *time_ot* sums the time spent weekly on shopping, paying bills, and driving others to and from activities. Models controlled for age, education, marital status, and presence of children—controls for hours spent at work and occupation were entered but were not significant and therefore were deleted from final models.

23. See Woodberry and Smith 1998, Wilcox 2004, Gallagher 2003, and Gallagher and Smith 1999.

24. Items in the Family Drain Scale:

My family kept me from spending enough time on my work.
My family kept me from becoming more involved in the community.
My family made me feel very tired or exhausted.
My family made me feel anxious or depressed.
My family kept me from spending enough time on myself.

Each item coded 1 = strongly disagree to 5 = strongly agree. Scale constructed through principal components factor analysis, varimax rotation.

25. Riley et al. (1994) outline this problem, identifying sources of what they call "structural lag," which has kept institutions from responding usefully not only to the increase in women's paid labor-force participation but also to other life-course changes, including the increasing health and longevity that have fundamentally transformed retirement in our society.

26. Chapter 5 outlines in more detail the critique of consumerism and careerism that local churches make; Bell 1958 and Mowrer 1958 claim that churches provided a similar critique in the 1950s. For a review of gender ideology and the family, see Sherkat and Ellison 1999, Christiano 2000, and Woodberry and Smith 1998.

27. Based on the following three items that loaded into a single factor, using principal components factor analysis (each item coded 1 = strongly disagree to 5 = strongly agree):

My work kept me from spending enough time with my family.
My work kept me from becoming more involved in the community.
My work kept me from spending enough time on myself.

28. Models are discussed in more detail in "Remaking Men's Work and Family Commitments: Religious Support for Scaling Back Strategies" by Penny Edgell, working paper, University of Minnesota, September 2002. Paper and models are available on request. For a discussion of scaling back, see Becker and Moen 1999.

29. Based on a logistic regression of the variable *eldcare*, coded 1 = yes, 0 = no, based on the following survey question: "Do you regularly spend time caring for an elderly or sick relative (not a child who is occasionally sick)?" Models controlled for age, education, marital status, presence of children, and church attendance—controls for hours spent at work and occupation were entered but were not significant and therefore were deleted from final models.

30. Based on a logistic regression on the variable *givehelp*, coded 1 = yes 0 = no, based on the following question: "Do you regularly give anyone informal help with these household tasks (yard work, laundry, accounting, child care, elder care, housecleaning, or shopping)?" Models controlled for age, education, marital status, and presence of children—controls for hours spent at work and occupation were entered but were not significant and therefore were deleted from final models.

31. Based on OLS regression on three items: *time_ft* sums the hours and minutes spent each week on meal preparation, dishes, laundry, and cleaning; *time_mt* sums the hours spent weekly on yard work, home repair, and car repair; *time_ot* sums the time spent weekly on shopping, paying bills, and driving others to and from activities. Models controlled for age, education, marital status, presence of children, hours spent at work, and occupation.

32. Based on the following three items that loaded into a single factor, using principal components factor analysis (each item coded 1 = strongly disagree to 5 = strongly agree):

My work kept me from spending enough time with my family.
My work kept me from becoming more involved in the community.
My work kept me from spending enough time on myself.

OLS regression including variables for age, education, occupation, hours worked, family status (married, presence of children), and church attendance.

33. Based on an OLS regression of a factor composed of the following three items, constructed through principal components factor analysis (1 = strongly disagree, 5 = strongly agree):

My work made me feel very tired or exhausted.
My work made me feel anxious or depressed.
My work gave me energy to accomplish more at home.

The regression equation included variables for age, education, occupation, hours worked, marital status, presence of children in the home, church attendance, the interaction of church attendance with marital status and with the presence of children, and conservative Protestant identity.

34. Based on an OLS regression on church attendance, using a seven-item attendance variable (attend: never, hardly ever except for holidays, less than once a month, about once a month, several times a month, once a week, more than once a week). Models controlled for age, education, marital status, presence and ages of children, religious salience, and religious identity (Catholic, conservative Protestant).

35. These two findings are based on logistic regression of two variables that capture whether the individual is involved in any ministry or regular organized church activity besides the Sunday worship service, and whether the individual reports that her children participate in any such ministry or activity. For details, see Becker and Hofmeister

2001. Models included controls for age, marital status, presence of children, education, and religious salience.

CHAPTER FOUR
STYLES OF RELIGIOUS INVOLVEMENT

1. Several works have discussed these particular changes in styles of religious commitment, including Bellah et al. 1985, Roof 1993, Tipton 1982, and Wuthnow 1998a and 1998b.

2. For a longer discussion, see Becker and Hofmeister 2001.

3. The original seven items are:

People should attend religious services together as a family.

Being a church member is an important way to become established in a community.

Going to religious services is an obligation.

Going to religious services is something you should do if it meets your needs.

An individual should arrive at his or her own religious beliefs independent of any church or synagogue.

Children should make their own decisions about whether to attend religious services.

Churches and synagogues play an important role in the moral education of children.

4. Although a sense of family-oriented religious commitment would not logically have to include an emphasis on the importance of expressing one's social establishment or the importance of participation in local community institutions, these intertwined relationships have been common in the United States since at least the 1950s, and both are linked together in structural location understandings of religious commitment. Cf. Bell 1958, Bendroth 2002, and Dobriner 1958a.

5. These factors emerged from a principal components analysis using varimax rotation with Kaiser normalization; the rotation converged in three iterations. These factors were initially developed for an analysis of men's and women's church attendance, use of church-based ministries, and religious volunteering (see Becker and Hofmeister 2001). Details of analysis are available on request.

6. Based on a question on the survey of community residents in which people were asked to say which is more important in preparing a child for life, teaching a child to obey his/her parents or teaching a child to think for himself/herself? Response options included: (a) teaching a child to obey, (b) teaching a child to think for him or herself, (c) both equally. Thirty-three (33) percent of those above the mean on the self-oriented scale chose either "obey" or "both equally" compared with 47 percent of those scoring above the mean on the family-oriented scale.

7. A full interpretation of the findings and the details of the statistical analyses are available in Becker and Hofmeister 2001. The results included the attitude scale items reported in box 4.1 as indicators of "family-oriented" and "self-oriented" beliefs. These scales were entered as variables in three separate logistic regressions predicting (1) whether a person attended church monthly or more, (2) whether a person was involved in a religious organization besides a local church, and (3) whether a person used or participated in any organized regularly occurring congregational ministry or activity.

Models included controls for age, gender, social class, religious salience, and religious identity (dummy variables for Catholic and conservative Protestant).

8. Results of a logistic regression on the variable *monthly or more church attendance*, where 1 = attend church monthly or more, weighted data used, sample weights constructed using 2000 census data to correct for oversampling of female and college-educated respondents.

9. The same pattern holds in analyses of other forms of religious involvement (religious saliency, participation in other kinds of organized religious activity). The model for church attendance is presented because this is the measure used by those who have studied structural location effects on religious involvement and because in this case it is a good proxy for other forms of religious participation.

10. These forms of analysis measure stable associations between two or more variables. In effect, they subdivide the data into social groups based on the variables entered into the equation as "predictors," calculate the "score" on the outcome variable for each subdivided group, and then calculate the probability that this set of outcome scores across groups is arrived at by chance.

11. See Hout and Fischer 2002.

12. This discussion draws on Wuthnow 1988, Warner 1993, and Hammond 1988 and 1992; cf. Becker 1999, chapter 9.

13. W. L. Warner 1961 and 1962, R. S. Warner 1993.

14. Bell 1958, p. 227.

15. Warner 1961, Christiano 2000, Ammerman and Roof 1995.

16. Bell 1958, Dobriner 1958a and 1958b, Hudnut-Beumler 1994.

17. Bendroth 2002, May 1999, Fairchild and Wynn 1961.

18. Warner 1961, Bell 1958, Fairchild and Wynn 1961.

19. Nash and Berger 1962, Fishburn 1991, Winter 1962.

20. For a treatment of the nostalgia for the 1950s, see Coontz 1992. Wuthnow (1998a) calls the patriarchy of 1950s religious familism a "domesticated" patriarchy. For treatments of the problems underlying the apparent calm of 1950s suburban life, see Bendroth 2002, Halberstam 1993, and May 1999.

CHAPTER FIVE
"THE PROBLEM WITH FAMILIES TODAY . . . "

1. Not only is there a widespread perception in our society that the family is in crisis, but Americans in general have grown much more willing, over the last twenty years, to affirm that there is a crisis in many of our major institutions, and many Americans believe that there is a broader moral and ethical crisis in our society that is causing widespread social malaise. Although the trends in these beliefs are easy to chart, the causes of the trends are much harder to identify. For a review, see Baker 2004.

2. Becker 1999.

3. Much of this is written from a "culture wars" perspective that emphasizes the differences between liberals and conservatives. For good overviews, see Hunter 1991, Bellah et al. 1991, and DiMaggio et al. 1996.

4. Struggles over the acceptance of gay members have plagued the Southern Baptist Conference (SBC), with denominational leaders imposing financial penalties on local

associations that will not expel "gay-friendly" congregations, and local pastors protesting the violation of local-church autonomy implied in the denomination's actions. Conflict over who has the authority to make decisions about women's roles in the church has also plagued the SBC, especially in the last few years. See "Stand on Gay-Friendly Churches May Cost Local Baptists" by Gayle White, February 9, 2001, *Atlanta Journal Constitution*, and "South Main Baptist Quits the Convention / Churches in Exodus over Doctrinal Divide" by Richard Vara, *Houston Chronicle*, January 22, 2001. Struggles over the roles of homosexuals in the church, and in particular the blessing of gay and lesbian unions, have also erupted in the United Methodist, Presbyterian, and Episcopal churches, intensifying over the last decade, as numerous articles in every major daily paper in the country attest.

5. See Wuthnow 1998b for a long exposition of the nature and sources of this changing style of voluntary commitment; c.f. Ammerman and Roof 1995.

6. See Becker 1998a for an extended discussion of culture work and the imposition of frames as congregations respond to racial changes in their communities. For other treatments of frames and religious responses to social change, see Ellingson et al. 2001 or Ammerman 1997. More general discussion of framing occurs in several literatures, but perhaps the most extended is the framing literature in social movement research, which draws on Erving Goffman's (1974) concept of "frame." The best review may be in the essays in Johnston and Klandermans 1995, especially the concluding essay by Johnston; see also Benford and Snow 2000. The distribution of common cultural frameworks of action within a field is one of the forces leading to institutional isomorphism; see Powell and DiMaggio 1991, especially the chapter by DiMaggio and the introduction. As Friedland and Alford (1991) argue, a source of variation and change within a field can be the borrowing of frames from other institutional arenas; cf. Stryker 1994 and Sewell 1992.

7. For example, the Catholic archdiocese that encompassed these four communities held a monthly meeting for directors of family ministry in the local parishes that was run by a woman whose job was to facilitate new ideas for how to run religious education programs for all ages.

8. See Hunter 1991 and Bellah et al. 1991. Ginsburg 1989 provides a good discussion of the different kinds of discussion that take place in local versus national discourse arenas on the abortion issue, providing an alternative perspective to the "culture wars" thesis.

9. See Gamson 1992. Five groups were conducted, one each in Seneca County, Liverpool, and Northside, and two groups in Tompkins County. A total of forty-seven pastors participated in these groups, including Catholic priests, pastors from a range of mainline Protestant denominations, and pastors from Holiness, Baptist, and independent congregations that span the range of evangelical groups in these four communities. The focus group meetings lasted an hour to an hour and a half and were recorded and transcribed verbatim.

10. Fieldwork was conducted by the principal investigator and a project team of four graduate students: Evelyn Bush, Pawan Dhingra, Heather Hofmeister, and Elaine Howard Ecklund.

11. For an excellent discussion of this phenomenon, see David Brooks's article "The Organization Kid" in the April 2001 *Atlantic Monthly*. Starting from birth, today's young people are scheduled into multiple supervised interactive arenas, a trend that

Brooks links to changes in styles of parenting and education dating from the mid-1980s. Cf. Robinson and Godbey 1997.

12. This figure does not denote "representativeness" in the statistical sense. Rather, it is included to show that the time-bind rhetoric comprises a dominant theme in the social discourse of area pastors. Focus groups are appropriate for getting at dominant versus marginal themes and in generating the kinds of variation around a central theme that this discussion highlights.

13. For example, see books by Jacobs and Gerson 2004, Hochschild 1997, and Robinson and Godbey 1997. Pastors often borrow cultural frames from secular sources (Witten 1993).

14. For an extensive review, see Becker and Hofmeister 2000.

15. For an excellent discussion of changes in commitment to voluntary organizations and to local communities of place, see Wuthnow 1998b; cf. Hammond 1988. On nostalgia for the "Ozzie and Harriet" family, see Coontz 1992, May 1999, or Skolnick 1991.

16. See Price (2001), whose studies suggest that the clergy have seen a decline in compensation relative to other professionals and an accompanying decline in public status.

17. It is no accident that soccer is spoken of with some bitterness by more than one pastor. Soccer became popular in the United States as a leisure activity after the loss of the kind of community arrangements for which these pastors are nostalgic. Soccer leagues for children are so popular and take up so much playing time on community fields that adult leagues are often organized early on weekend mornings, the only available time—directly conflicting with church and synagogue services.

18. In an area where Catholics are almost 40 percent of the population, they are part of the establishment.

19. The classic treatment is Rockwell's *Freedom from Want*, with the grandmother placing the huge turkey on the laden table, the grandfather standing by to carve it, and the excited children and grandchildren looking on.

20. Like many evangelical and fundamentalist churches, this congregation has religious education for both children and adults organized into age-graded, single-sex classes led by an adult of the same sex. This observation was conducted by a male research assistant.

21. Cf. Bartkowski 1997b, Wilcox 2004.

22. This fieldwork was conducted by a research assistant, Elaine Howard Ecklund, for a related project on Catholic laywomen's understandings of how their parishes have responded to changes in women's roles, and involved in-depth interviews with several Catholic priests in these four communities. See Ecklund 2003 for details of that research.

23. See Bellah et al. 1991, Hunter 1991, DiMaggio et al. 1996.

24. Local religious discourse is often not well understood using a "culture wars" framework; see Becker 1998a, Williams 1997.

25. See Bell 1958, Dobriner 1958a and 1958b, Fairchild and Wynn 1961, Fishburn 1991, Hudnut-Buemler 1994, Marler 1995, McDannell 1995, Mowrer 1958, Nash and Berger 1962, Seidler and Meyer 1989, Thomas 1956, and Warner 1961 and 1962. Not all Christian leaders were happy with this; see Winter 1962 or Berger 1959. Contemporary

sources suggest that rural and small-town churches were organized around a similar model of the family; see Lindstrom 1946 and Hunter 1947. Bendroth (1993) argues that in the 1950s there was a tension between evangelicals, who embraced a more nurturing or caring neopatriarchal family, and fundamentalists, who embraced a more authoritarian patriarchal family model. She argues that the evangelical expansion of the subsequent twenty-year period was linked to the more nurturing family model that had a broader appeal, being the model promoted by more mainstream religious institutions but also by the secular media in this period. For a more general discussion of the "anxiety" surrounding the suburban family lifestyle and the need to control and reintegrate children, see May 1999; for how churches responded, see Dobriner 1958b and Fairchild and Wynn 1961. See Holifield 1994 for a history of congregational forms. For a discussion of congregational ministry and suburbanization in the 1920s, with its accompanying expansion of Sunday School and women's programming, see Douglass 1970 and 1972.

26. Cf. Ingram and Clay 2000. This insight is related to a more general argument generated by the cognitive branch of institutional analysis (DiMaggio and Powell 1991) and also developed extensively by those who study social movement frames (Johnston and Klandermans 1995). Friedland and Alford (1991) argue that, to understand social action within a field, it is important to analyze how such action is anchored within the "cultural logic" that structures the field, while simultaneously understanding that individual agents have access to multiple fields with multiple logics that can be transposed across realms to provide a rationale for action within any given situation. The advantage of using the word *schema* is that it denotes a level of analysis that is more fundamental and anchoring and that can structure how other elements of culture are "borrowed" across arenas.

27. Bendroth (2002, 1993) makes the argument, in two fine historical studies of American Protestantism, that fundamentalist and evangelical Protestant traditions diverged in the late 1940s and through the 1960s in their ideology of family life, with evangelicals developing much of the emphasis on caring, nurturing, and loving paternal involvement that is central to evangelical discourse today (Smith 1998, Wilcox 2004). Cf. Nash and Berger 1962.

28. See Greenwood and Hinings 1996 for a more extended development of this argument about radical versus incremental organizational change. See Becker 1998b for an extended discussion of dominant versus alternative discourses (about gender and social class) within religious traditions, with a specific focus on religious popular culture.

29. For a discussion of this family model, see Lakoff 1996.

30. In the United Methodist Church (UMC), a reconciling congregation has taken an official stance of openness toward lesbian and gay members. The reconciling movement has become a controversial one in the UMC, and out of something more than 35,000 local congregations, 72 have voted to become reconciling churches (based on interview with a UMC pastor from Tompkins County, February 19, 2002; this number also corresponds to other reports, for example, Moon 2004). For an excellent description of two UMC congregations that confronted this decision and good background on the reconciling movement, see Moon 2004.

31. See Becker and Dhingra 2001.

CHAPTER SIX
THE PRACTICE OF FAMILY MINISTRY

1. See Williams 1996a for a good review of this distinction between implicit and explicit culture.

2. Essays in Bonnell and Hunt 1999 provide a good introduction to "practice theory," as does Ortner 1996; cf. Geertz 1973.

3. Goffman 1967. For a focus on ritual practice, see Turner 1974.

4. Cohen et al. 1972.

5. Morrill 1995; cf. Lichterman 1996.

6. Biernacki 1995.

7. DiMaggio 1991, Friedland and Alford 1991, Becker 1999.

8. For a review, read Emirbayer and Mische 1998.

9. Bonnell and Hunt 1999. Similar critiques of the new institutionalism have been made (DiMaggio and Powell 1991, Stinchcombe 1997).

10. For a review of "lived religion" approaches, see Halle 1997. For examples of qualitative studies, see Wuthnow 1994a and 1994b, Becker 1999, and Ellingson et al. 2001.

11. Becker 1997, 1998a, 1999; Ellingson et al. 2001, Wedam 1997.

12. See Becker 1997 and Wedam 1997; cf. Williams 1997.

13. Bendroth 2002, Dobriner 1958b, Ellwood 1997, May 1999, Whyte 1956; see Holifield 1994 for a discussion on the historical variation in the extent to which congregations have served as centers for sociability as well as religious practice.

14. Fishburn 1991, Nash and Berger 1962.

15. Nash and Berger 1962, Fishburn 1991, Prell 1988, Thomas 1956.

16. Fairchild and Wynn 1961, Thomas 1956.

17. Nash and Berger 1962, May 1999, Fishburn 1991, Dobriner 1958a.

18. In the fall of 1997, we ran an initial pastor focus group with four area pastors from a variety of Protestant traditions, which was designed to get feedback on survey topics and language, and interviewed the pastor of an African American congregation and the priest at a local parish for the same purpose. We subsequently pretested the original draft of our survey with four pastors (Catholic, Evangelical Methodist, Episcopal, and Presbyterian) recruited through personal networks who do not live in these four communities.

19. Dudley and Roozen 2001.

20. See Chaves 1998.

21. In all cases, conservative Protestants offer more programs and services on an informal/as-needed basis; others are more likely to have formal programs.

22. See Becker 1999 for a discussion of borrowing and niching in local religious ecologies.

23. This discussion draws heavily on Greenwood and Hinings 1996.

24. Many thanks to Evelyn Bush, who assisted in this data collection.

25. Chaves et al. 1999, Chaves 2004.

26. Cf. Wilcox et al. (2004). They also find that most formal family programming is organized around a traditional family model and point to institutional forces that lead to isomorphism in family-oriented programming across religious traditions. They raise

the question of whether more culturally specific ministry for families, and particularly nontraditional families, is provided through informal means.

CHAPTER SEVEN
RELIGIOUS FAMILISM AND SOCIAL CHANGE

1. This understanding of power is similar in some ways to Lukes's (1974) definition of the "third face of power" as the power to shape the ideas and desires of others so that they accord with one's own. Lukes understands this power as being, in all cases, an exercise in subverting others' interests and advancing one's own. Cultural power is in part the power to make others believe that their interests are consonant with one's own when this is not the case; cultural power hides the fact that dominant social arrangements advance some interests and undermine others. This is not so dissimilar to how many sociologists understand the power of cultural distinctions. Epstein (1988) understands cultural distinctions to be by nature invidious—that is, advancing some interests while undermining others (cf. Lamont 1992). Mary Douglas (1986) understands institutions in the same way: they are bundles of routinized practice that serve some interests while undermining others, all the while maintaining legitimacy by hiding the fact that they are, indeed, interested (cf. Weber 1978, discussions of legitimacy and authority, and Foucault 1978 on the medicalization of sexuality). My use of the term *cultural power* is close to Wuthnow's (1989) understanding of the ability to define a field of discourse and to propose figural action, or legitimate and appropriate ways to negotiate the world as the field of discourse defines it (cf. Becker 1998b). Wuthnow leaves aside the question of whether such power is always exercised in the service of interest, but my understanding is that the power to define ideals or cultural models of the world always involves the inclusion or advancement of some interests and the exclusion or thwarting of others, regardless of the motives of those proposing such models or arguments made about some models affirming a greater good that is somehow apart from interest.

2. See Smith 2003 for religion as a basis for identity; see Caplow et al. 1983 and Mueller and Johnson 1975 for religious participation as a sort of symbolic statement of respectability and morality.

3. See Becker 1997, 1999.

4. Cf. Wuthnow and Evans 2002.

5. Lehrer 1995 and 1996, Sherkat 2000.

6. Bourdieu (1977) argued that orthodoxy is an inherently evolving product, which changes owing to endogenous tension with a mutually defining heterodoxy. In Bourdieu's understanding, orthodoxy and heterodoxy are the products of culture-producing officials and elites. Bourdieu's model works well to explicate the evolution of official ideologies of the family within religious traditions as described by Bendroth's (2002) work on mainline Protestants, the numerous studies of contestation over gender roles and family ideologies in evangelical Protestantism (Bendroth 1993, Woodberry and Smith 1998), and studies of post–Vatican II changes in the Catholic church (Seidler and Meyer 1989, Dillon 1999). But the field of mainstream American religion is constituted by organizations at different levels of analysis, and at the local level, doxa (ideology) and praxis (practical daily activity) must both be taken into account.

7. Smith 2003, Becker and Dhingra 2001; also see Finke 2004.

8. See Becker 1999 for a discussion of mainstream religious institutions in the United States as perpetuating a white middle-class set of values and ways of doing things.

9. For a discussion of these changes, see the introduction to Ammerman and Roof 1995.

10. For discussions of family ideology and programming in African American churches, see Gilkes 1995; Freedman's (1993) ethnography of an urban African American congregation also finds a great deal of rhetoric both honoring fatherhood and seeking to bolster male members' investment in fathering.

11. See Swartz et al. 2004 for a discussion of the different cultural models of the family that they found in a study of immigrant communities in four states.

12. For a discussion of postdivorce trajectories, see Hetherington and Kelly 2002.

13. Hetherington and Kelly 2002, Amato 2000.

14. See Becker 1998a, 1998b, and 1999 for discussions of the institutional logic of local religious life and the two moral imperatives—"what is right" and "what is caring"— that form the heart of the religious logic in local religious communities.

REFERENCES

Abbott, Andrew. 1992. "What Do Cases Do?" In *What Is a Case? Exploring the Foundations of Social Inquiry*, ed. Charles C. Ragin and Howard S. Becker, pp. 53–83. New York: Cambridge University Press.

Airhart, Phyllis, and Margaret Bendroth, eds. 1996. *Faith Traditions and the Family.* Louisville: Westminster / John Knox Press.

Alexander, Jeffrey. 1988. *Action and Its Environments.* New York: Columbia University Press.

Alwin, Duane. 1986. "Religion and Parental Child-Rearing Orientations: Evidence of a Catholic-Protestant Convergence." *American Journal of Sociology* 92 (2): 412–40.

Amato, Paul R. 2000. "The Consequences of Divorce for Adults and Children." *Journal of Marriage and the Family* 62 (4): 1269–87.

Ammerman, Nancy Tatom. 1997. *Congregation and Community.* New Brunswick, NJ: Rutgers University Press.

———. 2003. "Religious Identities and Religious Institutions." In *Handbook of Sociology of Religion*, ed. Michelle Dillon, pp. 207–24. Cambridge: Cambridge University Press.

Ammerman, Nancy Tatom, and Wade Clark Roof, eds. 1995. *Work, Family, and Religion in Contemporary Society.* New York: Routledge.

Anderson, Herbert. 1999. "Between Rhetoric and Reality: Women and Men and Equal Partners in Home, Church, and Marketplace." *Journal of Family Ministry* 13: 12–24.

Argue, Amy, David R. Johnson, and Lynn K. White. 1999. "Age and Religiosity: Evidence from a Three-Wave Panel Analysis." *Journal for the Scientific Study of Religion* 38 (3): 423–35.

Bahr, Howard M., and Bruce A. Chadwick. 1985. "Religion and Family in Middletown, USA." *Journal of Marriage and the Family* 47 (May): 407–14.

Baker, Wayne. 2004. *America's Crisis of Values: Perception and Reality.* Princeton, NJ: Princeton University Press.

Bartkowski, John P. 1997a. "Debating Patriarchy: Discursive Disputes over Spousal Authority among Evangelical Family Commentators." *Journal for the Scientific Study of Religion* 36 (3): 393–410.

———. 1997b. *Gender Reinvented, Gender Reproduced: The Discourse and Negotiation of Spousal Relations within Contemporary Evangelicalism.* Ph.D. dissertation, University of Texas, Austin.

———. 2004. *The Promise Keepers: Servants, Soldiers, and Godly Men.* New Brunswick, NJ: Rutgers University Press.

Bass, Dorothy. 1994. "Congregations and the Bearing of Traditions." In *American Congregations*, ed. James P. Wind and James W. Lewis, 2: 169–91. Chicago: University of Chicago Press.

Becker, Penny Edgell. 1997. "'What Is Right' and 'What Is Caring': Identifying a Religious Logic in Local Congregations." In *Contemporary American Religion: An Ethnographic Reader*, ed. Penny Edgell Becker and Nancy L. Eiesland, pp. 121–46. Walnut Creek, CA: Alta Mira Press / Sage.

———. 1998a. "Making Inclusive Communities: Congregations and the 'Problem' of Race." *Social Problems* 45 (4): 451–72.

———. 1998b. "'Rational Amusement and Sound Instruction': Constructing the True Catholic Woman in the *Ave Maria*." *Religion and American Culture* 8 (1): 55–90.

———. 1999. *Congregations in Conflict: Cultural Models of Local Religious Life*. New York: Cambridge University Press.

———. 2000. "Boundaries and Silences in a Post-Feminist Sociology." *Sociology of Religion* 61 (4): 399–408.

Becker, Penny Edgell, and Pawan Dhingra. 2001. "Religious Involvement and Volunteering." *Sociology of Religion* 62 (3): 315–35.

Becker, Penny Edgell, and Heather Hofmeister. 2000. Work Hours and Community Involvement of Dual-Earner Couples: Building Social Capital or Competing for Time? Cornell University, Bronfenbrenner Life Course Center Working Paper #00–04.

———. 2001. "Work, Family, and Religious Involvement for Men and Women." *Journal for the Scientific Study of Religion* 40 (4): 707–22.

Becker, Penny Edgell, and Phyllis Moen. 1999. "Scaling Back: Dual-Earner Couples' Work-Family Strategies." *Journal of Marriage and the Family* 61: 995–1007.

Bell, Wendell. 1958. "Social Choice, Lifestyles, and Suburban Residence." In *The Suburban Community*, ed. William Dobriner, pp. 225–47. New York: G. P. Putnam's Sons.

Bellah, Robert N., Richard Madsen, William Sullivan, Ann Swidler, and Steven Tipton. 1985. *Habits of the Heart: Individualism and Commitment in American Society*. Berkeley and Los Angeles: University of California Press.

———. 1991. *The Good Society*. New York: Alfred A. Knopf.

Bem, Sandra Lipsitz. 1993. *The Lenses of Gender: Transforming the Debate on Sexual Inequality*. New Haven, CT: Yale University Press.

Bendroth, Margaret Lamberts. 1993. *Fundamentalism and Gender, 1875 to the Present*. New Haven, CT: Yale University Press.

———. 2002. *Growing Up Protestant: Parents, Children, and Mainline Churches*. New Brunswick, NJ: Rutgers University Press.

Benford, Robert D., and David A. Snow. 2000. "Framing Processes and Social Movements: An Overview and Assessment." *Annual Review of Sociology* 26: 611–39.

Berger, Peter L. 1959. "The Second Children's Crusade: Overemphasis on the Family in Suburbia's Churches Is Basically Subversive of the Christian Mission." *Christian Century*, December 2, pp. 1399–1400.

———. 1967. *The Sacred Canopy: Elements of a Sociological Theory of Religion*. Garden City, NY: Doubleday.

Biernacki, Richard. 1995. *The Fabrication of Labor: Germany and Britain, 1640–1914*. Berkeley and Los Angeles: University of California Press.

Bloch, Ruth H. 1978a. "American Feminine Ideals in Transition: The Rise of the Moral Mother, 1785–1815." *Feminist Studies* 4: 101–26.

Bloch, Ruth H. 1978b. "Untangling the Roots of Modern Sex Roles: A Survey of Four Centuries of Change." *Signs: Journal of Women in Culture and Society* 4 (2): 237–49.

Bonnell, Victoria, and Lynn Hunt. 1999. *Beyond the Cultural Turn: New Directions in the Study of Society and Culture*. Berkeley and Los Angeles: University of California Press.

Booth, Alan, David R. Johnson, Ann Branaman, and Alan Sica. 1995. "Belief and Behavior: Does Religion Matter in Today's Marriage?" *Journal of Marriage and the Family* 57 (August): 661–71.

Bourdieu, Pierre. 1977. *Outline of a Theory of Practice*, trans. Richard Nice. New York: Cambridge University Press.

Brooks, David. 2001. "The Organization Kid." *Atlantic Monthly*, April, pp. 40–54.

Browning, Don S., Bonnie J. Miller-McLemore, Pamela D. Couture, K. Brynolf Lyon, and Robert M. Franklin. 1997. *From Culture Wars to Common Ground: American Religion and the Family Debate*. Louisville: Westminster / John Knox Press.

Bruce, Steve. 1996. *Religion in the Modern World: From Cathedrals to Cults*. New York: Oxford University Press.

Cadge, Wendy. 2002. "Vital Conflicts: The Mainline Denominations Debate Homosexuality." In *The Quiet Hand of God: Faith-Based Activism and the Public Role of Mainline Protestantism*, ed. Robert Wuthnow and John H. Evans, pp. 265–86. Berkeley and Los Angeles: University of California Press.

Caplow, Theodore, Howard M. Bahr, and Bruce A. Chadwick. 1983. *All Faithful People: Change and Continuity in Middletown's Religion*. Minneapolis: University of Minnesota Press.

Casanova, Jose. 1994. *Public Religions in the Modern World*. Chicago: University of Chicago Press.

Chaves, Mark. 1994. "Secularization as Declining Religious Authority." *Social Forces* 72 (3): 749–74.

———. 1998. National Congregations Study. Data File and Codebook. Tucson: University of Arizona, Department of Sociology.

———. 2004. *Congregations in America*. Cambridge, MA: Harvard University Press.

Chaves, Mark, and Philip S. Gorski. 2001. "Religious Pluralism and Religious Participation." *Annual Review of Sociology* 27: 261–81.

Chaves, Mark, Mary Ellen Konieczny, Kraig Beyerlien, and Emily Barman. 1999. "The National Congregations Study: Background, Methods, and Selected Results." *Journal for the Scientific Study of Religion* 38 (4): 458–76.

Christiano, Kevin. 2000. "Religion and Family in Modern American Culture." In *Family, Religion, and Social Change in Diverse Societies*, ed. Sharon K. Houseknecht and Jerry G. Pankhurst, pp. 43–78. New York: Oxford University Press.

Cohen, Michael D., James G. March, and Johan P. Olsen. 1972. "A Garbage Can Model of Organizational Choice." *Administrative Science Quarterly* 17 (1): 1–25.

Coleman, James S. 1990. *Foundations of Social Theory*. Cambridge, MA: Harvard University Press.

Cook, Karen S., and Margaret Levi, eds. 1990. *The Limits of Rationality*. Chicago: University of Chicago Press.

Coontz, Stephanie. 1992. *The Way We Never Were: American Families and the Nostalgia Trap*. New York: Basic Books.

Cott, Nancy F. 2002. *Public Vows: A History of Marriage and the Nation*. Cambridge, MA: Harvard University Press.

D'Antonio, William. 1980. "Family and Religion: Exploring a Changing Relationship." *Journal for the Scientific Study of Religion* 19: 89–104.

———. 1983. "Family Life, Religion, and Societal Values and Structures." In *Families and Religions: Conflict and Change in Modern Society*, ed. William D'Antonio and Joan Aldous, pp. 81–108. Beverly Hills, CA: Sage.

D'Antonio, William, and Joan Aldous. 1983. *Families and Religions: Conflict and Change in Modern Societies*. Beverly Hills, CA: Sage.

Davidman, Lynn. 1991. *Tradition in a Rootless World.* Berkeley and Los Angeles: University of California Press.

Demmitt, Kevin P. 1992. "Loosening the Ties That Bind—The Accommodation of Dual-Earner Families in a Conservative Protestant Church." *Review of Religious Research* 34 (1): 3–19.

de Vaus, David, and Ian McAllister. 1987. "Gender Differences in Religion: A Test of the Structural Location Theory." *American Sociological Review* 52 (4): 472–81.

Dillon, Michelle. 1999. *Catholic Identity: Balancing Reason, Faith, and Power.* New York: Cambridge University Press.

DiMaggio, Paul J. 1991. "Constructing an Organizational Field as a Professional Project: U.S. Art Museums, 1920–1940." In *The New Institutionalism in Organizational Analysis,* ed. Walter W. Powell and Paul J. DiMaggio, pp. 267–92. Chicago: University of Chicago Press.

DiMaggio, Paul, John H. Evans, and Bethany Bryson. 1996. "Have Americans' Social Attitudes Become More Polarized?" *American Journal of Sociology* 102 (3): 690–755.

DiMaggio, Paul J., and Walter W. Powell. 1991. "Introduction." In *The New Institutionalism in Organizational Analysis,* ed. Walter W. Powell and Paul J. DiMaggio, pp. 1–40. Chicago: University of Chicago Press.

Dobriner, William. 1958a. "Local and Cosmopolitan as Contemporary Suburban Character Types." In *The Suburban Community,* ed. William Dobriner, pp. 132–46. New York: G. P. Putnam's Sons.

———, ed. 1958b. *The Suburban Community.* New York: G. P. Putnam's Sons.

Douglas, Ann. 1998. *The Feminization of American Culture.* New York: Noonday Press / Farrar, Straus and Giroux.

Douglas, Mary. 1986. *How Institutions Think.* Syracuse, NY: Syracuse University Press.

Douglass, H. Paul. 1970 [1925]. *The Suburban Trend.* New York: Arno Press.

———. 1972. *The Church as a Social Institution.* New York: Russell and Russell.

Dudley, Carl S., and David A. Roozen. 2001. *Faith Communities Today: A Report on Religion in the United States Today.* Hartford, CT: Hartford Institute for Religion Research at Hartford Seminary.

Durkheim, Emile. 1951. *Suicide.* New York: Free Press.

———. 1965 [1915]. *Elementary Forms of the Religious Life.* New York: Free Press.

Ebaugh, Helen Rose, and Janet Saltzman Chafetz, eds. 2000. *Religion and the New Immigrants: Continuities and Adaptations in Immigrant Congregations.* Walnut Creek, CA: AltaMira Press.

Eck, Diana. 2001. *A New Religious America: How a "Christian Country" Has Now Become the World's Most Religiously Diverse Nation.* San Francisco: HarperSanFrancisco.

Ecklund, Elaine Howard. 2003. "Catholic Women Negotiate Feminism: A Research Note." *Sociology of Religion* 64 (4): 515–24.

Eiesland, Nancy L. 2000. *A Particular Place: Urban Restructuring and Religious Ecology in a Southern Exurb.* New Brunswick, NJ: Rutgers University Press.

Ellingson, Stephen J., Nelson Tebbe, Martha van Haitsma, and Edward O. Laumann. 2001. "Religion and the Politics of Sexuality." *Journal of Contemporary Ethnography* 30 (1): 3–55.

Ellison, Christopher G. 1995. "Rational Choice Explanations of Individual Religious Behavior: Notes on the Problem of Social Embeddedness." *Journal for the Scientific Study of Religion* 34 (1): 89–97.

Ellwood, Robert S. 1997. *The Fifties Spiritual Marketplace: American Religion in a Decade of Conflict.* New Brunswick, NJ: Rutgers University Press.

Elster, Jon. 1990. "When Rationality Fails." In *The Limits of Rationality*, ed. Karen Schweers Cook and Margaret Levi, pp. 19–50. Chicago: University of Chicago Press.

Emirbayer, Mustafa, and Anne Mische. 1998. "What Is Agency?" *American Journal of Sociology* 103 (4): 962–1023.

Epstein, Cynthia Fuchs. 1988. *Deceptive Distinctions: Sex, Gender, and the Social Order.* New Haven, CT: Yale University Press.

Fairchild, Roy W., and John Charles Wynn. 1961. *Families in the Church: A Protestant Survey.* New York: Association Press.

Figart, Deborah M., and Lonnie Golden. 1998. "The Social Economics of Work Time." *Review of Social Economy* 56 (4): 411–23.

Finke, Roger. 2004. "Innovative Returns to Tradition: Using Core Teachings as the Foundation for Innovative Accommodation." *Journal for the Scientific Study of Religion* 43 (1): 19–34.

Finke, Roger, and Rodney Stark. 1992. *The Churching of America, 1776–1990: Winners and Losers in our Religious Economy.* New Brunswick, NJ: Rutgers University Press.

Firebaugh, Glenn, and Brian Harley. 1991. "Trends in U.S. Church Attendance: Secularization and Revival, or Merely Lifecycle Effects?" *Journal for the Scientific Study of Religion* 30 (4): 487–500.

Fishburn, Janet. 1991. *Confronting the Idolatry of Family: A New Vision of the Household of God.* Nashville: Abingdon Press.

Foucault, Michel. 1978. *The History of Sexuality*, vol. 1. Trans. Robert Hurley. New York: Pantheon.

Freedman, Samuel G. 1993. *Upon This Rock: The Miracles of a Black Church.* New York: HarperCollins.

Friedland, Roger, and Robert Alford. 1991. "Bringing Society Back In: Symbols, Practices, and Institutional Contradictions." In *The New Institutionalism in Organizational Analysis*, ed. William W. Powell and Paul J. DiMaggio, pp. 232–66. Chicago: University of Chicago Press.

Furstenberg, Frank. 1999. "Family Change and Family Diversity." In *Diversity and Its Discontents: Cultural Conflict and Common Ground in Contemporary American Society*, ed. Neil J. Smelser and Jeffrey C. Alexander, pp. 147–66. Princeton, NJ: Princeton University Press.

Gallagher, Sally K. 2003. *Evangelical Identity and Gendered Family Life.* New Brunswick, NJ: Rutgers University Press.

Gallagher, Sally K., and Christian Smith. 1999. "Symbolic Traditionalism and Pragmatic Egalitarianism: Contemporary Evangelicals, Family, and Gender." *Gender and Society* 13 (2): 211–33.

Gamson, William. 1992. *Talking Politics.* New York: Cambridge University Press.

Geertz, Clifford. 1973. *The Interpretation of Cultures.* New York: Basic Books.

Gerson, Kathleen. 2002. "Moral Dilemmas, Moral Strategies, and the Transformation of Gender: Lessons from Two Generations of Work and Family Change." *Gender and Society* 16 (1): 8–28.

Gesch, Lyn. 1995. "Responses to Changing Lifestyles." In *Work, Family, and Religion in Contemporary Society*, ed. Nancy Tatom Ammerman and Wade Clark Roof, pp. 123–36. New York: Routledge.

Giddens, Anthony. 1979. *Central Problems in Social Theory: Action, Structure, and Contradiction in Social Analysis.* London: Macmillan.

Gilkes, Cheryl Townsend. 1995. "The Storm and the Light: Church, Family, Work, and Social Crisis in the African-American Experience." In *Work, Family, and Religion in Contemporary Society,* ed. Nancy Tatom Ammerman and Wade Clark Roof, pp. 177–98. New York: Routledge.

Ginsburg, Faye. 1989. *Contested Lives: The Abortion Debate in an American Community.* Berkeley and Los Angeles: University of California Press.

Glenn, Norval D. 1987. "Social Trends in the United States: Evidence from Sample Surveys." *Public Opinion Quarterly* 51: s109–s126.

Glock, Charles, and Rodney Stark. 1965. *Religion and Society in Tension.* Chicago: Rand McNally.

Goffman, Erving. 1967. *Interaction Ritual: Essays on Face-to-Face Behavior.* Garden City, NY: Doubleday.

———. 1974. *Frame Analysis: An Essay on the Organization of Experience.* New York: Harper and Row.

Greenwald, Maureen Weiner. 1989. "Working-Class Feminism and the Family Wage Ideal: The Seattle Debate on Married Women's Right to Work, 1914–1920." *Journal of American History* 76 (1): 118–49.

Greenwood, Royston, and C. R. Hinings. 1996. "Understanding Radical Organizational Change: Bringing Together the Old and the New Institutionalism." *Academy of Management Review* 21 (4): 1022–45.

Hackett, David. 1995. "Gender and Religion in American Culture, 1870–1930." *Religion and American Culture* 5 (2): 127–57.

Hage, J. T. 1999. "Organizational Innovation and Organizational Change." *Annual Review of Sociology* 25: 597–622.

Halberstam, David. 1993. *The Fifties.* New York: Villard Books.

Halle, David, ed. 1997. *Lived Religion in America.* Princeton, NJ: Princeton University Press.

Hammond, Phillip E. 1988. "Religion and the Persistence of Identity." *Journal for the Scientific Study of Religion* 27 (1): 1–11.

———. 1992. *Religion and Personal Autonomy: The Third Disestablishment in America.* Columbia: University of South Carolina Press.

Hareven, Tamara. 1991. "The Home and the Family in Historical Perspective." *Social Research* 58 (1): 253–85.

Hart, Stephen. 1986. "Religion and Changes in Family Patterns." *Review of Religious Research* 28 (September): 51–70.

Hayghe, Howard V., and Suzanne M. Bianchi. 1994. "Married Mothers' Work Patterns: The Job-Family Compromise." *Monthly Labor Review,* June, pp. 24–30.

Helly, Dorothy O., and Susan M. Reverby, eds. 1992. *Gendered Domains: Rethinking Public and Private in Women's History.* Ithaca, NY: Cornell University Press.

Herberg, Will. 1960. *Protestant-Catholic-Jew.* Garden City, NJ: Anchor Books.

Hertel, Bradley R. 1995. "Work, Family, and Faith: Recent Trends." In *Work, Family, and Religion in Contemporary Society,* ed. Nancy Tatom Ammerman and Wade Clark Roof, pp. 81–122. New York: Routledge.

Hetherington, E. Mavis, and John Kelly. 2002. *For Better or for Worse: Divorce Reconsidered.* New York: W. W. Norton and Co.

Hochschild, Arlie Russell. 1989. *The Second Shift: Working Parents and the Revolution at Home.* New York: Viking Press.

———. 1997. *The Time Bind: When Work Becomes Home and Home Becomes Work.* New York: Metropolitan Books.

Hofmeister, Heather, and Penny Edgell. 2003. "Sunday Morning Rush Hour." In *It's about Time: Couples and Careers,* ed. Phyllis Moen, pp. 203–19. Ithaca, NY: Cornell University Press.

Holifield, E. Brooks. 1994. "Toward a History of American Congregations." In *American Congregations,* vol. 2., ed. James P. Wind and James W. Lewis, pp. 23–53. Chicago: University of Chicago Press.

Houseknecht, Sharon H., and Jerry G. Pankhurst, eds. 2000. *Family, Religion, and Social Change in Diverse Societies.* New York: Oxford University Press.

Hout, Michael, and Claude Fischer. 2002. "Americans with 'No Religion': Why Their Numbers Are Growing." *American Sociological Review* 67 (2): 165–90.

Hout, Michael, and Andrew Greeley. 1998. "What Church Officials' Reports Don't Show: Another Look at Church Attendance Data." *American Sociological Review* 639 (1): 113–19.

Hudnut-Buemler, James. 1994. *Looking for God in the Suburbs: The Religion of the American Dream and Its Critics, 1945–1965.* New Brunswick, NJ: Rutgers University Press.

Hull, Kathleen. 2001. "Wedding Rites / Marriage Rights: The Cultural Politics of Same-Sex Marriage." Ph.D. diss., Northwestern University.

———. 2003. "The Cultural Power of Law and the Cultural Enactment of Legality: The Case of Same-Sex Marriage." *Law and Social Inquiry* 28 (3): 629–57.

Hunter, Edwin A. 1947. *The Small Town and Country Church.* Nashville: Abingdon-Cokesbury Press.

Hunter, James Davison. 1991. *Culture Wars: The Struggle to Define America.* New York: Basic Books.

Ingram, Paul, and Karen Clay. 2000. "The Choice-within-Constraints Institutionalism and Implications for Sociology." *Annual Review of Sociology* 26: 525–46.

Jacobs, Jerry A., and Kathleen Gerson. 1998. "Who Are the Overworked Americans?" *Review of Social Economy* 56 (4): 442–59.

———. 2004. *The Time Divide: Work, Family, and Gender Inequality.* Cambridge, MA: Harvard University Press.

Jenkins, Kip. W. 1991. "Religion and Families." In *Family Research: A Sixty-Year Review, 1930–1990,* ed. Stephen J. Bahr, pp. 235–88. Lexington, MA: Lexington Books.

Jepperson, Ronald L. 1991. "Institutions, Institutional Effects, and Institutionalism." In *The New Institutionalism in Organizational Analysis,* ed. William W. Powell and Paul J. DiMaggio, pp. 143–63. Chicago: University of Chicago Press.

Johnston, Hank. 1995. "A Methodology for Frame Analysis: From Discourse to Cognitive Schemata." In *Social Movements and Culture,* ed. Hank Johnston and Bert Klandermans, pp. 217–46. Minneapolis: University of Minnesota Press.

Johnston, Hank, and Bert Klandermans, eds. 1995. *Social Movements and Culture.* Minneapolis: University of Minnesota Press.

Kimmel, Michael. 1996. *Manhood in America: A Cultural History.* New York: Free Press.

Kurtz, Lester. 1986. *The Politics of Heresy: The Modernist Crisis in Roman Catholicism.* Berkeley and Los Angeles: University of California Press.

Lakoff, George. 1996. *Moral Politics: What Conservatives Know That Liberals Don't.* Chicago: University of Chicago Press.

Lamont, Michele. 1992. *Money, Morals, and Manners: The Culture of the French and American Upper-Middle Class.* Chicago: University of Chicago Press.

Lehrer, Evelyn L. 1995. "The Effects of Religion on the Labor Supply of Married Women." *Social Science Research* 24: 1–21.

———. 1996. "The Role of the Husband's Religious Affiliation in the Economic and Demographic Behavior of Families." *Journal for the Scientific Study of Religion* 35 (June): 145–55.

Lichterman, Paul. 1996. *The Search for Political Community: American Activists Reinventing Commitment.* New York: Cambridge University Press.

Lincoln, C. Eric, and Lawrence H. Mamiya. 1990. *The Black Church in the African-American Experience.* Durham, NC: Duke University Press.

Lindstrom, David E. 1946. *Rural Life and the Church.* Champagne, IL: Garrard Press.

Luckmann, Thomas. 1967. *The Invisible Religion: The Problem of Religion in Modern Society.* New York: Macmillan.

Lukes, Steven. 1974. *Power: A Radical View.* London: MacMillan.

Lyon, K. Brynolf, and Archie Smith Jr., eds. 1998. *Tending the Flock: Congregations and Family Ministry.* Louisville: Westminster / John Knox Press.

Marler, Penny Long. 1995. "Lost in the Fifties: The Changing Family and the Nostalgic Church." In *Work, Family, and Religion in Contemporary Society,* ed. Nancy Tatom Ammerman and Wade Clark Roof, pp. 23–60. New York: Routledge.

Marty, Martin. 1976. *A Nation of Behavers.* Chicago: University of Chicago Press.

May, Elaine Tyler. 1999 [1988]. *Homeward Bound: American Families in the Cold War Era.* New York: Basic Books.

McDannell, Colleen. 1986. *The Christian Home in Victorian America, 1840–1900.* Bloomington: Indiana University Press.

———. 1995. *Material Christianity: Religion and Popular Culture in America.* New Haven, CT: Yale University Press.

McPherson, J. Miller, and Thomas Rotolo. 1996. "Testing a Dynamic Model of Social Composition: Diversity and Change in Voluntary Groups." *American Sociological Review* 61 (2): 179–202.

Meyerowitz, Joanne, ed. 1994. *Not June Cleaver: Women and Gender in Postwar America, 1945–1960.* Philadelphia: Temple University Press.

Miller, Donald. 1997. *Reinventing American Protestantism: Christianity in the New Millenium.* Berkeley and Los Angeles: University of California Press.

Moon, Dawne. 2004. *God, Sex, and Politics: Homosexuality and Everyday Theologies.* Chicago: University of Chicago Press.

Moran, Gerald F. 1992. "The Puritan Family and Religion: A Critical Reappraisal." In *Religion, Family, and the Life Course: Explorations in the Social History of Early America,* ed. Gerald F. Moran and Maris A. Vinovskis, pp. 11–58. Ann Arbor: University of Michigan Press.

Morgan, Edmund S. 1966. *The Puritan Family: Religion and Domestic Relations in Seventeenth-Century New England.* New York: Harper and Row.

Morrill, Calvin. 1995. *The Executive Way: Conflict Management in Corporations.* Chicago: University of Chicago Press.

Mowrer, Ernest R. 1958. "The Family in Suburbia." In *The Suburban Community*, ed. William Dobriner, pp. 147–64. New York: G. P. Putnam's Sons.

Mueller, Charles W., and Weldon T. Johnson. 1975. "Socioeconomic Status and Religious Participation." *American Sociological Review* 40: 785–800.

Myers, Scott M. 1996. "An Interactive Model of Religiosity Inheritance: The Importance of Family Context." *American Sociological Review* 61 (5): 858–66.

Nash, Dennison, and Peter Berger. 1962. "The Child, the Family, and the 'Religious Revival' in Suburbia." *Journal for the Scientific Study of Religion* 2 (1): 85–93.

Neitz, Mary Jo. 1987. *Charisma and Community: A Study of Religious Commitment within the Charismatic Renewal*. New Brunswick, NJ: Transaction Books.

Niebuhr, H. Richard. 1956 [1951]. *Christ and Culture*. New York: Harper and Row.

Nock, Steven L. 1998. *Marriage in Men's Lives*. New York: Oxford University Press.

Ortner, Sherry. 1996. *Making Gender: The Politics and Erotics of Culture*. Boston: Beacon Press.

Pearce, Lisa D., and William G. Axinn. 1998. "The Impact of Family Religious Life on the Quality of Mother-Child Relations." *American Sociological Review* 63 (6): 810–28.

Popper, Karl. 1959. *The Logic of Scientific Discovery*. New York: Basic Books.

Porterfield, Amanda. 1980. *Feminine Spirituality in America: From Sarah Edwards to Martha Graham*. Philadelphia: Temple University Press.

Powell, Walter W., and Paul J. DiMaggio, eds. 1991. *The New Institutionalism in Organizational Analysis*. Chicago: University of Chicago Press.

Prell, Riv-Ellen. 1988. *Recreating Judaism in America: An Anthropology of Contemporary Prayer*. Detroit: Wayne State University Press.

Price, Matthew. 2001. "Class and the Clergy: Are Ministers Falling Behind?" Paper presented at "Dissolving Boundaries: A Decade of Dialogue in the Study of Religion," a conference celebrating the centennial anniversary of the Center for the Study of Religion at Princeton University, May 4.

Riley, Matilda White, Robert L. Kahn, and Anne Foner, eds. 1994. *Age and Structural Lag: Society's Failure to Provide Meaningful Opportunities in Work, Family, and Leisure*. New York: J. Wiley.

Robinson, John P., and Geoffrey Godbey. 1997. *Time for Life: The Surprising Ways Americans Use Their Time*. University Park: Pennsylvania State University Press.

Roof, Wade Clark. 1993. *A Generation of Seekers*. San Francisco: Harper.

———. 1999. *Spiritual Marketplace: Baby Boomers and the Remaking of American Religion*. Princeton, NJ: Princeton University Press.

Roof, Wade Clark, and Lyn Gesch. 1995. "Boomers and the Culture of Choice." In *Work, Family, and Religion in Contemporary Society*, ed. Nancy Tatom Ammerman and Wade Clark Roof, pp. 61–80. New York: Routledge.

Schor, Juliet. 1991. *The Overworked American: The Unexpected Decline of Leisure*. New York: Basic Books.

Scott, Richard W. 1998. *Organizations: Rational, Natural, and Open Systems*. Upper Saddle River, NJ: Prentice Hall.

Seidler, John, and Katherine Meyer. 1989. *Conflict and Change in the Catholic Church*. New Brunswick, NJ: Rutgers University Press.

Sewell, William H., Jr. 1992. "A Theory of Structure: Duality, Agency, and Transformation." *American Journal of Sociology* 98: 1–29.

Sherkat, Darren. 1997. "Embedding Religious Choices: Preferences and Social Constraints into Rational Choice Theories of Religious Behavior." In *Rational Choice Theory and Religion: Summary and Assessment*, ed. Lawrence A. Young, pp. 65–85. New York: Routledge.

———. 1998. "Counter Culture or Continuity? Competing Influences on Baby Boomers' Religious Orientations and Participation." *Social Forces* 76 (3): 1087–1114.

———. 2000. " 'That They Be Keepers of the Home': The Effect of Conservative Religion on Early and Late Transitions into Housewifery." *Review of Religious Research* 41 (3): 344–58.

———. 2001. "Toward Synthesizing Social Psychological and Social Movement Theories: Integrating Rational Actor, Frame Analytic, and Structuration Theories." Paper presented at the Iowa Theory Workshop.

Sherkat, Darren, and Chris Ellison. 1999. "Recent Developments and Current Controversies in the Sociology of Religion." *Annual Review of Sociology* 25: 363–94.

Skolnick, Arlene. 1991. *Embattled Paradise: The American Family in an Age of Uncertainty.* New York: Basic Books.

Smith, Christian. 1998. *American Evangelicalism: Embattled and Thriving.* Chicago: University of Chicago Press.

———. 2003. *Moral, Believing Animals: Human Personhood and Culture.* Oxford University Press.

Smith, Tom W. 1987. "Classifying Protestant Denominations." *General Social Survey Methodological Report 43.* Chicago: National Opinion Research Center.

Spain, Daphne, and Suxanne Bianchi. 1996. *Balancing Act: Motherhood, Marriage, and Employment among American Women.* New York: Russell Sage Foundation.

Stacey, Judith. 1991. *Brave New Families: Stories of Domestic Upheaval in Late Twentieth-Century America.* New York: Basic Books.

Stark, Rodney, and Roger Finke. 2000. *Acts of Faith: Explaining the Human Side of Religion.* Berkeley and Los Angeles: University of California Press.

Steensland, Brian, Jerry Z. Park, Mark D. Regnerus, Lynn D. Robinson, W. Bradford Wilcox, and Robert D. Woodberry. 2000. "The Measure of American Religion: Toward Improving the State of the Art." *Social Forces* 79 (1): 291–318.

Stinchcombe, Arthur. 1997. "On the Virtues of the Old Institutionalism." *Annual Review of Sociology* 23: 1–18.

Stolzenberg, Ross M., Mary Blair-Loy, and Linda J. Waite. 1995. "Religious Participation in Early Adulthood: Age and Family Life-Cycle Effects on Church Membership." *American Sociological Review* 60 (1): 84–103.

Strang, David, and Sarah Soule. 1998. "Diffusion in Organizations and Social Movements: From Hybrid Corn to Poison Pills." *Annual Review of Sociology* 24: 265–90.

Stryker, Robin. 1994. "Rules, Resources, and Legitimacy Processes: Some Implications for Social Conflict, Order, and Change." *American Journal of Sociology* 99: 847–910.

Swartz, Teresa Toguchi, Erika Busse, and Debra Jozefowicz-Simbeni. 2004. "Passing On Privilege: Social Reproduction and Intergenerational Supports." Paper presented at the annual meeting of the Society for the Study of Social Problems, August, San Francisco.

Swidler, Ann. 1986. "Culture in Action: Symbols and Strategies." *American Sociological Review* 51: 273–86.

———. 2001a. *Talk of Love: How Culture Matters.* Chicago: University of Chicago Press.

————. 2001b. "What Anchors Cultural Practices." In *The Practice Turn in Contemporary Theory*, ed. Theodore R. Schatzki, Karen Knorr Cetina, and Eike von Savigny, pp. 74–92. London: Routledge.

Swidler, Ann, and Ronald L. Jepperson. 1994. "What Properties of Culture Should We Measure?" *Poetics* 22 (4): 359–71.

Thomas, John L. 1956. *The American Catholic Family*. Englewood Cliffs, NJ: Prentice-Hall.

Thornton, Arland. 1985. "Reciprocal Influences of Family and Religion in a Changing World." *Journal of Marriage and the Family* 47 (May): 381–94.

Thumma, Scott L. 1996. "The Kingdom, the Power, and the Glory: The Megachurch in Modern American Society." Ph.D. diss., Emory University.

Tipton, Steve. 1982. *Getting Saved from the Sixties*. Berkeley and Los Angeles: University of California Press.

Tocqueville, Alexis de. 2000. *Democracy in America*. Ed. and trans. Harvey C. Mansfield and Debra Winthrop. Chicago: University of Chicago Press.

Tolbert, Pamela, and Phyllis Moen. 1998. "Men's and Women's Definitions of 'Good' Jobs." *Work and Occupations* 25 (2): 168–94.

Treas, Judith. 1999. "Diversity in American Families." In *A Nation Divided: Diversity, Inequality, and Community in American Society*, ed. Phyllis Moen, Donna Dempster-McClain, and Henry A. Walker, pp. 245–59. Ithaca, NY: Cornell University Press.

Turner, Victor. 1974. *Dramas, Fields, and Metaphors*. Ithaca, NY: Cornell University Press.

Veroff, Joseph, Elizabeth Douvan, and Richard Kulka. 1981. *The Inner American: A Self-Portrait from 1957 to 1976*. New York: Basic Books.

Warner, R. Stephen. 1993. "Work in Progress toward a New Paradigm for the Sociological Study of Religion in the United States." *American Journal of Sociology* 98 (5): 1044–93.

————. 1999. "Changes in the Civic Role of Religion." In *Diversity and Its Discontents: Cultural Conflict and Common Ground in Contemporary American Society*, ed. Neil J. Smelser and Jeffrey C. Alexander, pp. 229–43. Princeton, NJ: Princeton University Press.

Warner, R. Stephen, and Judith G. Wittner, eds. 1998. *Gatherings in Diaspora: Religious Communities and the New Immigration*. New York: Cambridge University Press.

Warner, W. Lloyd. 1961. *The Family of God: A Symbolic Study of Christian Life in America*. New Haven, CT: Yale University Press.

————. 1962. *American Life*. Chicago: University of Chicago Press.

Weber, Max. 1978. *Economy and Society: An Outline of Interpretive Sociology*. Ed. Gnenther Roth and Claus Wittich. Berkeley and Los Angeles: University of California Press.

Weber, Max. 1998. *The Protestant Ethic and the Spirit of Capitalism*. Trans. Talcott Parsons, ed. Randall Collins. Los Angeles: Roxbury Publishing Co.

Wedam, Elfriede. 1997. "Splitting Interests or Common Causes: Styles of Moral Reasoning in Opposing Abortion." In *Contemporary American Religion: An Ethnographic Reader*, ed. Penny Edgell Becker and Nancy L. Eiesland, pp. 147–68. Newbury Park, CA: Alta Mira Press / Sage.

Welter, Barbara. 1976. *Dimity Convictions: The American Woman in the Nineteenth Century*. Athens: Ohio University Press.

Whyte, William Hollingsworth. 1956. *The Organization Man.* New York: Simon and Schuster.

Wilcox, W. Bradford. 2004. *Soft Patriarchs, New Men: How Christianity Shapes Fathers and Husbands.* Chicago: University of Chicago Press.

Wilcox, W. Bradford, Mark Chaves, and David Franz. 2004. "Focused on the Family? Religious Traditions, Family Discourse, and Pastoral Practice." *Journal for the Scientific Study of Religion* 43 (4): 491–504.

Williams, Rhys H. 1995. "Constructing the Public Good: Social Movements and Cultural Resources." *Social Problems* 42 (1): 124–44.

———. 1996a. "Introduction." *Sociology of Religion* 57 (1): 1–5, special issue on culture and religion.

———. 1996b. "Religion as Political Resource: Culture or Ideology?" *Journal for the Scientific Study of Religion* 35 (4): 368–78.

———, ed. 1997. *Culture Wars in American Politics: Critical Reviews of a Popular Myth.* New York: Aldine de Gruyter.

Williams, Rhys H. 1999. "Visions of the Good Society and the Religious Roots of American Political Culture." *Sociology of Religion* 60 (1): 1–34.

Williams, Rhys H., and Nicholas J. Demerath III. 1991. "Religion and Political Process in an American City." *American Sociological Review* 56: 417–31.

Wilson, John, and Darren E. Sherkat. 1994. "Returning to the Fold." *Journal for the Scientific Study of Religion* 33 (2): 148–61.

Winter, Gibson. 1962. *The Suburban Captivity of the Churches: An Analysis of the Protestant Responsibility in the Expanding Metropolis.* New York: Macmillan.

Witten, Marsha. 1993. *All Is Forgiven: The Secular Message of American Protestantism.* Princeton, NJ: Princeton University Press.

Woodberry, Robert D., and Christian S. Smith. 1998. "Fundamentalism et al.: Conservative Protestants in America." *Annual Review of Sociology* 24: 25–56.

Wuthnow, Robert. 1987. *Meaning and Moral Order: Explorations in Cultural Analysis.* Berkeley and Los Angeles: University of California Press.

———. 1988. *The Restructuring of American Religion: Society and Faith since World War II.* Princeton, NJ: Princeton University Press.

———. 1989. *Communities of Discourse.* Cambridge, MA: Harvard University Press.

———, ed. 1994a. *I Come Away Stronger.* Grand Rapids, MI: Eerdmans.

———. 1994b. *Sharing the Journey.* New York: Free Press.

Wuthnow, Robert. 1998a. *After Heaven: Spirituality in America since the 1950s.* Berkeley and Los Angeles: University of California Press.

———. 1998b. *Loose Connections: Joining Together in America's Fragmented Communities.* Cambridge, MA: Harvard University Press.

Wuthnow, Robert, and John H. Evans, eds. 2002. *The Quiet Hand of God: Faith-Based Activism and the Public Role of Mainline Protestantism.* Berkeley and Los Angeles: University of California Press.

Young, Lawrence A, ed. 1997. *Rational Choice Theory and Religion: Summary and Assessment.* New York: Routledge.

INDEX

PRINCETON STUDIES IN CULTURAL SOCIOLOGY